A Man of Distinction among Them

A Man of *Distinction* among *Them*

— ❧ —

Alexander McKee and the Ohio Country Frontier, 1754–1799

LARRY L. NELSON

THE KENT STATE UNIVERSITY PRESS

Kent, Ohio, and London

© 1999 by The Kent State University Press, Kent, Ohio 44242
All rights reserved
Library of Congress Catalog Card Number 98-43050
ISBN 0-87338-620-5
Manufactured in the United States of America

05 04 03 02 01 00 99   5 4 3 2 1

Material in chapter 1, "Cultural Mediation, Cultural Exchange,
and the Invention of the Ohio Frontier," was previously published in
Ohio History, volume 105, Winter–Spring 1996, and is reprinted with permission.

Library of Congress Cataloging-in-Publication Data
Nelson, Larry L. (Larry Lee), 1950–
A man of distinction among them / Alexander McKee and
the Ohio country frontier, 1754–1799 / Larry L. Nelson.
p.   cm.
Includes bibliographical references (p.).
ISBN 0-87338-620-5 (cloth : alk. paper) ∞
1. McKee, Alexander, ca. 1735–1799.   2. Indian agents—Northwest,
Old—Biography.   3. Indian agents—Canada—Biography.   4. Indians of
North America—Wars—1750–1815.   5. Northwest, Old—History—18th
century.   6. Great Britain. Indian Dept.—Officials and employees—
Biography.   I. Title.
E92.N45   1999
977'.01'092—dc21
[b]   98-43050

British Library Cataloging-in-Publication data are available.

For

Bill and Ardath

Contents

Preface

I first became interested in Alexander McKee while working for the Ohio Historical Society as the site manager at Fort Meigs State Memorial in Perrysburg. In 1988 I was asked to begin research on a proposed museum renovation project at another Ohio Historical Society property, Fort Recovery State Memorial in Mercer County, the site of Arthur St. Clair's 1791 defeat and the 1794 Battle of Fort Recovery. My initial research quickly revealed McKee's important role in both actions. Moreover, I was surprised to learn that McKee conducted his affairs during the 1790s Indian war period from his storehouse at the foot of the Maumee River Rapids, only a short distance from my office at Fort Meigs. Further investigation indicated his long involvement with the Ohio Country Indian nations and his prominent participation in Great Britain's attempt to win and then retain its imperial holdings throughout the Great Lakes region in the second half of the eighteenth century.

McKee was at the center of events along the Ohio frontier during the dozen or so years after the American Revolution that would broadly set the course of the region's history for many years to come. Indeed, these events would profoundly shape the destinies of the United States and Canada and of the area's native peoples for the next two centuries. This was nowhere more true than in his actions along the Maumee River during the 1790s. Anthony Wayne's victory over the confederated Indian nations at Fallen Timbers in 1794 and the subsequent Treaty of Greenville the following year secured uncontested sovereignty over the

Old Northwest for the United States. In the short term, the treaty terminated most Native American claims to the land, permitted the rapid, generally peaceful settlement of the region, and set the stage for the eventual admittance of Ohio, Michigan, Indiana, Illinois, and Wisconsin into the federal union. In the long term, the Old Northwest provided the natural resources, the water transportation systems, and the manufacturing basis that allowed the United States to emerge as a world industrial and economic power in the late nineteenth century and helped the nation maintain that status to the present day.

Alexander McKee was a pivotal figure in the events that would shape the region's future. McKee had been born and raised along the western border. He was the son of Thomas McKee, a well-known western Pennsylvania trader, and a Shawnee mother. Serving as a junior officer in the Pennsylvania Militia during the French and Indian War, McKee joined the British Indian Department under the tutelage of George Croghan in 1759. Acting as an interpreter and low-level diplomatic envoy to the western nations, he worked on the Crown's behalf during Pontiac's Rebellion, Bouquet's Expedition, and Dunmore's War. He also entered the fur trade during this period. By 1770 he had taken a wife from and established a home among the Shawnee bands that lived along the Scioto River Valley in present-day central Ohio. Sir William Johnson, the superintendent of Indian affairs for the Northern District, recognized the high esteem in which McKee was held among the Ohio Country tribes. When Croghan retired in 1771, Johnson appointed McKee to replace Croghan as Indian agent and to direct the Indian department commissary at Fort Pitt.

Remaining loyal to the British government during the Revolutionary era, McKee made his way to Detroit in 1778. Throughout the remainder of the war he engaged in a variety of military and diplomatic activities directed against the rebelling colonies. In 1778, McKee accompanied Henry Hamilton's expedition to Vincennes. Later he participated in Henry Bird's 1780 campaign into Kentucky and the 1782 foray along the Ohio River to Bryant's Station, which culminated in the defeat of American irregulars at the Battle of Blue Licks. Following the Revolution he became a prominent figure in local and colonial affairs, serving as a member of the Land Board of Hess, the provincial body that regulated settlement within Canada's lower–Detroit River region.

He also was appointed a justice with the local Court of Common Pleas and lieutenant colonel in the Essex County Militia of Upper Canada. During the 1790–1795 Ohio Country Indian wars, McKee played a central role in defining and implementing Upper Canada's diplomatic and military response. Throughout the crisis he was an energetic participant in Crown efforts to supply arms, ammunition, and provisions to the Maumee Valley tribes that opposed United States expansion into the region. Soon after the Battle of Fallen Timbers and the Treaty of Greenville, McKee was named deputy superintendent and inspector general of Indian affairs for Upper and Lower Canada, the second highest post dealing with Indian affairs in British North America and a position he would retain until his death in January 1799.

Despite McKee's important contributions to the history of the region, I was dismayed to find little in the secondary literature regarding his career. American historians seem to have neglected McKee for several reasons. First, he was a Tory during the Revolution. American leaders of great prestige during his lifetime, including Anthony Wayne, George Rogers Clark, and Daniel Boone, despised him as a traitor. That sensibility continued to follow McKee's reputation long after his death. As late as the mid-nineteenth century, the erstwhile biographer of American Loyalists, Lorenzo Sabine, would dismiss McKee by describing him simply as a person "of revengeful machinations" who used his position in the British Indian Department to "indulge his hatred towards the country he had deserted in the hour of peril." Secondly, McKee's reputation was further tarnished by his deep friendship and nearly lifelong association with Simon Girty, long reviled as the most vicious and treacherous border ruffian along the Ohio frontier.[1]

McKee's mixed-race parentage may also have caused historians to overlook his importance in the region's history. Commentators frequently have portrayed these "syn-ethnic" individuals as unscrupulous misfits and described them as outcasts unaccepted by either whites or natives. There is a long tradition of both popular and scholarly writing that deals with these people. But much of this literature either explicitly or tacitly incorporates a value system that is biased against them and employs several equally unflattering stereotypes to characterize their role along the frontier. Some of these stereotypes are as old as the frontier itself. Miscegenation was a common occurrence along the frontier, and the offspring of mixed-race unions were a visible and common part of border society. Peter Fontaine, a settler who lived in western Virginia in 1757, wrote to his brother complaining that "our traders have indeed their squaws, alias whores, at the Indian towns where they trade, but they leave their offspring like bulls or bears to be provided for at random by their mothers." The racially mixed children described by Fontaine were an accepted part of tribal life, yet whites frequently viewed children of dual Indian and European ancestry with a combination of suspicion and animosity. Indeed, the common wisdom maintained that these individuals inherited the worst characteristics present in each parent. As a result, an entire vocabulary, all of it pejorative and including terms such as "half-breed," "squaw-man," "mixed-blood," and "breed," came to be applied to these persons. White settlers occasionally portrayed them as the instigators of interracial friction. Fontaine, for one, claimed that "these bastards have been the leading men or war captains that have done us so much mischief." The more common view disparagingly dismissed them as disfranchised and alienated, having little influence or prestige in either the white or the Indian world.[2]

More recent scholarship has represented these individuals as tragic figures, inextricably caught between cultures. Able to move freely between Indian and European societies, they were, nonetheless, never fully accepted by either. Their lives display unresolved cultural ambiguity and a flawed sense of self-identity. They become persons who, despite what at times is an impressive record of personal achievement, are doomed to struggle throughout their lives in an unavailing attempt to find self validation and social approval. Isabel Thompson Kelsay, in her biography of the Mohawk leader Joseph Brant, for example, tells of the exiled Mohawk's anguished death as he lay in an English bed, in an English room, covered in a fine English blanket. He passed away, says Kelsay, casting a longing gaze upon his tomahawk and dagger, which hung on the wall in plain sight, but out of reach. Similarly, Paul A. Hutton has described William Wells, a white youth who was captured by the Miami Indians and who later became a United States Indian agent, as a "white Indian," a person who combined the characteristics of both European and native cultures in an uneasy alliance. During his entire life, he "swayed back and forth" between the two, "never sure to which he truly belonged." The indecision condemned Wells, claims Hutton, "For he could never be fully accepted by either society." Lastly, Anthony C. Wallace, in his classic study of Teedyuscung, a leader of the western Pennsylvania Delawares during the mid-eighteenth century, draws a portrait of an ambitious young Indian seduced by his own avarice into affecting European ways. Lured to white society in a self-interested quest to acquire wealth and prestige, Teedyuscung was rejected by Indian and white alike. Wallace urges his readers to think of the Delaware as a "man who tried to bridge in one lifetime the cleft between two worlds—the white man's world and the Indian world—and died an alien to both."[3]

Current scholarship has begun to employ a broadly interdisciplinary approach to study these individuals, seeing them as cultural "brokers," or "intermediaries," persons who were accepted by both the European and the Indian worlds and who were skilled at facilitating transactions between both cultures. This new methodology has produced several excellent studies of McKee's contemporaries, including Colin Calloway's "Simon Girty: Interpreter and Intermediary," and Nancy Hagedorn's "'Faithful, Knowing, and Prudent': Andrew Montour as Interpreter and Cultural Broker, 1740–1772." I have employed the same approach in this appraisal of McKee, with one important exception. Both Hagedorn and Calloway frame their understandings of their subjects through the use of sociologist Everett Stonequist's definition of "the marginal man," namely one "who through migration, education or marriage, or some other influence, leaves one social group or culture without making a satisfactory adjustment to another," consequently finding himself "on the margin of each, but a member of neither." I have discovered little that was "marginal" about McKee. Indeed, he seems to have possessed a mirrorlike quality that caused those with whom he dealt, whether they were Indian, British, American, trader, soldier, land speculator, or diplomat, to see themselves reflected in his personality. McKee enjoyed great success as a mediator because he had full access to and great influence with decision makers and elites on both sides of the cultural divide.[4]

The study that follows centers on McKee's life, but I also hope that it promotes a broad understanding of the region's cultural and political development, along with the attendant themes of race and class, during the mid- to late-eighteenth century. I have quoted frequently from the primary sources and have retained the spelling, capitalization, and punctuation found in the originals. Where I have felt that it was necessary to modify the source material to clarify its meaning, I have used brackets to indicate the change.

Authors accumulate debts, and I am no exception. Many people have contributed to this effort. David Skaggs and Ed Danziger at Bowling Green State University worked with me on this study when I submitted it as a doctoral dissertation and as I prepared it for publication. Mike Pratt at Heidelberg College and Rob Allen, formerly of the Claims and Historical Research Center, Department of Indian and Northern Affairs in Ottawa, Ontario, also commented on later drafts. This work was materially strengthened because of their observations and suggestions. Randy Buchman at Defiance College has been supportive of my interest in Ohio's frontier era for years and has sustained my efforts with his infectious enthusiasm and abiding love for the Maumee Valley's colonial history. Phil Hoffman of Westlake Village, California, was especially generous in sharing material that he has collected for a yet-unpublished biography of Simon Girty. Adam Sakel, my colleague at Fort Meigs State Memorial, created the maps used throughout the text.

The reference and archival librarians at the institutions where I conducted my research were, without exception, extremely helpful. At Bowling Green State University I especially benefited from the assistance of Bob Graham and his staff at the Institute for Great Lakes Research and Paul Yon and his staff at the Center for Archival Collections. The staffs at the Burton Collection of the Detroit Public Library, the Hiram Walker Museum (now Windsor's Community Museum), and the Ohio Historical Society should be held up for special commendation, as should Bob Garcia at Fort Malden National Historic Park in Amherstburg, Ontario, and John Harriman, Bryan Dunnigan, and their colleagues at the William C. Clements Library in Ann Arbor, Michigan. Earl Olmstead, the director of the Tusc-Kent Archives at the Tuscarawrus Campus of Kent State University, spent an entire day helping me with his extensive collection of Moravian and Ohio frontier materials. Tim Dubé, chief military archivist at the National Archives of Canada, aided me immeasurably by his prompt responses to many phone and mail inquiries. Further, he and his wife, Phyllis, opened their home and offered me unstinting hospitality during a one-week stay in Ottawa when I was completing my investigation. Lastly, I especially appreciate the assistance of Gary Ness, director of the Ohio Historical Society, and editor Robert Daugherty for giving permission to use in chapter one material that was originally published in *Ohio History*. To all, my heartfelt thanks.

Cultural Mediation, Cultural Exchange, and the Invention of the Ohio Frontier

There was little rest for Alexander McKee during the autumn of 1793. Over the course of the preceding three years, a loose confederation of Native Americans from along the Maumee River Valley had looked to their British allies for assistance. In their campaign to expel the United States from the Ohio Country, the northwestern tribes had already frustrated two American expeditions into the region. In October 1790, troops commanded by Josiah Harmar had retreated in disarray after they encountered unexpectedly stiff Indian resistance at the headwaters of the Maumee. In November of the following year, the confederated tribes had completely routed a second United States army led by Arthur St. Clair. Now, the tribes along the Maumee watched with mounting concern as a third force, with Anthony Wayne at its head, poised itself to strike at the native stronghold.[1]

McKee (ca. 1735–1799), a fur trader, land speculator, and agent with the British Indian Department, played an active role in lower Great Lakes Anglo-Indian affairs for nearly fifty years. Fathered by a white trader, but raised in part by his Shawnee mother, McKee was equally at home in either culture. He had lived among, traded with, and fought alongside many of the Ohio Country tribes. As tensions between the western tribes and the United States flared into open warfare during the 1790s, he met with tribal delegations at his post at the foot of the Maumee Rapids to discuss strategy, dispense gifts, and offer advice. He attempted to persuade the reluctant northern lake tribes, those living along the upper reaches of Lakes Michigan and Superior, to join the league. At the same time, he worked to isolate representatives from the accommodationist eastern Iroquois Confederacy who felt it would be in their interests to avoid armed conflict. He oversaw the shipment of military supplies and provisions from British officials at Detroit to his storehouse on the Maumee and coordinated covert British military assistance to the warring tribes. He entertained American envoys and received emissaries from the Crown. He directed spies, interrogated deserters, and exchanged prisoners. American ambition, native apprehension, and imperial aspiration converged at the British outpost along the rapids. In the center stood Alexander McKee.

McKee was a cultural mediator, a go-between who linked the native and European worlds. For much of the last half of the eighteenth century he exploited his familial affiliation and close economic ties to both communities to encourage trade, foster diplomatic relations, and forge a military alliance between the British government and the tribes of the Old Northwest. A shrewd, skilled negotiator and a loyal British partisan, McKee employed his abilities throughout his career to reconcile Crown and native political, military, and economic interests.[2]

McKee was not alone as a cultural mediator. Throughout the frontier era many others fulfilled similar roles. Perhaps the best known cultural mediator working within the Ohio Country was McKee's British Indian Department subordinate Simon Girty, the notorious Tory renegade. Other mediators included Matthew Elliott, Girty's and McKee's Indian department colleague; Andrew Montour, a translator and diplomatic envoy active in western Pennsylvania and eastern Ohio during the mid-eighteenth century; William Wells, a white youth who was captured and raised among the Indians and who fought against Arthur St. Clair in 1791 but who served as a spy and translator for Anthony Wayne at Fallen Timbers in 1794; John Slover, another captive who returned to white society and acted as Col. William Crawford's guide during his ill-fated expedition against the Ohio tribes in 1782 and who later narrated Hugh Brackenridge's famous account of the American

THE OHIO COUNTRY FRONTIER
1750–1800

commander's death at the hands of his Indian captors; and Abraham Kuhn, a Pennsylvania trader who married a Wyandot woman living near Lower Sandusky and who became known as "Chief Coon," a respected tribal statesman and advisor during the late 1780s.[3]

McKee and other cultural mediators played a central role in a complex process of cultural exchange that took place throughout the Great Lakes frontier. It is axiomatic that when two cultures meet, both are changed by the experience. But when two diverse peoples first come into contact, much of the encounter is mutually incomprehensible.

Differences of language, custom, and world view conspire to deprive both parties of opportunities for intelligible communication on all but the most basic level. As a result, cultures frequently resort to what historian Richard White has characterized as a process of creative and expedient misunderstandings. Individuals from each culture attempt to direct their efforts at communication to the perceived beliefs and social conventions of the other. That these initial perceptions are often false is of little consequence, for out of these misunderstandings arise shared perceptions regarding the meaning of the encounter. The form and significance of a cultural encounter, then, are predetermined only in small measure by the cultural imperatives brought to the meeting by each party. They are also mediated to a substantial degree through the negotiated manipulation of the encounter's specific circumstances. As members of both cultures interact, working relationships are established, and through these relationships a sense of common understanding emerges.[4]

As the encounter matures and becomes more complex, each party grows increasingly reliant upon the services of cultural mediators, individuals whose experiences have bridged both cultures. Always bilingual, usually related to both societies through birth, marriage, or adoption, and particularly adept at transacting the affairs of each in the world of the other, mediators become the specialized mediums through which cultures become interconnected. Historians Howard Lamar and Leonard Thompson have suggested that the frontier was a zone of cultural interpenetration, a region where indigenous peoples and intruders encountered one another and where, eventually, one or the other imposed a cultural hegemony over the entire area. But the Great Lakes frontier was also a zone of mutual reinvention. Europeans and natives alike voluntarily, indeed eagerly, adopted elements of each other's culture. Moreover, that adoption was always pragmatic, highly selective, and noncoercive. The Ohio frontier was a new creation. Fashioned by self-conscious choices of those engaged in the region's myriad forms of cultural interaction, the frontier contained readily identifiable elements from both Indian and white societies, combined in ways that were new and ingenious. Standing astride the cultural divide as they guided and shaped native and European interaction, McKee and other cultural mediators became creators as well as creations of the Ohio frontier.[5]

The new world invented by the process of cultural exchange was related to, yet distinct from, both native and European precedent. The Ohio Country was culturally diverse, an intricate social mosaic whose members asserted and defended a tangled web of interconnected national, regional, local, and individual agendas. European aims within the region were never unified, and white stratagems frequently collapsed along opposing national, religious, or economic lines. Indian allegiances were equally fragmented. Sovereign tribes and autonomous bands independently pursued their own self-interests through separate, often competing policies. But inter- and intraethnic cooperation also defined social reality along the Ohio frontier as much as inter- and intraethnic rivalry. Although cultural encounters were occasionally marked by violence, more commonly the very fabric of everyday life instigated a peaceful process of cultural interaction. The Great Lakes frontier became an open, assimilative world of shifting relationships in constant evolution. In this world, political loyalties and cultural values were fluid, pragmatic, and uncertain. National, ethnic, and even racial affiliation could become problematic. Social ambivalence and cultural interdependence were the natural by-products of the region's intercultural contact, trade, marriage, and diplomacy. Within this world, cultural mediators took on great importance. Able to transcend the boundaries of nation, race, and culture, mediators employed their skills to facilitate, and occasionally to direct, the course of native and European interaction.[6]

All cultural mediators share several characteristics. First, they live within a socially complex environment where opportunities for intercultural contact and exchange are likely to occur. Secondly, they occupy a position of centrality within that environment. Standing at the cultural intersections permits the broker to manipulate the terms under which interaction takes place. Cultural mediators also utilize first- and second-order societal resources. First-order resources are those directly controlled by the mediator. They can include commodities, such as trade goods or furs; specific forms of empowerment, such as the ability to enact or enforce trade regulations or the authority to grant access to tribal lands; and specialized skills or knowledge, such as facility in native and European languages and expertise in the ordinary social customs and highly conventionalized protocols required for trade and diplomacy. Contacts with other individuals, themselves often cultural brokers who have access to first-order assets, constitute second-order resources. First-order assets, when combined with an extensive network of family members, business associates, and personal friends, allowed a mediator to speak not only for Indians, but as an Indian; not only for Europeans, but as a European; not only for tribal authorities and colonial officials, but as one central to the decision-making process on both sides of the cultural line. The acquisition of first- and second-order resources accorded cultural mediators a position of great influence from which they could negotiate the price of goods, demand a desired quantity or insist on a high standard of quality for specific items, outlaw certain products or trading practices, prohibit or encourage trading activity at specified locations or throughout entire regions, and invite into or evict from their territory individual traders or groups of traders.[7]

The fur trade was the great engine of cultural transformation along the western border. Commerce in pelts supplied by Indians and trade goods exchanged by Europeans sparked the creation of the interconnected net of personal relationships, business partnerships, military alliances, and political accords that formed the institutional framework within which native and white encounters took place. Even on the Ohio Valley frontier, literally at the very edge of the British Empire, the fur trade was a powerful, sophisticated instrument of cultural and economic exchange. Embodiments of the frontier's cultural pluralism, mediators were at the center of this process.[8]

The fur trade provided an impressive array of goods destined for the western nations. In June 1766, the eastern trading firm of Baynton, Wharton, and Morgan invoiced Fort Pitt for a diverse inventory that included claret, rum, blankets, tobacco, gun flints, paint, wampum, hatchets, brass kettles, bar lead, thread, vermilion, lace, gun powder, bullet molds, hunting saddles, tin cups, jews harps, combs, knives, awls, muskets, bed lacing, shears, ribbon, pipes, looking glasses, razors, silver jewelry, needles, and articles of clothing that included ruffled shirts, plain shirts, calico shirts, leggings, matchcoats, gartering, and breechclouts. The following year, the Indian department commissary at the post reported that over twenty-six thousand pounds sterling worth of merchandise, including sixty-five hundred gallons of rum, had passed through the fort. He also calculated that over thirteen thousand gallons of rum had been distributed by unlicensed traders and that other sutlers had exchanged up to forty thousand pounds sterling worth of goods. In return, Fort Pitt had taken in 10,587 pounds of "Fall Skins," 104,016 pounds of "Summer Skins," and smaller amounts of pelts from otters, fishers, wolves, panthers, elk, and bear.[9]

At its most basic level, the fur trade permitted Indians simply to exchange traditional items of native manufacture for similar items made in Europe. Blankets, for instance, might replace pelts or woven mats; glass beads might be used instead of wampum in ceremonial belts; trade silver might substitute for jewelry made from shell or copper; kettles and pots of iron or brass would serve for those made earlier of fire-baked clay. But at a deeper, more subtle level, the acceptance and use of trade goods signaled a beginning of the process of cultural change that was at the heart of the invented frontier.[10]

European travelers within the Ohio back country often commented on the combination of native and European elements that made up Indian dress. Nicholas Cresswell, a young Englishman who dabbled in the Ohio fur trade just prior to the Revolution, visited Captain White-Eyes, a Delaware headman, at his village on the Upper Tuscarawas River in September 1775. The dress of the men at the village, noted Cresswell,

> is short, white linen or calico shirts which come a little below their hips without buttons at neck or wrists and in general ruffled and a great number of small brooches stuck in it. Silver plates about three inches broad round the wrists of their arms, silver wheels in their ears, which are stretched long enough for the tip of the ear to touch the shoulder, silver rings in their noses, Breechclouts and Mockeysons with a match-coat that serves them for a bed at night. . . . The women wear the same sort of shirts as the men. Wear their hair long, curled down the back in silver plates, if they can afford it, if not tied in a club with red gartering. No rings in the nose but plenty in the ears. Both men and women paint with Vermilion and other colours mixed with Bear's Oil and adorn themselves with any tawdry thing they think pretty.[11]

Other observers made an explicit connection between appearance and the frontier's ambiguous sense of cultural identity. In 1742, the Moravian benefactor and missionary, Count Nicholas Ludwig von Zinzendorf, met with Andrew Montour near Shamokin, Pennsylvania.

Zinzendorf had found Montour, the son of a French woman and an Oneida war chief, wearing a sky-colored coat of fine cloth and a black cordovan neckband decorated with silver bugles, a red damask lapelled waistcoat, breeches, shoes, stockings, and a hat. The Moravian claimed that although Montour's ears were "braided with brass and other wire like a handle on a basket" and he wore "an Indianish broad ring of bear fat and paint" on his face, his appearance was remarkably European, and when addressed in French, the interpreter responded cordially in English.[12]

It was not just Indians who adopted white articles of clothing. Whites quickly sought out and acquired Indian modes of dress, which they found practical and eminently suited to the frontier environment. In the spring of 1775, Cresswell traveled from Fort Pitt to Harwood's (Harrod's) Landing, an isolated settlement on the Kentucky River, and then back again. His traveling companions, whom he described as a "motley, rascally, and ragged crew," consisted of "two Englishmen, two Irishmen, one Welshman, two Dutchmen, two Virginians, two Mary-landers, one Swede, one African Negro, and a Mulatto." "I believe there is but two pair of Breeches in the company," remarked Cresswell, "one belonging to Mr. Tilling and the other to myself. The rest wear breech-clouts, leggings and hunting shirts, which have never been washed only by the rain since they were made."[13]

The party's native garb was no mere costume. Culturally, Cresswell and the men in his party were no longer completely European. Nor, despite their clothing, had they become Indian. Rather, they had se-lectively adopted elements from native culture and retained others of their own to reinvent themselves in response to the region's intercultural contact. The men's appearance reflected an emerging frontier identity in which national allegiance was blurred and ethnic affiliation diffused. Cresswell himself was aware of how his experiences along the frontier had affected his sense of self-identity. In August 1775 he employed an Indian woman to make a pair of moccasins, leggings, and other clothing that he hoped to wear on his next trip to the Ohio Country. His selection of native attire was not haphazard. Rather, it was informed by a finely honed appreciation for the frontier's evolving cultural values. Warned by another English trader that his Indian clients would be offended by a white man coming among them wearing a hunting shirt, he also ordered a calico shirt "made in the Indian fashion." When he wore his new clothes for the first time, "Trimmed with Silver Brooches and Arm-plates," he claimed, "I scarcely know myself."[14]

The inventive process of reciprocal, discretionary cultural exchange occasionally led to unexpected juxtapositions of the native and European worlds. Margaret Handley Erskine, a captive who lived with the Ohio Shawnee from 1779 until 1784, became fond of the wife of a village chief, Blue Pocket, during her time with the tribe. Erskine remembered Blue Pocket's wife, a "half French woman of Detroit," as a woman who enjoyed living in great style in a luxurious house furnished with curtained beds and silver spoons. The Indian party that captured a young Englishman, Thomas Ridout, along the Ohio River in 1787, gave their prisoner a breakfast of chocolate and flour cakes as they made their way back to their villages on the Maumee River in northwest Ohio. After reaching the Maumee, Ridout lived with an "old Chief" named Kakinathucca, his wife Metsigemewa, and an African slave. On Ridout's first day with his new family, Metsigemewa prepared breakfast by using bear's fat to fry venison in an iron skillet, boiling water in a copper kettle, and brewing tea sweetened with maple sugar in a yellow-ware teapot. When finished, she served the meal on pewter plates and in yellow cups and saucers that matched the teapot. David Jones, a Presbyterian missionary who traveled to Indian villages throughout east-central Ohio in 1772 and 1773, enjoyed a meal of fat buffalo, beaver tails, and chocolate with his Indian hosts, while Nicholas Cresswell drank tea with Captain White-Eyes and Captain Wingenund in their cabin at Kanaughtonhead (Gnadenhutten) in 1775.[15]

Native food choices reflected direct contact with Europeans through the fur trade, gift giving, military action (the chocolate that Ridout was given after his capture had been taken at the same time he was), and a selective adoption of European crops and agricultural practices. Lt. John Boyer, an officer who served with General Anthony Wayne along the Auglaize and Maumee Rivers in the summer of 1794, commented that Indian gardens within the region produced "vegetables of every kind in abundance" and that corn fields measuring "not less than one thousand acres" stretched for miles along the rich river flood plains near the Glaize, a large Indian settlement located at the confluence of the two rivers. Wayne himself was amazed at the area's highly cultivated gardens and noted that he had never "before beheld such immense fields of corn, in any part of America, from Canada to Florida." In addition to the traditional selection of corn, beans, and squash, Indian fields throughout the Ohio frontier frequently contained European crops such as turnips, cabbage, pumpkins, cucumbers, "Irish" potatoes (a Meso-American staple transported to the Old World by the Spanish during the sixteenth century, spread throughout Europe in the seventeenth century, and then introduced into Ohio by the French and English in the eighteenth century), and African foods such as watermelons and muskmelons. "Regular and thrifty" orchards adjacent to Indian homes produced a cornucopia of fruits. Moreover, some tribes also raised livestock. Oliver Spencer, a captive who lived at the Glaize until 1794, claimed that the Indians along the Maumee River kept neither cattle, hogs, nor sheep. But the Moravian missionary David Zeisberger noted that several tribal bands in eastern Ohio were raising cattle because they had become "very fond of milk and butter," while his colleague John Heckewelder recorded that Indians also owned chickens and semidomesticated pigs.[16]

In addition to agricultural practices, the process of selective cultural reinvention revealed itself in other areas of the Ohio frontier's economy. When the missionary David Jones began his journey into Ohio in 1773, he traveled well supplied with trade goods and other useful items. Jones hoped to barter with the region's Indians for provisions and other supplies as he moved deep within the Ohio back country, believing that "these Indians as yet have not the use of money." Jones, though, was badly mistaken. The evangelist learned that nearly every good or service he required during his trip could be purchased only with cash. At a small settlement north of the Hocking River, Jones bought milk for himself and corn for his horse "at a very expensive price." Later, he was forced to pay twenty-five dollars for a horse and six dollars for a guide to escort him from the Muskingum River to the Ohio, even though, as Jones later discovered, the guide "knew not the course." When he tried to retain the services of a translator for five pounds a month, the translator easily dickered the price up to seven pounds, causing Jones to comment that the region's Indians, "From the greatest to the least, seem mercenary and excessively greedy of gain." Complaining that meat could not be purchased at any price and that milk was selling at ninepence a quart and butter for two shillings a pound, Jones ended his journey "much discouraged . . . by hardships and want of provisions."[17]

Other changes within the region's economy were widely reflected throughout the Ohio Country. By the early 1770s, many of the Indian communities located along the Tuscarawas and Muskingum Rivers had adapted to a cash economy by becoming market-based centers for the exchange of goods and services. When Jones purchased milk and corn while on his journey, he did so from a Shawnee woman whom Jones described as the chief of a small, mixed band of Delaware and Shawnee families. The woman, claimed the missionary, was "esteemed very rich," and she frequently boarded travelers in a small cabin usually occupied by her African slaves. Moreover, she also kept a sizable herd of cattle in order to produce both milk and beef for sale to her guests. Likewise, in 1804, the French traveler Constantin Francois Volney reported that the Miami chief Little Turtle kept a cow and made butter at his home near Fort Wayne, but that he did not "indulge himself in these things, but reserves them for the whites."[18]

Cultural mediators, usually European men who had married Indian women and who maintained either a permanent or semipermanent residence among the western tribes, also played an active part in the region's transformed economy. Jones remarked that Richard Conner, a trader from Maryland, had established "sort of a tavern" for the convenience of travelers on the upper Muskingum. Likewise, John Irwine kept a considerable inventory of goods at Chillicothe, a Shawnee village near present-day Frankfort in south-central Ohio. Irwine sold his wares to travelers from a log building he rented from another Indian who resided in the town. Chillicothe was also the home of Moses Henry, a Lancaster trader and gunsmith who pursued both occupations for native and European clients at the village. Henry lived "in a comfortable manner, having plenty of good beef, pork, milk, &c.," claimed Jones. "His generosity to me was singular, and equal to my highest wishes."[19]

Commercial establishments such as these were common throughout the Ohio frontier. The Glaize, a community comprised of seven distinct Shawnee, Delaware, and Miami villages, was clustered around a centrally located trader's town placed at the confluence of the Maumee and Auglaize Rivers. Residents of this commercial district included Englishman George Ironside, who maintained a substantial log dwelling and warehouse at the community, and a French baker named Pirault who supplied bread to both Europeans and Indians. Other entrepreneurs included John Kinzie, a British silversmith; trader James Girty, Simon Girty's younger brother; and two Americans, Henry Ball and Polly Meadows, who had been captured after Arthur St. Clair's defeat in 1791. Meadows supported herself by taking in laundry and sewing, while Ball found employment ferrying goods and individuals to the Maumee Rapids, some forty miles downriver. The same type of commercial center, made up of French and English artisans, mechanics, and traders also existed at Kekionga, a multivillage Miami settlement located at the headwaters of the Maumee River in present-day Fort Wayne, Indiana.[20]

The process of intercultural exchange also led to an evolution in both the appearance as well as the function of Ohio frontier communities. As early as the 1750s, European travelers within the Ohio Country noted that the region's Indians lived in structures similar to European log cabins. One of the earliest descriptions of these dwellings was made by James Smith, an eighteen year old who had been captured by a group of Caughnewagas and Delawares in western Pennsylvania in 1755. During the winter of 1755–56, Smith was with a mixed band of Caughnewagas, Delawares, and Wyandots when they constructed such a building near the mouth of the Black River, west of present-day Cleveland. To construct the cabin, they

cut logs about fifteen feet long, and laid these logs upon each other, and drove posts in the ground at each end to keep them together; the posts they tied together at the top with bark, and by this means raised a wall fifteen feet long, and about four feet high, and in the same manner they raised another wall opposite to this, at about twelve feet distance; then they drove forks in the ground in the center of each end, and laid a strong pole from end to end on these forks; and from these walls to the poles, they set up poles instead of rafters, and on these they tied small poles in place of laths; and a cover was made of lynn bark, which will run [i.e., will keep out water] even in the winter season.

At the end of these walls they set up split timber, so that they had timber all around, excepting a door at each end. At the top, in place of a chimney, they left an open place, and for bedding they laid down the aforesaid kind of bark, on which they spread bear skins. From end to end of this hut along the middle there were fires, which the squaws made of dry split wood, and the holes or open places that appeared, the squaws stopped with moss, which they collected from old logs; and at the door they hung bear skin, and notwithstanding the winters are hard here, our lodging was much better than what I expected.

It may be that this type of structure represented an adaptation of the traditional native longhouse form to European construction techniques and materials.[21]

Indian-built log structures never completely replaced longhouses and bark-covered wigwams. The Moravian mission at Schoenbrunn, for example, contained about sixty log houses, as well as a substantial number of "huts and lodges." But as the century progressed, log homes became increasingly common across the frontier. By the 1770s, many native log homes had taken on a distinctively European character. David Zeisberger remarked that the Moravian Delawares who lived in eastern Ohio, "Coming much in contact with the whites, as they do not live more than a hundred miles from Pittsburgh," had learned to build "proper and comfortable" hewed log homes. In some cases they even had hired whites to come to their villages and build the structures for them. William Albert Galloway, who spent his youth during the nineteenth century with the Shawnee after their removal to Missouri, claimed that the Ohio tribes purchased axes, saws, and augers for this purpose from French and English traders throughout the frontier era.[22]

Finely made hewed log homes could be found in Indian communities across the Ohio Country. Zeisberger described Gekelemukpechunk (Newcomerstown) as "a large and flourishing town of about one hundred houses, mostly built of logs." When Rev. David McClure visited Netawatwes, a village leader who lived there in September 1772, he commented that "some of the houses are well built, with hewed logs, with stone chimnies, chambers & sellers. These I was told were built by the english captives in the time of the French wars." Although Netawatwes's home was the largest in the village, it certainly was rivaled by another, owned by the village shaman. According to McClure, a stone-lined cellar, a staircase leading to the second story, a well-built stone chimney and fireplace, closets, and a first floor divided into several smaller rooms gave the building the appearance of an English dwelling.[23]

It was not just Indian homes that resembled English buildings. Entire villages took on the appearance of European settlements. Nicholas Cresswell described Schoenbrunn as a "pretty town . . . regularly laid out in three spacious streets which meet in the center, where there is a large meeting house built of logs." Cultural transmission, though, remained selective. Many Indian villages retained the organic and, to European eyes, seemingly haphazard placement of structures traditionally seen in native communities. David Zeisberger noted that when they built their towns, the Indians rarely considered a "regular plan." David Jones echoed that observation. Commenting on the arrangement of buildings at Chillicothe, he remarked that there was no more "regularity observed in this particular than in their morals, for any man erects his house as fancy directs.[24]

Mutual transculturation was also reflected in the social customs and institutions that made up the fabric of everyday life along the Ohio frontier. In early September 1775, Cresswell was at Coshocton where he witnessed an Indian dance. According to the trader, the Indians made their music with "an old Keg with one head knocked out and covered with a skin and beat with sticks." Caught up in the excitement of the moment, Cresswell, who had been "painted by my Squaw in the most elegant manner," stripped off all of his clothing except for his shirt, breechclout, leggings and moccasins. Joining the dance, he moved around the campfire "whooping and hallooing" with the "most uncouth and antic postures imaginable." While Cresswell danced across the cultural divide, his Indian associates also used music to redefine their place within frontier society. At Newcomerstown three days after the dance, Cresswell listened while an Indian made "tolerable good music" playing an old tin violin. The following evening the trader was at Gnadenhutten. Visiting the village's chapel, Cresswell watched an Indian convert play the congregation's spinet piano during the Moravian worship service.[25]

Everyday social conventions also showed the influence of cultural reinvention. David Zeisberger noted that when Indians greeted one another, they did so by shaking hands. Charles Johnston was with a group of settlers floating down the Ohio River in 1790 when his boat was ambushed by Indians lying in wait near the shore. The attackers quickly overpowered the vessel, killing several of Johnston's companions and wounding others. The survivors were herded toward one end of the boat as the Indians boarded, killed the wounded, stripped the dead, and threw the bodies overboard. Johnston was convinced that he and the others were about to be summarily executed. To his immense surprise, the war party's leader approached Johnston, took the frightened American's right hand and forearm in both of his hands and after pumping them vigorously, exclaimed, "How-d'ye-do! How-d'ye-do!" Later, as he was being led to his captor's home in northern Ohio, Johnston commented that all the Indians they met had "caught the common salutation" and greeted each other by shaking hands and exchanging howd'ye-dos. The custom seemed to have been of recent origin. James Smith explicitly noted that in the 1750s the Indians with whom he was familiar did not use "how do you do," but relied instead on greetings in their own language that translated into exchanges such as, "You are my friend; Truly friend, I am your friend," and "Cousin, you yet exist; Certainly I do."[26]

Intercultural contact led Europeans to incorporate Indian words and phrases such as "squaw" and "succotash" into their vocabularies. Native Americans throughout the Ohio Country were equally quick to selectively adopt European expressions and figures of speech. Charles Johnston noted that while only two of the Indians in his party could speak or understand his language, virtually all of them cursed in English. Oliver Spencer remembered that when a packhorse carrying a heavy load collapsed along a trail and refused to go further, the horse's Indian owner "began in broken English to curse him, and after loading the poor animal with all the opprobrious epithets he could think of, left him lying in the path." Likewise, Col. William Christian, an officer in the Virginia Militia, reported that during the 1774 Battle of Point Pleasant, Indian warriors came close to the American lines and "damn'd our men often for Sons-of-Bitches."[27]

James Smith claimed that the Indians "never did curse or swear, until the whites learned them." Furthermore, he also stated that the Ohio Indians would frequently use European expletives without understanding their meaning. While Smith was living with the Ohio tribes, Tecaughretanego, one of his Caughnewaga companions, became angered and used the phrase "God damn it" in Smith's presence. The outburst offended Smith and when he explained that the expression meant "calling upon the great spirit to punish the object" that his friend was displeased with, his companion first became embarrassed and then confused. "He stood there for some time amazed," said Smith,

> and then said if this be the meaning of these words, what sort of people are the whites? When the traders were among us these words seemed

to be intermixed with all their discourse. . . . He said the traders applied these words not only wickedly, but often times very foolishly and contrary to sense or reason. He said, he remembered once of a trader's accidentally breaking his gun lock, and on the occasion calling out aloud God damn it—surely said he the gun lock was not an object worthy of punishment for Owaneeyo, or the Great Spirit; he also observed the traders often used this expression when they were in a good humour and not displeased with any thing. I acknowledged that the traders used this expression very often, in a most irrational, inconsistent, and impious manner, yet I still asserted that I had given the true meaning of these words. He replied, if so, the traders are as bad as Oonasahroona, or the underground inhabitants, which is the name they give the devils.[28]

Social institutions, as well as social customs, were reinvented in the wake of the region's intercultural contact. Native marriages were less permanent, though no less solemn, than white unions. According to John Heckewelder, when Indians entered into marriage it was understood by both partners that they would not live together any longer "than suits their pleasure or convenience." "The husband may put away his wife whenever he pleases," claimed the evangelist, "and the woman may in like manner abandon her husband." European men, particularly traders and merchants who resided in the Ohio Country, frequently adopted the Indian mode of marriage and took Indian wives in the Indian fashion.[29]

Other Europeans occasionally attributed the transitory nature of Indian marriages and the traders' readiness to enter into such unions to a widespread licentiousness among the Indians and a general degradation of moral standards along the frontier. David Jones, for example, claimed that Indian women "are purchased [by their husbands] by the night, week, month or winter, so that they depend on fornication for a living," and he stated that the Europeans he came into contact with at Pickaweeke, a small Shawnee village situated along the Scioto River, were chiefly "robbers," "villains," and "scoundrels" who were "guilty of theft and robbery without any apology or redress." Nicholas Cresswell likewise described the settlers living near Fort Pitt as "nothing but whores and rogues." Indians, however, and the Europeans who married them, understood the marriage pact differently.[30]

Kinship was one of the fundamental relationships of native culture. Many of the activities and social relationships that made up village life, as well as the trading partnerships and diplomatic allegiances that defined a band's place within the broader scope of native society, were predicated upon familial affiliation. Marriage permitted Indians to extend political and economic ties to the white world; strengthen their alliances with other Indians; and carefully regulate the process through which Europeans became fully accepted, integrated, and participating members of Indian society. These intercultural marriages allowed tribal bands to enforce social customs and impose standards of behavior and formalized social obligations on their new European members. Moreover, because trade acted as a means to preserve peaceful relations, both between natives and whites and between tribal bands, these marriages stabilized the broad intercultural bond between Indians and Europeans that guaranteed the supply of trade goods necessary to maintain inter- and intracultural alliances. Whites benefited from these arrangements as well. The power of the marriages to cement economic and diplomatic relationships was self-evident to Capt. Hector McLean, the British commander at Fort Malden (Amherstburg, Ontario) in 1799. According to McLean, either "marriage or concubinage" connected most of the officers attached to the British Indian Department at the post to the Ohio Valley Shawnee. Likewise, the Indian woman who accompanied Nicholas Cresswell while he traveled through Ohio in 1775 made his clothing, acted as a translator, tended his horses, prepared his camp, and undoubtedly arranged for him to meet the tribal leaders with whom he frequently dealt. Cresswell was well aware of the importance of this woman to his success. "However base it may appear to conscientious people," he noted, "it is absolutely necessary to take a temporary wife if they have to travel amongst the Indians." Even the normally judgmental missionary David McClure conceded that "the greater part of the Indian traders keep a squaw and some of them a white woman, as a temporary wife. They allege the good policy of it, as necessary to a successful trade." The transculturation of the Ohio Country, therefore, was based upon the exchange of individuals as well as goods, ideas, and customs.[31]

Alexander McKee's father, Thomas McKee, a western Pennsylvania Indian trader and sometime agent with the British Indian Department, died near his trading post along the Susquehanna River in 1769. Four years later, John Parrish, a Quaker missionary from Philadelphia, and two companions traveled through western Pennsylvania and into the Ohio Country. Their journey was, in part, a social one, an opportunity too long delayed to renew friendships and strengthen acquaintances throughout the region. On July 26, in a small settlement west of the Ohio River, Parrish had the extraordinary good fortune to run into an old and dear friend, Thomas McKee. At their meeting, McKee, after inquiring about the health of his friends, gave Parrish and his companions a "hearty welcome," invited them to accompany him, and escorted the group to his home.

Throughout the following week, Parrish and his friends were entertained with great hospitality. McKee's Indian wife lavished her attention on them, saw to their every comfort, and prepared their meals from the best provisions available at the town. By August 3, it was time to return. McKee, having business to transact in Pittsburgh, decided to accompany the Quaker and his friends to the frontier outpost. As they traveled up the Ohio River, they paused at Alexander McKee's trading post and acquired the provisions to continue their journey. The party then continued to Pittsburgh where, according to Parrish, McKee met with all of the town's "men of note."[32]

This Thomas McKee was an Indian, a Delaware who, as a token of respect for his friend Thomas McKee, had taken the trader's name and retained it after his death. James Kenny, a Pittsburgh trader, recorded the names of many such Indians, including Jimmy Wilson, John Armstrong, Sir William Johnson, William Turnum, and John Doubty, as they bartered for provisions at his establishment. European traders found Indian names notoriously difficult to pronounce, and it is likely that many Indians used European names only to facilitate their dealings with Kenny and the other merchants within the region. On one occasion, for example, Kenny noted that when a young Indian man "having no English name" came to trade, "I gave him my name, which he said he would keep." Thomas McKee's acceptance of his friend's name, though, appears to be more than a matter of mere convenience.[33]

McKee bore the outward sign of a deeper cultural reality. The Ohio frontier was a place of great cultural restlessness, a setting where personal identity reflected the impermanence of one's ethnic, national, or racial affiliation. McKee was part of a world that permitted individuals to cross racial and ethnic barriers both symbolically and literally with a considerable degree of intimacy and completeness. Indeed, it was a world that allowed certain individuals to be either Indian or European at their discretion. The eastern woodland Indians had long used the "mourning war" to retaliate against their enemies. The mourning war was fought using small-scale raids to acquire either Indian or European captives. These prisoners later would be adopted into the tribe that had captured them to replace other tribal members who had died from disease or combat. After James Smith's capture, he was bathed, dressed in Indian clothing, painted in Indian fashion, and brought before a council of village leaders. Eventually, one of the tribal elders arose and said "My son, you are now flesh of our flesh, and bone of our bone."

> By the ceremony which was performed this day, every drop of white blood was washed out of your veins; you are taken into the Caughnewaga nation, and initiated into a warlike tribe; you are adopted into a great family, and now received with great seriousness and solemnity in the room and place of a great man; after what has passed this day, you are now one of us by an old strong law and custom—My son, you have now nothing to fear, we are now under the same obligations to love, support and defend you that we are to love and to defend one another, therefore you are to consider yourself as one of our people.

Smith at first doubted the truth of what he had been told, but later commented that "from that day I never knew them to make any distinction between me and themselves in any respect whatever." This evolving, fluid sense of personal identity, shared by both Indians and Europeans, reflected the culturally complex and pragmatic nature of the Ohio frontier. Personal identity could be expediently reinvented as circumstance required. For many who lived in the Ohio back country, racial and ethnic affiliation became a temporary response to altered personal relationships, shifting political contexts, and emerging economic opportunities.[34]

Indians and Europeans alike, then, had transformed the Ohio Country and, with it, themselves. An overtly negotiated process of selective cultural exchange defined much of the encounter between Native Americans and whites along the Ohio frontier and fashioned the region into a zone of mutual reinvention. Cultural mediators were at the heart of this exchange. For much of the early frontier era, the process of transculturation permitted both parties to reconcile their differences and allowed each to engage the other peacefully and profitably and with a degree of understanding otherwise impossible.

Relations between Europeans and natives throughout the Ohio hinterlands were always complex, comprised of an interwoven net of competing and often contradictory interests. Intercultural contact also fostered cultural continuity as well as cultural change. Native Americans and Europeans alike were keenly aware of their own self-interests, and much of the cultural change seen along the Ohio frontier can be viewed as concessions inconsequential to a central core of traditional cultural values. The fur trade had engendered a process of cultural encounter that encouraged mutual cultural change and ethnic diffusion, but the quest for land created a second process of encounter, one that demanded mutual cultural stability and sharply drawn ethnic distinctions and required cultural resistance instead of accommodation.[35]

The colonial era was a period of intermittent warfare throughout the Ohio Country as France, England, and the United States, each in its turn, sought to wrest control of the region from its indigenous population and extract the wealth promised by vast reserves of land and resources. To a considerable degree, this conflict was part of a larger contest fought between the European powers and not a struggle explicitly waged between Indians and whites. Nonetheless, it was the Ohio Country's native peoples who bore a disproportionate share of the violence unleashed by these wars. A Delaware friend of John Heckewelder told him that the English and the Americans were like a pair of scissors. Scissors were constructed of two knives that when brought together appeared as if they should destroy each other, but in reality damaged only that which was caught between them. "It is not each other that they want to destroy, but us, poor Indians, that are between them," claimed Heckewelder's friend. "By this means they get our land, and when that is obtained, the scissors are closed again, and laid by for further use." Native Americans along the Ohio frontier responded to the conflict in a variety of ways, sometimes allying themselves with one or another of the belligerents as they did during the Seven Years War and the War of 1812; sometimes seeking neutrality as many of the Ohio nations did during the opening years of the American Revolution; sometimes acting as surrogates for one of the combatants as in the 1790s Indian Wars; and by occasionally forming an exclusively native military response to European encroachment as was done during Pontiac's Rebellion and Dunmore's War. Yet despite the outward diversity reflected both in these responses and in the conflicts that prompted them, each was based upon an assertion of political sovereignty, territorial self-determination, and cultural autonomy expressed along clearly defined racial lines. The contest for suzerainty over the Ohio Country frontier was marked by unambiguous ethnic loyalty. From the outset of the Seven Years War to the end of the War of 1812, Native Americans throughout the lower Great Lakes region waged a protracted, rancorous, and often violent resistance against European and Euro-American intrusions into their homeland. Cultural mediators also stood at the center of this process.[36]

Through their familiarity with both Indian and white decision makers, their facility in language, and their knowledge of the ceremonies that accompanied diplomatic transactions, cultural brokers fashioned the political understandings that shaped the course of diplomatic and military affairs within the region. Cultural mediators served as translators at negotiations between Indians and whites, and they saw that the proceedings conformed to the almost liturgical rituals of diplomatic discourse. Brokers facilitated formal negotiations and arranged for informal discussions away from the council fire. And by exploiting their personal relationships to colonial and tribal authorities, mediators occasionally could bring a measure of integrity and trust to meetings that frequently were marked by overt self-interest and mutual suspicion.[37]

Cultural mediators also served as participants in the military contests that raged across the frontier. Mediators arranged for logistical support, evaluated intelligence, defined objectives, and instructed their allies in tactics. All of the European powers selectively employed the irregular tactics used by native warriors, and France, England, and the United States fielded ranger units throughout the colonial era. Native forces also borrowed from European tactics and occasionally fought using the formal, linear methods usually used on the continent. In the summer of 1780, George Rogers Clark and Benjamin Logan led a force of Virginia regulars and Kentucky backwoodsmen against Piqua and Chillicothe, two Shawnee villages located along the upper Great Miami River in west-central Ohio. The Shawnees had learned of the Americans' advance and had abandoned and burned Chillicothe before Clark's arrival, electing to engage the invaders at Piqua, a few miles away. As the

American army entered the second village, they found the Shawnees defending a well-engineered fortified blockhouse protected by a log stockade and earthen defensive works. As Clark pressed the offensive, the defenders "opened the only gate of the fort . . . & marched out & took position on the flat below, & formed into a single line." The Shawnees continued to keep the attackers at bay with well-timed volleys until Clark deployed his artillery, forcing the Indians to withdraw. Cultural mediators also accompanied raiding parties; they participated in combat and interceded on the behalf of prisoners, seeing to their safety and often arranging for their subsequent release. When the Englishman Thomas Ridout was captured by a Shawnee war party, a white man "about twenty-two years of age, who had been taken prisoner when a lad and had been adopted, and was now a chief among the Shawanese," approached Ridout immediately after his capture. The otherwise un-identified mediator "stood up and said to me in English, 'Don't be afraid, sir, you are in no danger, but are given to a good man, a chief of the Shawanese, who will not hurt you; but after some time will take you to Detroit, where you may ransom yourself. Come and take your breakfast.'" Later, both Simon Girty and Alexander McKee helped British officials at Fort Lernoult secure Ridout's release.[38]

Through their skill in facilitating intercultural contact, cultural mediators were indispensable in establishing and maintaining the delicate linkages between Europeans and Indians on the Great Lakes frontier. Reflecting as well as manipulating the cultural ambiguity of the region, McKee and others like him shaped the course of Anglo-Indian relations throughout the colonial era. Like his contemporaries, Alexander McKee was intimately connected to the cultural and political fluidity of the region and was adept at transforming his personal sense of cultural diversity into a shared perspective of common cause between the British Empire and the nations of the Old Northwest. Within the Ohio Country, persons like McKee found both place and purpose as cultural mediators.[39]

What distinguished McKee from his fellow mediators was his unique sense of place and his distinct articulation of purpose. More than any of his fellow brokers, McKee coupled his sense of place within the lower Great Lakes Region with a wider appreciation of the frontier's place within the British realm. Neither Simon Girty nor Matthew Elliott, the two Indian department colleagues whose careers most closely paralleled his own, took much interest in the world beyond the Ohio Country, and both conducted their dealings with the Great Lakes tribes with indifference to events that transpired beyond their immediate experience. Only McKee's vision of the Great Lakes frontier transcended the Ohio Country and placed the region within the broader reaches of the British Empire. Girty and Elliott mediated local interests where they intersected with those of the Crown. McKee mediated imperial interests where they meshed with those of the Ohio Country. McKee's activities were determined also by personal allegiance to the British Crown, genuine sympathy for the Ohio Country Indians, and a keen appreciation for how his relationship with both parties influenced his economic standing. His close relations with crown and tribal officials brought him opportunities to direct and manipulate the course of cultural contact for both his own benefit and that of his clients. Cultural centrality, informed by loyalty to the Crown, shaped by an intimate understanding of the western nations, and filtered through the lens of self-interest, defined his career and made him one of the most powerful figures to bridge the Indian/white cultural divide along the Ohio frontier.[40]

CHAPTER TWO

From the Susquehanna to the Ohio, 1735–1763

When he was a young man, Alexander McKee was a fully participating and fully accepted member of Ohio Country Indian society. The central-Ohio Shawnees regarded him completely as one of their own. He spoke their language, followed their customs, and observed their rituals. They were his family. In peace they were business partners; in war they were allies. He looked after their well-being and they his. At his death in 1799, McKee was a fully participating and fully accepted member of Upper Canada's landed gentry. The governing aristocracy regarded him completely as one of their own. He spoke their language, followed their customs, and observed their rituals. They were his family. In peace they were business partners; in war they were allies. He looked after their well-being and they his. This slow transformation in character, this gradual evolution in self-perception, is the key to understanding his actions throughout his career along the Ohio frontier.

McKee was born about 1735 in the Pennsylvania backwoods of the Susquehanna Valley. His father, Thomas McKee (born c. 1695), was the first of three generations of McKees active in imperial Indian affairs along the northern frontier. Thomas arrived in America with his father, Alexander (died 1740), from County Antrim, Ireland, after 1707. Alexander, a veteran of the Battle of the Boyne, began to farm along the Pennsylvania frontier in Lancaster County soon after he arrived.

Thomas established himself in the western Indian trade while in his thirties or early forties. Licensed as a trader by Pennsylvania in 1744 and 1747, he already had erected a post along the Susquehanna River near present-day Dalmatia, in 1740. By 1742 he had established a second site, McKee's Post, near present-day Dauphin and was trading at Big Island, at the mouth of the Juniata River, on the south branch of the Susquehanna.[1]

In 1747 and 1748, McKee organized a small company of rangers to protect the western region of Lancaster County during King George's War. In 1755, after the outbreak of the French and Indian War, he raised a second company of volunteers and commanded a small garrison, McKee's Fort, at Hunters Mill. Beginning with the commencement of hostilities, McKee's career became increasingly entwined with that of George Croghan, one of western Pennsylvania's most flamboyant land speculators and fur traders. Throughout the ensuing years, Croghan enlisted McKee's help in a variety of business and diplomatic enterprises in which McKee's long experience in the Indian trade proved useful. Following his career with Croghan, in 1763 McKee accepted an appointment to the post of Justice of the Peace and presided over cases held in Northampton, Berks, and Lancaster Counties. He died at his home at McKee's Falls in 1769.[2]

Less is known of Alexander's mother. It is certain that Thomas married a woman who lived with a mixed band of Shawnees, Delawares, and Iroquois on the Susquehanna River, near present-day Lock Haven. In January 1743, McKee attended a council at the village, located opposite his storehouse on Big Island. He had traded with this band for some time and considered the village headman, Johnny Shikellamy, a personal friend. Although when he arrived, McKee greeted the Indians with the customary courtesies, their reception of him was noticeably cool. As the council began, the leader of a returning Iroquois war party related that while he and his band traveled through Virginia they had been ambushed by a group of whites. Four of the Indians had died in the attack. The action greatly disturbed the Shawnees and several at the meeting suggested the deaths might be avenged by striking at whites living along the Pennsylvania frontier. McKee, who was fluent in several Indian languages and who understood the proceedings, became justifiably alarmed. Acting through "an Old Shawna, with whom he was best acquainted," he managed to discourage the band from taking

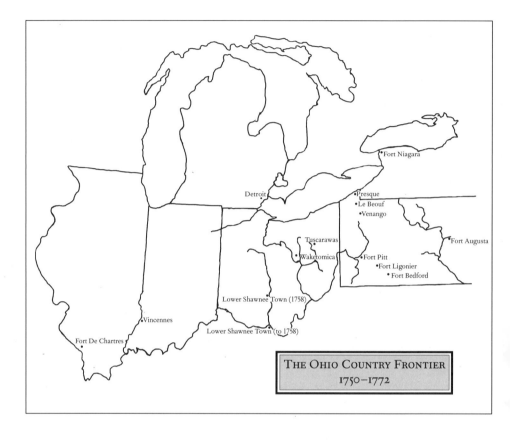

Detroit

Fort Niagara

Presque
Le Beouf
Venango

Tuscarawas

Waketomica

Fort Pitt
Fort Ligonier
Fort Bedford

Fort Augusta

Lower Shawnee Town (1758)

Vincennes

Lower Shawnee Town (to 1758)

Fort De Chartres

THE OHIO COUNTRY FRONTIER
1750–1772

part in any retaliatory raids, but several of the Shawnees remained
noticeably upset. Later that evening, a white woman who had been captured as an infant in North Carolina and later adopted by the tribe approached McKee with a warning. Some of the warriors, she claimed,
planned to kill the trader as he left the village the following day. Leaving
his goods behind, McKee and the woman escaped that evening, traveling three days and three nights to avoid capture. Later, this woman became his wife. One source incorrectly identifies the woman as the sister
of Tanacharison, the Iroquois Half King. A second tradition passed
down through the McKee family during the last quarter of the nineteenth century claims that the woman was Tecumapease, an older sister
of Tecumseh's. An affidavit filed with the deputy register of Lancaster
County after Thomas's death lists her simply as Mary McKee.[3]

Mary McKee had become completely assimilated into the Shawnee culture during her captivity. Five years after she and Thomas escaped, the Moravian missionary J. C. F. Cammerhoff, who traveled along the Pennsylvania frontier stopped at McKee's home on January 13, 1748. Cammerhoff noted that the McKees "received us with much kindness and hospitality." "McKee is an extensive Indian trader," wrote the evangelist, observing that he "bears a good name among them, and drives a brisk trade with the Allegheny Country. His wife, who was brought up among the Indians, speaks but little English." Even as late as 1756, Canaghquiesa, an Oneida chief, referred to Mary simply as McKee's "Shawanese squaw."[4]

Mary McKee is the woman who raised Alexander as her son, beginning when he was an adolescent. It is less certain whether Mary McKee was Alexander's biological mother. After Thomas's death in 1769, Alexander filed petitions in December 1769 and August 1773 with the Lancaster County Orphans Court in which he declared that he was the eldest of his father's six children and that Thomas had died without a will. As a consequence, Alexander became the executor of Thomas's estate. In 1778, Alexander openly aligned himself with the British cause during the American Revolution and escaped from Pittsburgh to British-controlled Detroit. After his defection, Patriot authorities charged him with treason, and the state government eventually confiscated his property throughout Pennsylvania. In May 1779, Alexander's younger brother, James, informed the authorities in Lancaster that at least some of Alexander's lands had been seized improperly. James claimed that his mother and father were not married at the time of Alexander's birth. As a result, James argued that he, and not Alexander, should have inherited the property in question, and therefore it should not have been taken by the state. In December 1780, the Supreme Court of Pennsylvania decided the case in James's favor and awarded him possession of Thomas's plantation in Paxton Township, Lancaster County. Because James's claim to the family property based on Alexander's illegitimacy was not only asserted, but also successfully argued before the state's Supreme Court, it seems likely that the allegation was a truthful, albeit convenient, method of circumventing the forfeiture based on the charge of treason. James's testimony, while admittedly in his own self-interest, suggests that either Alexander was born to Thomas and Mary before their marriage was formalized, or he was the offspring of a passing relationship between Thomas and an unnamed Indian woman.[5]

Like the circumstances of his birth, little is known of Alexander's early years. It is possible that in the life of his father and grandfather he discerned a family tradition of loyalty to the Crown and a willingness to articulate that loyalty through service in the institutions of the realm, such as the military and the courts. Perhaps, too, from his father he learned to bargain tough, to depend on his wits, and to use any means at his disposal to extract advantage from whatever circumstance fate brought his way. One disillusioned business partner described the traders working in western Pennsylvania as a "sett of the most debased banditti that ever infested a government." That Alexander also received an education superior to that of many of his contemporaries is suggested by the legible script, standard spelling, and cogent composition of his later correspondence. But beyond this, the record is silent. The specifics of his youth, though, are perhaps less important than the general influences that shaped the world in which he was raised.[6]

The Pennsylvania frontier, like the Great Lakes frontier that it anticipated, was a close-knit community composed of an intricate network of individuals linked by family and trade. The frontier of Alexander McKee's youth was defined by an intimate web of such relationships, comprised of persons who easily traversed the boundaries imposed by race, nationality, and culture. Peter Chartier was part of this world. The son of a French-Canadian trader and a Shawnee woman, Chartier was raised among the Shawnee, eventually married within the tribe, and traded extensively among the Indian bands that lived in Lancaster County. Chartier's contemporary, French Margaret, descended from French-Canadian stock, married into the Mohawk nation and exercised great personal influence within that nation throughout her life. During the French and Indian War she concealed English prisoners from the French and aided their escape. Madame Montour, another resident of the western Pennsylvania border, was also a French-Canadian captured as a youth and raised among the Iroquois. She acted as an interpreter at conferences between the Iroquois and the governor of New York and used her considerable prestige among her tribe to define diplomatic and military responses to both European and native initiatives.

Madame Montour's son, Andrew, played an equally central role in native-European relations. He served as an interpreter, accompanied Conrad Weiser and George Croghan on trade and diplomatic missions to western Pennsylvania and the Ohio Country, helped defend Fort Necessity under George Washington's command in 1754, and led Indians who fought for the Crown during the French and Indian War and Pontiac's Rebellion. Individuals like Chartier, French Margaret, and the Montours were common in the world in which Alexander McKee was brought up, a world in which cultural lines were indistinct, national allegiances diffuse, and racial affiliations fluid. The western Pennsylvania frontier provided ample role models and opportunities for those like McKee, perceptive enough to realize the possibilities inherent in such an environment and nimble enough to negotiate the region's social and cultural complexities.[7]

Like his father, Alexander McKee enlisted in the military at the outbreak of the French and Indian War. In August 1756, after serving briefly as a volunteer with the local militia at his father's store at Dauphin, he was appointed ensign in Capt. Elisha Saltar's company of the Augusta Regiment, the Third Battalion of the Provincial Militia. The regiment, commanded by Maj. (later Col.) James Burd, a Scottish-born resident of Philadelphia, spent much of 1756 constructing Fort Augusta, near Thomas McKee's trading post on the upper Susquehanna. The French held Fort Duquesne, located at the Forks of the Ohio River (the site of present-day Pittsburgh), at the beginning of the war. Two British expeditions, one under George Washington in 1754, the second under Edward Braddock in 1755, failed to bring the outpost under Crown control. A third attempt was begun in 1757 by troops commanded by John Forbes. Rather than attack the French fortification from the south, as had Washington and Braddock, Forbes cut a road nearly due west, running from Chambersburg, through Raystown (Bedford), Loyal Hanna (Ligonier), and on to the Ohio River. Burd's regiment joined the Forbes campaign in the spring of 1758 and helped construct the roadway, build fortifications, and stockpile rations and supplies. McKee also served as a scout for the expedition as it moved slowly westward.[8]

In September 1758, frustrated by his lack of progress, Forbes's subordinate, Henry Bouquet, permitted Maj. James Grant of the Seventy-

Seventh Regiment of Highlanders to lead a reconnaissance in force against the enemy stronghold. Grant, with over eight hundred men, including McKee, advanced against Duquesne on September 14. Bouquet had ordered Grant to approach the French post silently, after dark, and reconnoiter the enemy position. If he saw Indians or French soldiers outside the fort, and if they appeared to be vulnerable, he was to attack them with bayonet after midnight. But if Grant was discovered, he was to "think only of retreating." Grant approached Fort Duquesne and spent the night as ordered, quietly taking the measure of the enemy fortress. Believing that the post was only lightly defended, he disregarded his orders. At daybreak he posted his troops in an ambush and sent two hundred Highlanders, with drums beating and pipes playing, straight at the enemy gates. More than eight hundred French troops and native allies responded to the alarm in a ferocious counterattack that cut through the English lines. French resistance quickly put the English party to flight after inflicting approximately three hundred casualties. McKee was one of the wounded, and although no record of his actions during the engagement survive, one participant, Daniel Clark, claimed that "the Pennsylvanians ran at the first fire." Despite the setback, Forbes eventually captured the French post, which he renamed Fort Pitt, the following November. Following the capture, McKee's regiment spent the remainder of its enlistment guarding communications between Carlisle and the forks.[9]

The period following McKee's military service was marked by gradual transition. The war had brought him into contact with people and events whose influence reached far beyond the Pennsylvania backwoods. For the next eighteen years, although he remained a resident of the Pennsylvania frontier, McKee was slowly drawn into the world of those whose prestige and power extended eastward across the continent and into the courts of Europe. Surprisingly, his entrance into the world of international affairs was accompanied not by the polished demeanor and refined manners of the British officer corps, but by the thick brogue and easy conviviality of George Croghan.

Hostilities had virtually ruined the substantial fur trading enterprise built by Croghan along the western Pennsylvania border in the late 1740s and early 1750s. Deeply in debt and threatened with arrest by his creditors, the Irish trader returned east in 1756, offering his services to Sir William Johnson, the superintendent of Indian affairs for the northern colonies. Johnson was quick to appreciate Croghan's considerable talents in dealing with the Indians and named him to the post of deputy agent in June. Before the end of 1758, Croghan was once more on the Pennsylvania border, accompanying Forbes's expedition to the Forks of the Ohio. In 1759, he was living at Fort Pitt and acting under the direct orders of the ailing commander's second in command, the Swiss mercenary Henry Bouquet.[10]

Bouquet instructed Croghan to help the Crown bring the Great Lakes tribes under British influence by reestablishing and then extending the fur trade into the region. An exclusive British trade would serve to open diplomatic channels with the western nations; increase native dependence on British goods and, thus, the British alliance; diminish the influence of French traders who still intrigued throughout the area; and solidify British claims to the western country asserted in the wake of Forbes's victory at the forks. In January 1759, Bouquet called McKee to Fort Pitt and requested that he remain with the army and serve as an interpreter. McKee claimed he was unwilling to submit "to the drudgery of it," and he declined the invitation.[11]

Free of his military obligation, Alexander turned to his father to help him find employment. Thomas McKee had become one of Croghan's assistants in 1755. Undoubtedly with Thomas's approval, and probably with his encouragement, Alexander joined with the glib Irishman in early 1759. In April, he and Croghan escorted twenty-eight horses laden with Indian goods and military supplies bound from Carlisle to Fort Pitt. They and their cargo arrived safely at the British garrison on June 18. Croghan immediately sent an invitation to the area tribes, asking them to come to a conference at the fort for the purpose of acknowledging the peace, receiving their gifts, and learning of British intentions in the region. The meeting, held the following month, did not totally allay native concerns, but it did establish the British presence in the region and affirmed Croghan's importance to British plans for the area.[12]

The meeting was the first of many that McKee would attend, either as Croghan's assistant or as an official representative of the Crown. From April 6 through 12, 1760, McKee was present at a second conference at the post. The meeting, between Croghan and a large band of Shawnees, Delawares, and Miamis from the Ohio Country, plus

Mohawks and other Iroquois from the east, confirmed the allegiance of the previously hostile tribes. Further, the Indians requested that Croghan allow British traders to travel to the Ohio Country villages to conduct business there. The conference ended with a generous distribution of rum and Croghan's promise to "take fast hold of the Chain of friendship with both my Hands." McKee's participation during the meeting was limited, as befited one who, although raised among and familiar with the Great Lakes tribes, was new to the rarified and formal atmosphere of diplomatic discourse.[13]

British military efforts had met with further success following the fall of Fort Duquesne. Fort Niagara had surrendered in July 1759 and Fort Carillon the following month. In September, Quebec capitulated after a long siege. By May 1760, the French had given up efforts to retake the town, and by early summer British commander in chief Maj. Gen. Jeffrey Amherst was threatening Montreal. Faced with the prospect of military defeat, Pierre Reguad de Vaudreuil, the governor general of New France, surrendered Canada to Great Britain on September 7, 1760. Soon after the cessation of hostilities, Amherst ordered Maj. Robert Rogers, who had won widespread fame during the war for his exploits as a frontier ranger, to lead a detachment of men from Fort Pitt to Detroit and secure the city for the British. Rogers was to collect any arms that remained in the town, administer the oath of allegiance to the city's populace, establish trading relations with the Indians who lived in the vicinity, and escort French officers back to Fort Pitt where they would be questioned and paroled. Both McKee and Croghan accompanied Rogers on the mission.[14]

Leaving Pittsburgh on October 10, Rogers and his men slowly rowed along the southern shore of Lake Erie, occasionally encountering bands of Indians with whom they exchanged gifts and informed of the impending peace. Throughout the journey, Croghan and McKee were ordered to stay close to Rogers and inform him of any intelligence they might glean during these meetings. Arriving at Detroit on November 11, 1760, Rogers stopped at a grassy glade a short distance from the French post, formed his command, and marched the final half mile to his destination. There, he accepted the French surrender and hoisted the British colors. About seven hundred Indians who witnessed the brief ceremony "gave a shout," an action, that, according to Rogers, "expressed their satisfaction at our generosity in not putting them to death." By early December, the detachment had disarmed the local militia and had heard their oath of loyalty to the British Crown. Rogers also successfully established trade relations with the local Indians. Linking the Detroit area nations to the British through trade was an important step in securing the town for the Crown. Rogers and the British command feared French machinations among the western tribes. Rogers had learned that the French were meeting with the southern Cherokees in an attempt to undermine the British victory. By establishing trade relationships with these tribes, Rogers hoped to diminish French influence while drawing the Indians deeper into the British sphere of influence. On December 7, Rogers urged Bouquet to encourage Pittsburgh traders to come to the Detroit region as quickly as possible. The traders, claimed Rogers, "Will be the very way to Prevent them Indians in that fort from Joining the Cherokees the French had already called."[15]

McKee's role during Rogers's negotiations with the Detroit tribes was limited. It is certain that he and Croghan served as liaisons between the British officer and Pittsburgh trading interests. McKee undoubtedly served as a translator during the proceedings as well. His skill in Indian languages was well known throughout the western theater by this time, and even Bouquet acknowledged that there are "only a few of those [Indians] on the Lakes whose Linguage Mr. McKee does not understand."[16]

On December 7, Rogers sent McKee to retrieve several French officers and soldiers who were being held at the Lower Shawnee Town, located at the Pickaway Plains near present-day Circleville, Ohio, sixty miles north of the confluence of the Ohio and Scioto Rivers. The Lower Shawnee Town was one of the largest Indian villages in Ohio, a regional center for the fur trade, and the principal home to the Ohio Shawnee. Originally, the village had been located at the confluence of the Ohio and Scioto Rivers. When Christopher Gist, an agent for the Ohio Company and one of the area's first English explorers, visited the site in 1750–51 he described a village of about 300 men [1,200 persons] and 140 houses clustered on both banks of the Ohio, surrounding "a Kind of State-House of about 90 Feet long, with a light Cover of Bark in which they hold their Councils." In the spring of 1758, the Ohio River flooded to nearly fifty feet above its normal depth, destroying much of the town. Soon after, the Shawnees relocated to the Pickaway Plains. Croghan claimed that the village had been England's firm ally during King George's War, but during the present conflict the Indians who lived there had become Britain's inveterate enemies.[17]

McKee traveled to the village with Pierre Antoine, Chevalier de Hertal, the commander of the French garrison at Detroit. McKee was to acquire the prisoners, acquaint the Shawnees with the French surrender, and give the "Oath of Fidelitie" to any French traders he might meet along the way. Hertel and the other French soldiers were then to be delivered to Crown authorities at Fort Pitt. Although Hertel became ill along the way and twelve of the eighteen French prisoners either deserted or were too sick to make the journey, McKee, the French commander, and six French soldiers arrived safely in Fort Pitt on February 12, 1761.

After his return, McKee continued to aid Croghan in his bid to reestablish the Crown in the fur trade and, with it, his own fortunes. In 1760, English traders, most of whom operated from Pittsburgh but who spent much of their time living with the Indian nations, were permitted to enter the Ohio Country. Croghan enlarged his staff and apparently acquired a financial interest in the stores of several other Pittsburgh traders. By February 1761, Croghan had employed four assistants, one gunsmith and assistant, one blacksmith, one doctor, and two interpreters. Yet the end of hostilities brought obstacles as well as opportunities to the Irish trader. In the spring of 1761, Amherst, alarmed at the continuing expenses associated with the Indian Department, ordered Croghan to reduce his costs and cut his staff. Accordingly, Croghan dismissed all of his assistants except McKee.[18]

Despite the reductions, Croghan refused to be deterred from his single-minded quest for profits. At Fort Pitt he became an outspoken opponent of the illicit traffic in liquor. But many suspected his motives were not altruistic. John Langdale, a Quaker and a competitor, claimed that as official regulations dried up the rum trade elsewhere in town, the restrictions were openly flouted at William Trent and Andrew Levy's establishment. Langdale suspected that Croghan and McKee had "assumed the direction" of the store and were not only giving the Indians rum (Langdale had seen several kegs carried into the trading post), but were also paying for their furs with generous amounts of powder and lead, two commodities supposedly tightly controlled by official regulations. Langdale complained that while he and the other traders labored under a "scrupleous exactness" of the town's general orders, Croghan had "made an Engine . . . whereby to draw all ye trade to one Store."[19]

As Croghan attempted to recoup his loses, ominous signs of a pervasive discontent among the western tribes began to filter back to the Irish agent. Natives who lived along the western frontier had watched with growing anger when, at the end of hostilities, British troops had not withdrawn from the area. Indeed, at posts such as Detroit, Niagara, and Fort Pitt, the English garrisons had been strengthened and had become deeply entrenched. Making matters worse, Amherst's Indian policy, designed to bring economy to the imperial administration of western Indian affairs, served instead to infuriate the western nations. Amherst banned the giving of presents to the tribes and placed severe restrictions on the distribution of gun powder and lead. Quickly, Indians throughout the Great Lakes frontier understood that they were to be denied the traditional tokens of friendship dictated by custom among allies, cut off from the crucial provisions they and their families needed to survive the winter, and treated as conquered subjects throughout the land that they considered their own. As early as July 1761, Croghan had learned of a Seneca plot to unite the western tribes against the British. The scheme, once exposed, evaporated. Yet throughout the remainder of the year and into the following one, disturbing reports continued to trickle in from the west, hinting at native unrest.[20]

A worried Sir William Johnson instituted a fundamental shift in imperial policy toward the western tribes. During the war, British agents had labored to create a sustained native alliance that could be used against the French. Now, that very alliance seemed beyond imperial control and was actively plotting against the Crown. Johnson ordered that the Indian department direct its resources toward creating and nurturing conflict among the Great Lakes Indians, thereby preventing establishment of a coherent union.[21]

On September 28, 1762, an "Indian of Good Character amongst all the Western Nations" visited McKee at his home in Pittsburgh. He warned of a large, secret conference held by the chiefs and principal warriors of the Wyandots, Chippewas (Ojibwas), Ottawas, and Potawatomis near Detroit. "This Man says I may depend on it that they were Meditating something against us," reported McKee. "I asked him several questions, but he flatly refused telling me any further." Two days later "three Men of the Six Nations whom I have ever found to be friends to the British Interest" confirmed the intelligence and claimed that French officers along the Wabash River were supplying the western tribes with powder and ball and encouraging them to attack the English.[22]

The reports were two among many that had grown so threatening and so frequent that by early October, Croghan decided to send McKee to live among his relatives at the Upper and Lower Shawnee Towns to gather intelligence. "The French," claimed Croghan, had been "endeavoring to Poison the minds of several of the Western Nations of Indians in Prejudice to His Majesty's Subjects," and they were attempting to "Stir up all these Nations to Murder." McKee was to travel to the Shawnee villages, request the return of several white prisoners promised the previous year, and determine what the Indians knew of the council that, supposedly, had been held near Detroit. "From your General acquaintance with this Nation," wrote Croghan in his instructions to McKee, "I make no doubt if they are Acquainted with the plan (if any) you will be able to find out the Secret."[23]

Croghan's instructions to McKee were noteworthy for their explicitness about the speeches McKee was to deliver and the diplomatic protocols he was to follow. McKee's speeches were carefully scripted, and Croghan also told his assistant to follow each oration with an exchange of "strings" and "belts." These strings and belts were made of wampum, woven strands of colored beads. Wampum had many uses in native diplomacy. The color, pattern, and size of the strands served as general indications of the purpose of the proceedings in which they were used and signaled that the meeting was formal in nature and required careful deliberation and a formal reply. Strings were regarded as less important than belts, and large belts were understood to be more important than small ones. By accepting a string or belt, the listener acknowledged the acceptance of a message, while the refusal to accept a strand might indicate the rejection of a specific proposal. Belts could be refused, dropped, or even thrown back at the presenter, each indicating the degree of displeasure felt by the listener. McKee also would have been expected to be familiar with and perform the numerous ritualistic amenities that accompanied diplomatic exchanges. These meetings typically began with an exchange of gifts; the metaphorical wiping of tears from the eyes of both parties so that neither was blinded by passion; the unplugging of the ears so that both parties might hear the undistorted words of the other; and the cleansing of the throat so that each might speak honestly and openly. If a death had recently occurred, the bereaved might be comforted by figuratively "covering the bones of the dead" with goods. These and other similar ceremonies of purification and reconciliation formed the actual and symbolic arena in which diplomacy took place. Croghan's obvious concern that McKee master these intricacies was a reflection of the mission's importance and not a comment about McKee's readiness. The expedition shows McKee's growing maturity and capability within the Indian department, a willingness on Croghan's part to trust his assistant on assignments of increased responsibility, and McKee's continuing education in the formalized structure of diplomacy.[24]

Leaving Pittsburgh on October 12, accompanied by Frederick Post, a Moravian missionary, McKee stopped first at Tuscarawas, a Delaware town along the Tuscarawas River, and then at Waketomica, a Shawnee village along the upper Muskingum, before he arrived at the Lower Shawnee Town on October 27. While en route, McKee encountered a second Moravian missionary, John Heckewelder, who was returning from a journey to the tribes in the Muskingum Valley. Heckewelder reported widespread violence directed against white traders in the Ohio region. Of the nine traders who were living along the Muskinghum and Cuyahoga Rivers, seven had been killed and the remainder forced to flee for their lives. Furthermore, Indians had also killed sixteen members of an eighteen-man trading expedition to Sandusky. Despite Heckewelder's "earnest remonstrances," McKee and Post continued onward to their destination. McKee's lack of caution astounded Heckewelder, who considered McKee both foolhardy and "totally ignorant of the real state of affairs." According to the missionary, McKee did not understand the grave danger that he and Post were in until after he arrived at the Lower Town.[25]

McKee's reception at the village was cordial. When he was given an opportunity to address the band, McKee requested the return of the prisoners still held by the tribe. The village leaders responded by claiming that many of the captives were ill and that some were temporarily away from the settlement, but all that wished to return would be brought to Pittsburgh in the spring. Publicly, McKee accepted this answer, but privately he wrote Croghan claiming that the Shawnees were reluctant to deliver their prisoners because they believed that after they had done so, the English would be free to attack them.[26]

On November 1, fifteen Miami Indians arrived in camp and held a private council with the Shawnees. The following day, three of the visitors told McKee that the rumors of a secret meeting held in Detroit to plot the overthrow of the British were true. The Senecas and the Delawares had agreed to strike at the English and had secretly sent a "large belt with a Bloody Hatchet" across the Great Lakes region to solicit the support of the outlying tribes. The Shawnees had given the Miamis the belt with the instruction to keep its existence an absolute secret. Because the tribe still regarded the English as their friends, they had come to the Lower Shawnee Town to return the belt. Further, they claimed that no tribe except the Shawnee was willing to join in the plan.[27]

Shortly after he obtained this information, McKee returned home, arriving in Pittsburgh on November 31. The temporary failure of the Senecas, Shawnees, and Delawares to broaden their alliance did little to calm colonial officials within the town. Bouquet was somewhat relieved, claiming that "the distant Nations having refused to join in that Scheme; The whole will vanish into Smoke & will only Serve as a Warning for us to be very vigilant." Croghan, though, remained disturbed. The western agent was convinced that open hostilities, even if postponed for the moment, were inevitable. Angrily, he placed the blame for the present situation squarely on Amherst and his restrictive policies. Complaining bitterly to Bouquet, Croghan wrote that the general's frugality was the direct cause of the Indian's present "Poverty and Messerray." The result was widespread native resentment against the British. "I have Made use of all the arguments I was Master of & used all the Influence I had to perswade them that thire Jelouses & Suspisions of us are Rong," he claimed, but the time was drawing near, he felt, when nothing would prevent a general Indian uprising. Desperately hoping to prevent open warfare, Croghan immediately sent McKee back to Ohio to winter with the Shawnees.[28]

Traveling with Thomas Smallman, another Pittsburgh trader who was escorting a shipment of goods to the Shawnee village, McKee arrived at the Lower Town on January 24, 1763. Many of the men in the village were away hunting and did not return until February 10; on February 11, McKee asked to speak to the village leaders in council and reminded them of their promise to deliver their English captives in the spring. The Shawnees again pledged that they would lose no time in collecting the prisoners and in determining when and where the exchange would take place.[29]

On February 26, McKee received a letter from Croghan telling him of the February 10 Treaty of Paris that officially ended hostilities between France and England. Under the agreement, France ceded Canada to Great Britain. Croghan instructed McKee to acquaint the Shawnees with the treaty and its provisions. The Indians were stunned, then outraged at the news. The following day, four village leaders demanded to know by what right the French had given the English Indian land. McKee could only answer that England claimed only the parts of the continent occupied by France during the war and taken by military measures. McKee's feeble answer satisfied no one among the Indians, and they bluntly told him that the "English would soon be too great a People in this Country." Curtly, the Shawnees informed McKee that the tribe would be unable to carry out the planned prisoner exchange until after a tribal delegation had traveled to Pittsburgh to find out the terms of the treaty for themselves. On March 10, McKee started for Fort Pitt, arriving on April 2. He had been able to persuade the Shawnees to relinquish eight prisoners, though two of them had left McKee and returned to the Shawnee village after only one night. Yet despite this small gesture of good will on the part of the Indians, few on the frontier expected the peace to last for any appreciable time. The provisions of the treaty, once widely known throughout the Great Lakes frontier, demanded that the Indians harden their diplomatic stance toward the British. The British responded in kind. "It seems from Mr. McKee's return that the Shawnee are no longer so well disposed as they were last autumn," observed the commander at Fort Pitt, Capt. Simeon Ecuyer. "[They] will be here in a few days with 5 prisoners escorted by 100 beggars. We have resolved to receive them very coldly."[30]

The Indian delegation, composed of three headmen and 125 warriors, met with Ecuyer on April 16. Opening the conference by presenting the commander with twelve bundles of skins so that the returned captives might "patch their Shoes as the[y] Travel Home to their

Friends," the Shawnee professed their friendship for the British. They also admitted being uneasy about the continued British occupation of the region but hoped that negotiation and diplomacy could settle their differences. "Our Chiefs formerly cleared the road to this Post," they claimed, "but as some Tree's may have fallen since then, our Warriors now Join with us to clear it; and make it more level & smooth for you & us to Travel." Ecuyer remained unmoved, and the following day bluntly told the assembled Indians that the French had ceded the region to the British, that his troops would continue to be garrisoned at Fort Pitt, and within a short time other English troops would also occupy the now abandoned French posts within the region. The council ended the following day with both Ecuyer and the Shawnees promising their continued friendship, but clearly the meeting had done little to alleviate the Ohio tribe's suspicions.[31]

At Fort Pitt, Croghan watched in alarm as, for the second time within ten years, it appeared he would be ruined by violence on the frontier. Although he had been unable to prevail upon Amherst personally to change his policies, Croghan used the opportunity given him by the peace between France and Great Britain to travel to England on his own. There, he hoped to discuss his views for improving the Indian department with his British business and political associates. Placing McKee in charge of affairs at his post at Fort Pitt during his absence, Croghan left on May 2, 1763, stopping briefly at Johnson Hall in New York and in Philadelphia before he ventured on to England. He did not return to his storehouse at the forks of the Ohio until March 1765.[32]

Croghan's departure would prove to be a great opportunity for McKee who would now play a major role in Indian affairs at the western outpost. The previous eight years had been a period of initiation for Croghan's young assistant. Much as a neophyte is introduced to the veiled esotery of a fraternal brotherhood, Croghan and the military had shown McKee the inner workings of the imperial bureaucracy as it sought to direct Indian affairs along the western border. They had made McKee aware of its specialized ceremonies and schooled him in its peculiar modes of speech. He had been instructed in its mysteries. From Croghan, he learned how regulations could be bent for personal enrichment and how policy could be cynically manipulated to protect the interests of the Crown. He had demonstrated his proficiency in the tasks assigned him and, as importantly, had proven himself trustworthy, willing and capable of keeping the secrets of the order.

In 1763, McKee enjoyed a familiar relationship with many of the western tribes and a familial one with the Shawnees who lived in the Scioto and Ohio River Valleys. Kinship and economic ties fully integrated him into the lives of the native communities. Slowly, though, McKee's relationship with Croghan was pulling him away from the frontier and into the broader world of imperial affairs. McKee's sympathies were divided, distributed between the Crown and the Ohio Country nations. But his loyalties were not ideological. Rather, they were tied directly to his relationship with Croghan, on one hand, and his family and friends among the western tribes, on the other. His loyalties were defined by personal relationships and a sense of place that reached little beyond the Pittsburgh hinterland.

McKee had benefited immensely from his association with Croghan. Nonetheless, the Irish trader's enormous reputation and larger-than-life persona frequently had caused McKee's contributions to be overshadowed. Croghan's abrupt departure for England during a time of crisis and McKee's willingness to accept the duties imposed by the Crown in Croghan's absence would serve both to bring him to the attention of the Indian department's senior hierarchy and to draw him further into a relationship with the British government based on national allegiance and ethnic affiliation. Almost imperceptibly, events would cause McKee to fashion a broader based, ideologically defined sense of loyalty to the British Empire. McKee assumed his duties at a time when British officials at Fort Pitt were casting a wary eye toward the vast, unbroken wilderness west of the Ohio River. Native disaffection was real. Although Crown officials did not yet realize it, native leaders of considerable power and prestige were openly advocating armed resistance. By May 1763, McKee had completed his initiation by instruction. Ahead lay his initiation by ordeal.

CHAPTER THREE

—— 🐾 ——

From Commissary to Agent: Indian Affairs, Land Speculation, and the Fur Trade, 1764–1772

————

The generalized Indian discontent in the Ohio Country was strength-ened and given focus by the teachings of Neolin, the Delaware prophet. Neolin was the most recent and influential in a long line of nativistic-revivalist Indian teachers active in the Great Lakes region beginning about 1735. These spiritual leaders sought to turn their followers away from European influences and return to a life free of trade goods, rum, settlers, and Christianity. Fueled by the pervasive cultural disruption and economic dislocation caused by nearly a decade of open warfare along the Pennsylvania and Ohio Country border, Neolin's teachings had attracted a sizable following by the fall of 1761. Neolin's doctrine was political as well as spiritual. As early as 1761, the prophet was cau-tioning his audience that war with the British was inevitable. Guided in part by Neolin's message and seeking to expel the British from the Great Lakes region, a loose coalition of Ottawa, Chippewa, Potawatomi, Huron, Shawnee, and Delaware tribal members from the Detroit re-gion persuaded an Ottawa chief, Pontiac, to undertake the leadership of a plot to drive the British from Fort Detroit. In early May 1763, Pontiac's forces began a protracted siege of the British garrison that would last until October 31. Although Pontiac's attempt to dislodge the British installation was ultimately unsuccessful, his actions encouraged other tribes throughout the Great Lakes area to strike at white settlers and the British military. By midsummer, native forces had destroyed the garrisons at Venango, LeBoeuf, and Presque Isle, invested Forts Niagara and Pitt, and embroiled the frontier in a general uprising.[1]

Unaware of the events transpiring at Detroit, the small community around Fort Pitt endured a peaceful, though tense, early spring. On May 27, a large party of Mingoes, displaced Iroquois who lived throughout the eastern Great Lakes region, came to trade at James Kenny's post. Kenny noted that the Indian delegation seemed to be unusually hasty in conducting their business, and when they were finished, they attempted to buy as much powder and ball as they could. After they left Kenny's establishment, one of the Indians, Turtle's Heart, went to see McKee. Turtle's Heart urged the agent to flee the area at once. Detroit, along with several other British outposts, he confided, had been attacked. Ottawas and Chippewas were preparing to attack Fort Pitt as well. According to Turtle's Heart, if McKee would not leave within four days, then he would be killed.[2]

Concerned, McKee reported the incident to the post commander, Simeon Ecuyer. Ecuyer responded by sending McKee to Turtle's Heart's village, located a few miles from the fort, to gather further intelligence. The band had left the area before McKee arrived, but shortly after their departure they took several horses and a keg of rum from a home near Bushy Run and stole fifty pounds at gunpoint from a settler named Coleman who lived on the Bedford Road running east of Fort Pitt. On June 1, King Beaver, Shingas, Weindohela, and Daniel and William Anderson, Delaware headmen from along the Tuscarawas River, also met with McKee; they carried warnings of violence near Detroit and throughout the Ohio Country. All the British at Detroit, at Sandusky, and at the mouth of the Maumee River were dead, they claimed, as were smaller groups of traders scattered across the frontier. They had brought the warning to Fort Pitt because "we thought your King had made Peace with us, & all the Western Nations of Indians; for Our Parts we Joined it heartily and Desired to hold it always good," stated the Delaware delegation, and they were not ready to be drawn into a war not of their making. As Turtle's Heart had done, the

Delawares also urged McKee seek a place of safety and to "Avoid the Road & Every [place] where Indians Resort." The Indian report was confirmed by Thomas Calhoun, a trader whom the Delawares had escorted to the fort for his own safety. Many British still survived in the west, said Calhoun, but Detroit and the western posts were under siege, and the danger to Fort Pitt was real. The warning was not wasted. Ecuyer began at once to strengthen the fort with what few personnel were available. Within two days, other whites fleeing the Ohio Country also verified Turtle Heart's report, and scouts from Fort Pitt discovered two soldiers a short distance from the garrison who had been killed and scalped.[3]

During the first week of June, the fort became the target of increased harassment from hostile Indians in the area. Although a concerted attack against Fort Pitt failed to materialize, roving enemy bands hampered Ecuyer's ability to communicate with the surviving British posts to the East. Moreover, he continued to receive a steady stream of reports from the western frontier that detailed the extent of the Indian uprising. He also continued to strengthen the defensive posture of his post. Sixteen pieces of artillery were mounted and placed in battery; the fort's earthworks were strengthened; and a hospital, safely shielded from musket fire, was constructed in the garrison's interior. On June 16, four Shawnees approached the fort and asked to speak with McKee. The Indians informed him that their band, apparently at McKee's earlier request, was protecting several English traders who had been stranded by the outbreak of violence in the Ohio backwoods. The traders, they promised, would be taken care of until the war was over. They also told McKee that it was the Delawares in the Muskingum Valley who were actively plotting against the fort. The following day, the same group reappeared and told McKee that all the tribes in the region, including their own band, had now joined in the plan to attack the garrison. The Shawnees had agreed because they felt pressured by the other tribes in the alliance. "They were afraid to refuse taking up the Hatchet," the Shawnees claimed, "as so many Nations had done it before it came to them." The group also urged McKee to flee the post and seek safety at the Lower Town. McKee refused. Ecuyer reported that McKee gave the Indians' information "great credit" but personally dismissed the reports as the work of "rascals" and "vagabonds." "I have seen but few Indians around us up to the present time," he wrote to Bouquet. "However it may be, let them come when they wish. The post is in good shape."[4]

The attack came on June 22. Appearing suddenly at the edge of the woods that surrounded the garrison, the Indian force assaulted the fort on all sides, killing one militiaman and wounding another. Small arms fire from the post's defenders and several rounds from the fort's cannon kept the attackers at bay. During the assault, McKee participated in the fort's defense, killing at least one Indian.[5]

At midnight on the evening of June 23, Turtle's Heart and Mamaltee, a Delaware chief, approached the fort and called to McKee, telling him that they wished to meet with the agent. The following morning, the two Indians again warned McKee that a large party of Indians was poised to destroy the garrison. The two Delawares also claimed that they had prevailed upon the group to temporarily postpone the attack. The Indians told Ecuyer, after he had joined the group, that he and his men should immediately abandon the post and retreat to the eastern outposts. Angered at the suggestion, the commander advised the Indians that he was confident of his garrison's ability to defend itself. "I now tell you that I will not abandon this post," he responded. "I have warriors, Provisions, and ammunition plenty to defend it against all the Indians in the woods, and shall never abandon it as long as a white man lives in America. . . . This is our Home. You have attacked us without reason or provocation, you have murdered and plundered our warriors and Traders, you have took our Horses & Cattle & at the same time, you tell us your hearts are good towards your Brother the English. How can I have faith in you and believe you are sincere." As the meeting ended, McKee gave the Indian delegation a few gifts, including some provisions, a little rum, and a small British flag that the Indians could fly if they wished to speak to the garrison again. But William Trent, an English trader at the post, also noted that, perhaps unbeknownst to McKee, "Out of our regard to them, we gave them two Blankets and an Handkerchief out of the Small Pox Hospital. I hope it will have the desired effect."[6]

Throughout the remainder of June and July, McKee met with Indian groups and individuals as they passed near the fort. On June 25, a lone Shawnee warned him that a large body of hostile Indians was marching toward Fort Pitt and planned to attack the post. On July 3, four Ottawas from near Detroit informed him that they wished to end the hostilities between themselves and the English. Flying British colors, the Indians ritualistically concluded a peace between their band and the British garrison. The following day, ten other Ottawas attempted to take a British soldier prisoner while some of their number spoke with McKee. On July 21, a Shawnee chief advised McKee that the siege of Detroit was ended and that hostilities throughout the region would soon be concluded. Amidst the bewildering array of native responses, Ecuyer continued to keep the post in a strong defensive posture. A second attack came on the afternoon of July 28. Lasting five days and nights, the battle resulted in no deaths among the Americans, although Ecuyer and six others were wounded. The English captain estimated that his men had inflicted over twenty casualties among the Indians. The siege was lifted, but not because of Ecuyer's staunch defense. Rather, the British military response to the investment provided the Shawnees and Delawares with a greater opportunity to defeat the Crown away from the garrison.[7]

The previous June, when it became clear that Fort Pitt was surrounded, Jeffrey Amherst had ordered Col. Henry Bouquet to prepare a force to march to the beleaguered outpost's relief. Assembled and provisioned by mid-July, Bouquet and his army began their expedition on July 18, marching from Carlisle and moving westward over the remains of the road cut by Forbes only a few years before. Learning of Bouquet's advance, the Indians near Fort Pitt broke off the attack and moved east, hoping to engage and destroy the English column. The Indians and Bouquet met one another on the afternoon of August 5, about twelve miles from Fort Pitt and near a small stream known as Bushy Run. The Indian attack against the British was ferocious, lasting throughout the day, into the night, and throughout the following morning. Surrounded, Bouquet and his army were desperate. Shortly after dawn of the second day, the center of the British line appeared to falter and give way. Pressing their advantage, the Indian force charged the weakening position and watched as it seemed to disintegrate before the onslaught. As the line gave way the Indians continued to push the retreating British back. The "retreat," though, was a ruse, a cleverly executed maneuver designed to lure the Indians into a deadly trap. As the Indians pushed the center of the British line to the rear, the sides closed around the unsuspecting attackers while other British companies, hidden by the crest of a hill, moved to close off their line of retreat. The tribes that participated in the battle were routed, and the loose confederacy that made up the Indian resistance in the Upper Ohio vicinity, while not crushed, was driven into temporary submission. Without further interference, Bouquet arrived at Fort Pitt on August 10.[8]

At first glance, the events that surrounded the siege of Fort Pitt, and McKee's role within them, appear almost incomprehensibly confused, with Indians divulging intelligence, offering aid, suing for peace, and perpetrating violence seemingly at the same time. Yet these actions become understandable when seen as reflections of the cultural and political ambiguity of the Great Lakes frontier. The Indian resistance centered at Detroit was never unified and grew less so as it moved away from its western seat of power. The actions of the western Pennsylvania and eastern Ohio tribes mirrored the diversity of native diplomatic and military responses as individual tribes and bands sought to cope with the changing, fluid nature of their relations with both the English and each other.

The English at Fort Pitt had also responded to the crisis in ways that reflected the diversity of cultural perspectives within their ranks. Ever since the conquest of 1763, British authorities had regarded the region's Indians as subjects of the Crown. Thus, imperial officials viewed the rebellion as treason and the natives who participated in it as traitors. Ecuyer's military actions are understandable as a legitimate response to an armed challenge against British political hegemony in the region. William Trent's distribution of blankets contaminated by smallpox to the warring tribes was also informed by his perception of the rebellion as an insurrection against Crown authority. Trent's actions were driven by an ideologically defined sense of national allegiance and were framed within a context that demanded swift and severe retribution for acts of sedition. Unlike Ecuyer and Trent, McKee had sought to exploit his bonds of family and friendship with the western tribes. Significantly, virtually every incident that McKee mediated between the Indians and the British post during the siege was based to a considerable degree on his personal relationships with the region's Indians. His actions during this period can be seen as culturally determined responses in which personal allegiances defined his role as a cultural intermediary, eclipsing loyalties based on racial or national affiliation.

Bouquet's success at Bushy Run imposed a temporary lull in the hostilities near Fort Pitt. Elsewhere in the western theater, the violence continued. Pontiac's forces still surrounded Detroit and controlled much of the area near Niagara. The Indian movement was showing signs of dwindling momentum, however. By early fall, several tribes had left the confederacy, and in October French officials from Fort de Chartres bluntly informed Pontiac that France would no longer supply covert aid to the warring tribes. By December, the rebellion appeared to have come to an end. On December 1, Sir William Johnson sent McKee a detailed communique that explicitly outlined his responsibilities as negotiator and translator for the Crown. The memorandum was undoubtedly, in part, a response to McKee's actions during the Fort Pitt crisis. There is no hint of censure or displeasure at McKee's conduct in the document. But clearly, the letter, entitled "Instructions for Alexander McKee, Gentleman and Assistant Deputy," was intended to impose an ideological and procedural rigor upon McKee's future actions. Indeed, Johnson's use of the term "Gentleman" to describe McKee was an overt indication that the superintendent sought to have McKee identify himself with the broader social values of the British realm. Johnson urged McKee to use his "best endeavors to conciliate and fix to the British Interest all the several Nations and Tribes of Indians who may fall within the reach of your Influence," and to persuade those tribes that wavered in their allegiances to join the British alliance. Significantly, McKee was warned to "conduct your proceedings as to have an Eye only to the Good of his Majesty's Service," and "avoid entering into the Views of any particular Government, Person, or party." In addition, McKee's instructions ordered him to receive the permission of the commanding officer at Fort Pitt before "treating" or holding conferences with the tribes that had taken up arms against the Crown. The letter also urged him to use any means at his disposal to keep arms and ammunition from the western tribes, advised him to keep a written journal regarding all his transactions, and required him to submit periodically a written record of his actions to Johnson for his inspection.[9]

Bouquet and his army remained at Fort Pitt throughout the winter and into the spring of 1764. But despite the military's presence, as the weather moderated, roving bands of Delaware and Shawnee from the Muskingum Valley renewed their campaign of violence against the white settlements scattered across the western Pennsylvania frontier. The continuing raids prompted retaliatory action from whites throughout the region. In December 1763, a mob of fifty-seven whites from

Paxton murdered six Conestoga Indians who lived on the Susquehanna River near Lancaster. The Conestogas had been longtime residents of the area, were known to be peaceful, and had not taken part in the war. The remainder of the band, about fourteen in number and consisting mostly of women and children, attempted to flee but were detained by the local sheriff who confined them in the community's jail. McKee was nearby, visiting his father, when the violence erupted. Thomas reported that when the mob discovered where the survivors were housed, they "broke open the Work house and in a most inhuman Manner butchered the whole, sparing neither Women or Children, an Action I look upon not inferior to any of the Cruelties committed by the Savages since the Commencement of the late or present War."[10]

Convinced that quick and decisive action against the warring tribes was needed to end the violence, Sir Thomas Gage, who had replaced Amherst as commander in chief, ordered Bouquet to prepare an expeditionary force with which to awe the Ohio Indians. At the same time, Gage ordered a second expedition, led by Col. John Bradstreet, to march to Detroit. Bradstreet quickly reached his objective and concluded a peace on September 7. While on the march, he had accepted the return of several prisoners from a band of Shawnees and Delawares that lived near Sandusky. On September 12, Bouquet sent McKee to Sandusky to help with these prisoners, but he cautioned Bradstreet to "send him back to me as he is well acquainted with the Shawnese Language and will be useful to me in any future Business I may have with that Nation." McKee, though, had managed to travel only about fifty miles from Fort Pitt when he discovered the head of another messenger, sent out by Bouquet a few days before him, impaled on a pole set in the middle of the road. A second messenger, who had accompanied the first, was nowhere to be found, and McKee presumed he had been taken prisoner. Judging the road too insecure for travel, McKee returned to Fort Pitt.[11]

Throughout the remainder of the summer, Bouquet prepared his new army and laid plans to invade the Ohio Country. Although recruiting and logistical concerns delayed the anticipated campaign, by early autumn Bouquet's force of nearly fifteen hundred regular and provincial troops was assembled, equipped, and provisioned. On October 1, it began its advance against the western tribes. McKee traveled with Bouquet, serving as his chief translator and negotiator.[12]

The western nations were greatly concerned over the show of force marshalled by Bouquet, whose reputation had soared in the wake of his victory at Bushy Run. In mid-September, a delegation of Ohio Country tribes came to Fort Pitt to ascertain the army's intentions. "I must now consider You as a people whose Promises I can no more trust," Bouquet told the Indians. "I have had it in my Power to put you all to Death, and you deserved it." He had not done so, he claimed, because a "Door open to Mercy" still existed. He demanded that the Indians leave two of their number as hostages with the Americans and sent the remainder of the delegation back to their villages. There, they were to warn their people that Bouquet would soon travel into the Ohio Country, and he would then expect the Indians to deliver up all their captives. A second delegation approached Bouquet one day after the expedition departed from Fort Pitt. Bouquet told these Indians that he had been sent into Ohio to "take revenge of the Murders committed by the Delawares & Shawnese." But he also claimed that "if the Chiefs of the Delawares & Shawnees have any thing to say to me I will hear them at Tuscarawas, & if they are inclined sincerely for Peace, I will tell them in that place what they are to Do to obtain it."[13]

Marching directly to the seat of Indian power, Bouquet established his camp at Tuscarawas (near present-day Bolivar, Ohio), on the upper Muskingum, in mid-October. McKee reported that the Indians seemed "very frightened," and within a few days, Indian delegations had met with the British commander to sue for peace. On October 17, a delegation of Senecas, Delawares, and Shawnees met with Bouquet, claiming to "take fast Hold of the Chain of Friendship" and promising to return all the captives in their possession within a short time. On October 20, Bouquet replied that he remained unconvinced of the Indians' good intentions, and before he would continue with the negotiations, he demanded that the Indians return all white prisoners in their possession within twelve days. Then, breaking off the negotiations, he and his army moved even deeper into enemy territory, eventually stopping at the forks of the Muskingum where the army could control the strategically vital area between the Scioto and Muskingum Rivers. The warring tribes began to comply with Bouquet's demands at once.[14]

Within days, Indians and their prisoners were flowing into the encampment. As the captives were brought into camp, William Smith, a member of the expedition, recalled "fathers and mothers recognizing

English artist Benjamin West created this view of Henry Bouquet's negotiation with the western nations at Tuscarawas in 1764. Although not drawn from life, the central figure standing behind the writing table is clearly Henry Bouquet. The figure standing immediately to his left may represent McKee, Bouquet's translator and chief negotiator. His status as a cross-cultural mediator is emphasized by his location—literally between the army and the Indian delegation—and by his close proximity to the burning council fire, a symbol of the peace toward which both sides are proceeding. His dual cultural affiliation is also suggested by his European-style military uniform, to which he has added thigh-high leggings, typically worn by Indians of the period. The Indian at right is ending his oration by offering a belt of wampum. *William L. Clements Library.*

and clasping their once-lost babes; husbands hanging round the necks of newly-recovered wives and sisters and brothers unexpectedly meeting together after long separation, scarce able to speak the same language or, for some time, to be sure that they were children of the same parents." At the same time, other families who had expected to be reunited and had learned instead that the missing member was dead "stiffened into living monuments of horror and woe." The Indians suffered as greatly. As they turned over their captives, many of whom had been adopted into their families, they wept, provided them with corn, skins, and horses, and other goods, and personally asked Bouquet to see to their safety and comfort. McKee also noted that the Senecas and Delawares had been eager to conclude the negotiations, but the Shawnees had behaved insolently throughout the proceedings. As the deliberations closed, Bouquet, satisfied of the Indians' goodwill, took possession of over two hundred returned captives and instructed the warring chiefs to proceed to Sir William Johnson's estate in New York to conclude a formal peace. His mission accomplished, Bouquet returned home, arriving at Fort Pitt on November 28.[15]

While Bouquet forged a peace in the Ohio Country, George Croghan completed his business in England. The continuing hostilities in the Great Lakes region had deeply disturbed the British Board of Trade, the agency charged with overseeing the Crown's interests in the western country. As the violence increased during 1763 and 1764, the board proved willing to consider Croghan's plans for a reorganization of the Indian department. With his personal fortunes in the balance, Croghan's considerable persuasive talents were at their height. By June 1764, the Board had agreed to administer western Indian affairs with an elaborate new system based almost entirely on Croghan's recommendations. Under the new arrangement, the management of Indian affairs was to be conducted independently, without military interference. The Board created two departments, the northern and the southern, placing each under the direction of a superintendent. Sir William Johnson, named to head the northern department, supervised three deputies who, in turn, watched over the trade at thirteen posts. An interpreter and a gunsmith were to man each post and be inspected periodically by a deputy agent. A commissary, also stationed at each post, watched over the trade and enforced the prices set by the superintendent.[16]

After gaining approval for the new regulations, Croghan returned to America in the late fall of 1764. Informing McKee of his arrival on December 6, the agent praised his assistant for his actions during the siege of Fort Pitt, noting that "it gives me no Small Pleasure to hear your Conduct has been generally approved of by all the Gentlemen of the army in So critical Affair." After advising McKee of the new system for regulating Indian affairs, Croghan asked him to inform the tribes around Fort Pitt that he would soon return to the military post to reestablish the fur trade in the region. "You are under no necessity of acquainting any officer what Instructions you receive from me," reminded Croghan. "All you need Say is that I have desired you acquaint the Indians of my Arrival, and that I shall be there about the last of the Holydays."[17]

Croghan's haughty demeanor immediately placed him at odds with Bouquet. Noting that Croghan's obviously self-interested motives were "too conspicuous to need any comment," the commander complained that matters of great importance to the western frontier seemed to have been entrusted to a man who was "Illiterate, imprudent, and Ill bred." Indeed, Bouquet felt that the new regulations for the Indian department would do little but "destroy the Harmony which ought to Subsist between the different branches of the Service."[18]

Croghan returned to Fort Pitt on February 28. Two weeks earlier, McKee had sent an invitation to the Ohio nations, asking them to come to the British post and meet with Croghan to learn of the new regulations that would govern the western trade. The Ohio Country tribes were slow to assemble, but by early May, nearly six hundred representatives from the Delaware, Shawnee, Seneca, Munsee, and Wyandot nations living at Sandusky had gathered at the English garrison. Meeting with the delegation from May 9 through May 11, McKee and the post commander, Maj. William Murray, reaffirmed their friendship with the western nations and reopened trade at the post. "When first your brethren, the English settled here," claimed McKee, "they kindled a council fire for all the Nations of Indians to the sun-setting; but for two years past, this fire has been neglected and was near going out. Now Brethren, I put some good dry wood on your council fire, that it may blaze up to the sky, so that all nations may see it and come here to smoke with their brethren, the English, in peace." The meeting's conclusion signaled that, for the moment, relations between the British and the Ohio nations had returned to a semblance of normality.[19]

Croghan, however, was interested in more than just strengthening ties between the Crown and the Indians that lived near Fort Pitt. Croghan's instructions from the Board of Trade also required him to extend the fur trade deep into the Illinois Country. Great Britain had acquired the territory, which included the area north of the Ohio River as far west as the Mississippi, at the conclusion of the war with France in 1763. But the violence perpetrated by the western Indian nations and continuing machinations from French trading interests had prevented Britain from taking possession of the area. Croghan hoped to travel as far west as Fort de Chartres, an abandoned French post on the Mississippi River, in present-day western Illinois, and reopen the trade. Not only would this trade secure the area natives' loyalty to the Crown, it would also substantially contribute to Croghan's financial well-being. In order to accomplish his task, Croghan was eager to secure the assistance of the Ohio Country Shawnees, whom the trader felt exerted considerable influence over the Mississippi tribes.[20]

Leaving McKee in charge of his affairs at Fort Pitt, Croghan left Pittsburgh on March 15 and traveled down the Ohio River with two bateaux and an entourage that included a sizable delegation of Senecas, Delawares, and Shawnees. By June 6 the company had reached the mouth of the Wabash River. The party lingered at the camp for a second day, planning to begin their final descent to Fort de Chartres on June 8. At daybreak on June 8, Croghan's camp was attacked by a party of eighty Kickapoos and Mascoutins, Algonquian tribes that ranged widely throughout the Mississippi basin. Two of Croghan's employees were killed, as were three members of the Shawnee delegation, Big Hole, Wapecawpa, and a "Shawnee who speaks but little English named John." During the attack, another Shawnee was wounded but managed to hide in the woods until the assault was over. Once the fight had ended, he came out of hiding and approached the attackers. He "made a very bold speech," reprimanding the attackers and telling them that all the Ohio Country tribes would unite and take revenge for these unwarranted and cowardly killings.[21]

The speech terrified the far-western tribes who were ill prepared to open hostilities against their eastern neighbors. Quickly they rounded up the survivors and led them on an arduous seven-day overland journey to Vincennes, a small settlement of eighty or ninety French families situated along the Wabash River in present-day southern Indiana. After resting a few days, the survivors were moved again to Ouiatenon, a Kickapoo village located on the upper Wabash River, a few miles west of its confluence with the Tippecanoe. On July 1, the French sent the Kickapoos a speech and a belt and requested the Indians burn Croghan and destroy the remainder of his party. The Kickapoos declined the belt, confiding to Croghan that they had done so because they dreaded the possibility of a war with the Ohio Country nations and were unwilling to do anything that might make an already bad situation worse. For the first time since his capture, Croghan sensed an advantage. He told the Indians that the problem could be rectified by opening trade to the British, evicting the French, and allowing him to personally intercede with the Ohio tribes to prevent further violence. Pressing his case, Croghan continued to meet with tribal leaders until July 8, when the Kickapoos finally agreed unconditionally to Croghan's wishes. "The Indians agree to our taking possession of the Illinois," wrote a jubilant Croghan to McKee, adding that "my success is entirely due to my misfortune in being taken and plundered." Next, Croghan planned to go to Detroit to conclude his negotiations with the Mississippian tribes. While Croghan traveled to Detroit, the Kickapoos and their allies sent four speeches and four pipes of reconciliation to McKee. Croghan told his assistant to inform the Ohio nations that the far-western tribes wished to remain at peace and become faithful allies of the Crown. McKee was to deliver the pipes and attempt to dissuade the Shawnees from making war on the Kickapoos. Croghan and McKee's diplomacy was successful, and in August McKee reported that although the Ohio Shawnees remained disturbed by the deaths of their people, they agreed to take no action against the far-western nations until after Croghan returned to Fort Pitt and they had discussed the matter personally with him.[22]

Croghan's journey to the Illinois Country was an enormous triumph and served to vindicate dramatically the new Indian policy that he had recommended to the Board of Trade. In March 1766, Sir William Johnson responded to the organizational changes authorized for the Indian Department by naming McKee commissary for Fort Pitt. The appointment reflected McKee's continuing success in dealing with the western tribes, his growing maturity in his interactions with the imperial bureaucracy, and the increasing regard in which he was held by the upper echelon of the Indian department. Informing McKee of his new position, Johnson emphasized that "the inspection of Trade, Correcting abuses, Redressing Grievances, gaining intelligence of all ill designs, and securing the Friendship of the Indians" were to be his principal duties. The office of commissary was one of considerable responsibility. McKee would directly supervise two other Indian department employees, an interpreter, and a gunsmith. Further, he was required to keep a detailed record of his actions and to submit a copy of it to the Deputy Agent for the Western District (Croghan) "every three months, or oft'ner if the Service Requires it."[23]

At the heart of his new responsibilities was the regulation of the Indian trade. The provisions of the Royal Proclamation of 1763 prohibited white settlement west of the crest of the Alleghenies and decreed that trade with the Indians was to be conducted only by traders licensed by the Crown. Individual traders were no longer permitted to go among the tribes. Trade was to be conducted under the Crown's direct supervision only at government posts located along the western border. As commissary, McKee personally oversaw the extensive western fur trade that originated from Fort Pitt and surrounding areas. As part of his duties, he regulated the price of trade goods and attempted to curb the notoriously irregular business practices of the western trade community.[24]

With the power to regulate, McKee also gained the power to manipulate. The new trade system, which required Indians in the region to carry their furs to the eastern posts in order to receive payment, was the object of bitter complaints among the western tribes who objected to the inherent inconvenience of the plan. In the fall of 1766, McKee responded to these complaints by allowing Baynton, Wharton and Morgan, a firm in which both he and Croghan held a financial interest, to establish a trading post among McKee's family and friends at the Lower Shawnee Town, along the Scioto River. Several traders in the Pittsburgh area, apparently after protesting to McKee and getting no response, wrote directly to Johnson claiming that the new post would lead to their ruin. In a none too subtle demand that Johnson rein in his subordinate, the traders stated that they were "confident . . . that whatever directions you are pleased to give for this purpose [the removal of the trading house], will be punctually and justly Executed." The post was finally closed after an inquiry from Gage.[25]

McKee also monitored the actions of unlicensed traders who were operating illegally within the Ohio region and the movements of settlers who, despite prohibitions to the contrary, were slowly expanding into the western Pennsylvania backwoods. Land-hungry whites and unscrupulous traders were constant sources of trouble to McKee and other Crown officials. Peace of a sort had come to the Pennsylvania frontier, but sporadic, localized conflict that resulted from the actions of these two groups remained an ever-present threat to the continued stability of the region. In February 1767, McKee reported that trade violations were rampant in the area and that four Indians had been robbed and murdered by persons who, though unidentified, were suspected to be area traders. Two weeks later, he related that the area tribes were greatly concerned by reports that more than one thousand Virginians planned to forcibly evict a Delaware community on Red Stone Creek near Fort Pitt and establish their own settlement. In September, McKee sent word to Johnson that ten Chippewas from Saginaw Bay had murdered eleven traders while in the Ohio Country and then had plundered their goods.²⁶

These incidents reflected great unrest among the western tribes, and McKee, according to Croghan, was "in Great Distress for fair of an Indian Warr." McKee immediately sent his translator, Andrew Montour, to live among the tribes, to gather intelligence and to discover their intentions. Within a few days, Croghan ordered McKee to the Lower Shawnee Town for the same reason. Indian resentment was widespread throughout the lower Great Lakes region, reported McKee. A consensus for armed resistance, however, was not present. During December, Croghan personally made a tour throughout the Ohio Country and went to Detroit to placate the tribes while McKee hosted a conference at Fort Pitt. Gifts, promises, and skilled diplomacy on the part of both men ended the crisis peacefully.²⁷

The fragile rapprochement was quickly broken. On January 10 and 11, 1768, Frederick Stump, a settler living near Middleburg in central Pennsylvania, and his servant, John Ironcutter, brutally murdered and scalped ten Indians. Moreover, while Stump was being detained by the local authorities in order to be questioned about the crime, his neighbors stormed the jail and spirited him away. The crime and the government's inability to take effective action in its wake sent waves of indignation throughout the western tribes. Four messengers sent by the

Shawnees and Delawares who lived on the Susquehanna River carried news of the crime to the Ohio tribes on January 27. In mid-February, McKee noted that the Ohio Indians were much alarmed by the affair. The fact that Stump had scalped his victims, he claimed, indicated to the western nations that the act was a declaration of war by the British against the Indians. McKee attempted to calm the Indians and urged Croghan to come to Fort Pitt as quickly as possible. Most of the Ohio Shawnee and Delaware headmen were already at the post, wrote McKee, waiting to meet with Croghan before they decided on a course of action. Within a few days, Croghan had prepared a message of condolence for McKee to personally carry to the western tribes, and he ordered gifts worth three thousand pounds sterling to be distributed among the different nations. Croghan, McKee, and two commissioners sent by John Penn, the governor of Pennsylvania, met with over eleven hundred Indian delegates at Fort Pitt from April 26 through May 9. During the council, McKee read a message from Penn in which the governor claimed that the murders had been "the imprudent act of a few foolish people." Hoping that "no black clouds might arise over our heads to prevent us from seeing the sun rise and set over us" in friendship, Penn promised that the affair would be settled with the "strictest justice." Croghan, McKee, and the others in attendance reiterated these sentiments throughout the remainder of the meeting. Anger over the incident was not easily quenched, and Indian discontent continued throughout the spring; but once again, diplomacy, gifts, and promises restored the tenuous peace.[28]

Native frustration within the Upper Ohio Valley was further fueled by Sir William Johnson's actions in 1768. Johnson had concluded an agreement with the eastern Iroquois at Fort Stanwix, in New York, by which the Iroquois ceded lands along the Ohio Valley to the Crown. The British government, in turn, opened the region to purchase and settlement. The land, however, was occupied not by the Iroquois, but by the Ohio Country Shawnees and Delawares, who recognized neither the eastern confederacy's claim to the land nor their right to negotiate on behalf of the western tribes. The Iroquois' questionable dealings and the British government's willingness to exploit its clouded title to the area exacerbated the friction between white newcomers and the Indians. Predictably, as whites moved into the newly opened land, incidents involving violence between surveyors, speculators, traders, settlers, and the Ohio Country tribes were not long in following. Unfortunately, at the very time a strong Indian department bureaucracy guided by a clearly articulated Indian policy might have done much to quiet events along the border, the British government retreated from its responsibility to regulate Indian affairs along the Great Lakes frontier. Faced with a growing financial crisis in the wake of the Seven Years War, Whitehall abdicated control of the Indian trade in April 1768. Although the new policy abolished McKee's position as Indian department commissary, he quickly found employment once again as an assistant to Croghan, who retained his position as deputy agent.[29]

If British policy had been too restrictive before the retrenchment, now the lack of Crown supervision within the region allowed a variety of abuses perpetrated by an increasing tide of white settlers to go unchallenged. More and more, McKee began to divide his time between his family at the Lower Shawnee Town and Croghan's post at Pittsburgh. As before, he attempted to learn of plots against the Crown, the depth of native disaffection, and the machinations of the other tribes in the region. Likewise, he continued to exploit his bonds of kinship and trade with the western tribes to strengthen their allegiance to the British. In September 1769, McKee traveled to the Susquehanna to settle his father's estate. Writing to Croghan, he noted that the Ohio tribes were angry over the actions of the Six Nations. He also claimed that many of the Ohio tribes were turning against the British because of the great numbers of Pennsylvanians, Virginians, and Marylanders who, although unauthorized to do so, were entering the land adjacent to the Ohio River and surveying the area for settlement. In some cases, these surveyors had proceeded as far as seventy miles below Fort Pitt. Encouraged by support from clandestine French and Spanish trading interests in the region, some of the younger warriors were calling for armed resistance. They were opposed by the older chiefs of the Shawnees and Delawares, but the young men, claimed McKee, said they "may as well die like men as be kicked about like dogs." Some of the Senecas who lived near Fort Pitt began to kill cattle, steal horses, and plunder houses, but McKee admitted that some of the whites who lived near the town acted as poorly to their Indian neighbors and seemed "to wish for a quarrel as much as the Indians." As a result of these insults, the Shawnees and Delawares built a large council house on the Scioto and invited the Wabash Indians, the Hurons, the Ottawas, Potawatomis,

Chippewas, and Senecas to attend a general council the following spring. The intention, McKee had learned, was to form a confederacy between the Great Lakes, Mississippi, and southern nations against the English.[30]

McKee continued to receive intelligence throughout the winter. In February 1770, he met with a large delegation of Shawnee and Delaware chiefs who had waited impatiently for his return to Fort Pitt. The conspiracy in the west was gaining strength, they reported. The northern tribes had ended their traditional enmity between themselves and the southern nations, making the formation of a lasting confederacy all the more possible. While McKee noted that the delegation with which he met insisted upon their peaceful intentions, he also noted that all the tribes within the area had accumulated enormous stockpiles of powder and ball. Croghan was convinced that the intelligence bode ill for the fortunes of the Crown. Writing to Sir William Johnson on May 10, Croghan predicted that if the plot reported by McKee was true, then it was only a matter of time before widespread violence engulfed the south, and if and when the Wabash nations and the tribes north of Detroit joined in the conspiracy, then "no negotiations, nor presents though ever so great will prevent their making a trial of their strength." Only time, he claimed, would show the truth of the matter.[31]

That May, two Pittsburgh residents named Pendergrass and Elliot entered into an agreement with a drunken Indian and claimed that the agreement allowed them to begin a settlement on the west side of the Ohio River, opposite Fort Pitt. McKee understood at once that when the arrangement and the circumstances under which it was concluded became widely known, it would infuriate the area's tribes and increase tensions within the region. McKee spoke to the military authorities at Fort Pitt who immediately moved to suppress the agreement, correctly claiming that it was an infringement of the Crown's prerogative. Pittsburgh endured an uneasy summer. Then, in August, McKee learned that the anticipated meeting at the Scioto had taken place, but fewer Indians than expected had attended. Beyond that, he was unable to learn anything more of the proceedings.[32]

In March 1771, three Indians who had spent the last year living with the Shawnees and Delawares brought a report of what had transpired on the Scioto. The informants told McKee that the Six Nations had instigated the conspiracy by telling the Ohio tribes that they had never sold any land south of the Ohio River to the English and that the settlers who now resided in the area had stolen their land from the Indians. The Six Nations had then suggested the Ohio tribes form an alliance with the Mississippi tribes, to better defend their land; the Ohio nations were given four years to accomplish the task. However, the Ohio tribes had moved far more quickly than anticipated, and the three informants reported that the Delawares, Shawnees, Hurons, Ottawas, Potawatomis, Chippewas, Miamis, Ouiatanons, Piankeshaws, Kickapoos, and Mascoutins were "all of one Mind and determined to strike the English." The news stunned both Croghan and McKee. As soon as the three informants departed, Croghan sent for an old friend, a Shawnee living at Logstown whose honesty he completely trusted. After telling the Shawnee what he had learned and chiding his friend for his secrecy, Croghan asked him to verify the report. The informants had told the truth, said the Shawnee. War was inevitable, and he promised, as a token of his friendship for the Irish trader, that as soon as he learned the specifics of the plot, he would tell Croghan when the attack was to take place. "I love the English and wish there was to be no War," he stated. "By telling you this I have put my Life in your Hands, for if the Indians Knew that I have told you they would Kill me."[33]

McKee began at once to make plans to travel to the Scioto and attempt to undermine the plot. Leaving Pittsburgh on April 20, McKee arrived at the central Ohio Shawnee villages in late spring. As early as 1770, Croghan had suggested that to defeat the conspiracy, if it existed, the English needed to divide the plotters and sow discord among them. Thomas King, an Oneida envoy in Croghan's pay, had spent a considerable amount of time that spring at the Scioto villages where he spoke against the Six Nations and cautioned the Ohio tribes against joining in an alliance with them. McKee continued to hammer away at this theme as he met with tribal leaders throughout July. None of the Indians denied the plot, and all claimed it was the Iroquois, acting through the Senecas, who had instigated it. But McKee continued to claim that the Senecas were liars and the English were the Ohio nations' only friends. Seeing that King's speeches had "thrown the western Indians into great Confusion," and that as a result the Senecas were now "despised," he openly reprimanded the Shawnees for their conduct and forced the Miamis to acknowledge that their behavior towards the English was inappropriate among friends. Thomas King had supplied the wedge, and McKee drove it home. By midsummer he had created enough doubt, shame, and mutual suspicion that the plot collapsed.[34]

The Shawnees had been among the most eager of the Ohio tribes to forge a military alliance with the Senecas. With the fall of the conspiracy, McKee reported that their standing among the western nations was greatly diminished. He also noted that the Wabash Indians were still behaving arrogantly and perhaps posed a threat to the English garrisons near Fort de Chartres. The Miamis, he said, were the best disposed among the western tribes, followed closely by the Delawares, but he had little doubt that had the plot been put into action, both would have acted against the English. Trading abuses, unauthorized settlement, and too much liquor all continued as sources of discontent among the Ohio tribes, but for now, the immediate crisis was over. McKee returned to Pittsburgh on August 24.[35]

Despite the intensity of his diplomacy among the Ohio nations in 1770 and 1771, McKee's work for Croghan took only a portion of his time. Because his official duties concerning Indian diplomacy and the regulation of the fur trade were over, he was able to devote his efforts to personal matters. Following the successful outcome of Bouquet's expedition to the Ohio Country, Bouquet granted McKee fourteen hundred acres of land at the mouth of Chartiers Creek (present-day McKee's Rocks), in western Pennsylvania, in consideration of McKee's role in the expedition. The gift marked McKee's first substantial land acquisition in the west. In the ensuing years, he would become involved in several schemes, mostly at Croghan's instigation, concerned with western land speculation.[36]

Immediately before the Treaty of Fort Stanwix was signed, Croghan acquired 127,000 acres of land from the Indians before title to it could be claimed by the Crown. To conceal the extent of his purchases from British officials, Croghan placed title to the new land in the names of several associates, including McKee, who eventually returned title back to him. McKee also dealt on his own behalf. By 1778 he had either purchased or inherited several properties, including an estate on the Susquehanna in Lancaster County; two homes and several lots in Pittsburgh; 6,102 acres of land south of Fort Pitt, on the Ohio River; and 2,000 more on the Elkhorn River in Kentucky.[37]

The Treaty of Fort Stanwix also lured others interested in western lands into the Ohio Valley. Croghan's and McKee's knowledge of western affairs made them invaluable sources of information for those who also wished to acquire property beyond Fort Pitt. In October 1770, the Virginia land speculator, George Washington, stopped at McKee's home during a trip down the Ohio to inspect land in the Ohio Valley. While there, Washington dined with McKee, Croghan, and Robert Hamilton, an officer at Fort Pitt, and presumably they discussed his prospects in the western country.[38]

During the late 1760s and early 1770s, McKee also entered the fur trade as a private trader, joining in a profitable partnership with another Pittsburgh resident, Alexander Ross. He used the proceeds to develop his property north of Pittsburgh, where he built a large and imposing estate, Fairview, that overlooked the Ohio River. Prosperous by frontier standards and highly visible as a result of his continuing association with Croghan, McKee became active in local politics as well, accepting the position of justice of the peace for newly formed Bedford County in 1771. Despite his increasingly strong links to white society, McKee also remained tied to the western tribes. In 1768 or 1769, McKee married a woman living in the Lower Shawnee Town, and in 1769 or 1770, she bore his first child, Thomas. Little is known of McKee's wife. John Johnston, a United States Indian agent at Piqua, Ohio, in the early nineteenth century, understood that she was an Indian, and by his marriage McKee became related to the Shawnee war chief, Blue Jacket. An unattributed marginal note in the McKee Family Genealogical file at Fort Malden suggests that her name was Charlotte Brown, raising the possibility that, like his mother, she may have been a white captive raised among the tribe. McKee's wife and child continued to live among the Indians in the Scioto Valley, while Alexander divided his time between Pittsburgh and the central Ohio backwoods.[39]

The 1760s had seen McKee rise rapidly in stature along the western frontier. While still closely associated with Croghan, McKee matured and developed his own identity as a responsible and respected Crown official and businessman. His growing affiliation with the institutions of the realm had brought him land, power, and modest wealth. At the same time, his ability to control the western trade and his marriage into the local Shawnee community had helped him forge links with the Great Lakes tribes that had never been stronger. In a letter to Sir William Johnson, Croghan boasted that "the Shawnas whome I well know wold Tell him anything they Knew as they Consider him as one of thire own people." In both worlds, McKee had acquired admiration and respect and was regarded by natives and whites alike as a potent figure who bridged the two cultures.[40]

In November 1771, Croghan resigned from the Indian department. The past few years had been financially troublesome as Crown duties had prevented him from devoting his full attention to several potentially profitable enterprises. In seeking a replacement, Johnson turned to McKee, the person who "next to Mr. Croghan is not only best acquainted with, but has the most influence over these Indians," naming him to the post of deputy agent, pro tempore in December.[41]

McKee's influence among both the western tribes and Crown officials was substantial, but his appointment had come at a time when increasing suspicion and hostility defined the relationship between natives and whites along the western Pennsylvania border. In the months to come, his considerable skills as a mediator would be severely tested.

CHAPTER FOUR

Dunmore's War,
1772–1774

The early 1770s were a particularly frustating time for McKee. His abilities as a cultural mediator were honed to an almost surgical edge during this period, but those abilities, no matter how well developed or expertly employed, had limits. By 1774, McKee would be in the middle of events that he could neither fully control nor significantly influence. As a result, he would be forced to reassess his obligations to the western nations and redefine his relationship to the Crown. McKee's appointment as deputy agent came at a time when the British government was incapable of providing effective leadership in western affairs. Following the French and Indian War, Great Britain had tried without success to impose a tax upon the colonies that would both defray the cost of England's military expenditures taken on America's behalf and provide for the colonies' continued defense. The colonies, except for Quebec, had met these measures with stiff political resistance and occasional violence. As a result, the Crown continued to labor under an immense fiscal burden incurred during the War for Empire from which it could find little relief.[1]

The financial reductions that had cost McKee his post as commissary in 1768 had been one response to the national debt. The bureaucratic realignment that had accompanied that measure also returned the responsibility for western Indian affairs to the military. Despite these added duties, the depleted treasury and the possibility of domestic violence along the eastern seaboard forced the government to withdraw its troops—and with them any real foundation for the application of effective imperial authority—from the western posts in 1772. As early as 1768 Gage had claimed that if the British had no garrison at Fort de Chartres, then there would be no need for one at Fort Pitt. Writing to Lord Hillsborough in June of that year, Gage insisted that the British occupation of Fort Pitt should "depend upon having or not having a Military Establishment at the Illinois." Furthermore, he also observed that if the far-western post was ever abandoned, then he would "not hesitate a Moment" to recommend the abandonment of Fort Pitt as well.[2]

Imperial officials agreed. Driven by the deepening financial crisis, British authorities ordered the destruction of Fort de Chartres in December 1771. The task was completed in early summer 1772, and as promised, Gage then ordered the reduction of Fort Pitt on August 31. In his orders, Gage instructed the post's commander, Capt. Charles Edmunstone, to transport all ordnance and other valuable supplies east to Philadelphia. Equipment and supplies that either could not be transported or that Edmonstone deemed not worth the effort were to be destroyed. Further, Edmonstone was also to destroy the buildings and the earthworks "in such a manner as it shall afford no defense for an Enemy." Among the buildings scheduled to be razed was a small brick outbuilding situated outside the fort's main defensive earthworks. In September, McKee wrote to Gage claiming that he had made several improvements to the building to facilitate its use as a place to conduct business with the area's Indians, and he asked that the building be preserved for that purpose. Gage agreed, and the small structure was saved. By December, the military had substantially, though not entirely, completed the reduction of the remainder of the western outpost and pulled its troops out of the garrison. Only minimal garrisons remained at Niagara, Michilimackinac, and Detroit to monitor events throughout the Great Lakes region. The result was predictable. Unaddressed grievances over uncontrolled white settlement on Indian lands, unrestricted trading practices, and escalating intercolonial competition fostered by rekindled political aspiration and territorial ambition in the Ohio Country combined to create a climate of suspicion and violence.[3]

The collapse of imperial resolve along the western frontier led to an inevitable lessening of administrative discipline within the Indian department and a corresponding weakening of bureaucratic oversight throughout the region. McKee's own actions during the period also significantly contributed to the rapid deterioration of affairs within the area. When he was appointed deputy agent, McKee became, by default, the highest ranking Crown official concerned solely with the administration of Indian affairs within the region. The importance of his post was further enhanced by the withdrawal of British troops from Fort Pitt in December 1772. Yet despite the increased significance that had been placed on his office by the course of events, McKee displayed growing signs of indifference toward his official duties.

The early 1770s had seen a marked increase in McKee's family obligations and a major expansion of his involvement in personal entrepreneurial ventures. Perhaps as well during this time, he became disillusioned about the Crown's reduced commitment to an active role in the region's affairs. By 1772, his relationship with the Indian department had grown distant, apathetic, and indifferent. In May, when Sir William Johnson recommended McKee for promotion, he admitted to Gage that he had not heard from McKee "for some time." Johnson believed McKee was living with his Indian relatives, but it was apparent that Sir William was unsure of the agent's exact whereabouts.[4]

The following month Johnson complained directly to Croghan, protesting that although McKee had been appointed "to transact business with the Indians in that Quarter," and that Johnson had "expected long since to have heard from him on that Head," the superintendent had "not had a line from him Since which leaves me a good deal in the dark with what is passing now in that Quarter." Sir William instructed Croghan to contact McKee, "If he is in them parts," and order him to report to the superintendent immediately. Sir William also requested that McKee travel to the Shawnee camps along the Scioto River to observe events and report any disaffection among the tribe.[5]

As Sir William suspected, McKee was already at the Scioto Shawnee villages, living with his family in a small settlement, Wockachaalli, or Crooked Nose's Place, about three miles from Chillicothe, east of Paint Creek. The settlement was small, newly plotted, and according to the Presbyterian missionary David Jones who visited McKee there in

January 1773, not much land was cleared. But Jones also reported that he found some of the finest horses he had seen in the Ohio Country at the village, along with cattle of equal quality. McKee and his family, said Jones, were earning their living mostly by trading in livestock. McKee did not respond to Johnson until after his return to Pittsburgh in mid-August. In early September, nearly nine months after his last communication, he wrote to Sir William with an account of his activities. He reported no overt complaints against the Crown, but he related that several meetings had taken place between representatives of the Shawnees, the Six Nations, the tribes along the Wabash, and the "Nations of the Misisipi."[6]

The information troubled Johnson. For several years the Indian department had heard rumors that Gaustarax, a disaffected Seneca, was attempting to form another confederacy of western tribes to strike at the English. McKee had been unable to discover the exact nature of the talks that had taken place along the Scioto. Nonetheless, he remained suspicious, reporting that there "appeared a Good deal of Disingenuity in the Conduct of the Indians," and he suspected the western tribes were up to "some bad purpose."[7]

McKee remained at Fort Pitt throughout October, where he and Croghan entertained Reverend Jones. In November, the deputy agent returned to the Scioto to attempt to cement the loyalty of the Shawnees to the Crown. He informed the tribe of Great Britain's sincere desire to maintain amicable relations with them and announced that the abandonment and razing of Fort Pitt was a "singular Mark of our Sincerity towards them." But he also warned that continued good relations would depend on "their own Good Conduct, as well as the Good Government of their Foolish Young Men," who for several years had harassed whites along the Ohio frontier.[8]

McKee also asked the village headmen about their meetings with the western nations the previous fall. The chiefs claimed the visits were nothing more than an effort to establish peaceful relations with tribes as far west as the Missouri River. But McKee noted that when two emissaries who had been to the Mississippi returned to camp, the tribe showed "a Degree of more Chagrin than could be expected would proceed the declared intention." Whatever the tribe's true objectives, McKee predicted that the coming spring would "shew the Issue of their Determination." McKee also reported that the Shawnee were genuinely pleased with the proposed demolition of Fort Pitt and that the tribe planned to visit Pittsburgh the following spring to express their appreciation and demonstrate their commitment to the new era of peaceful relations that the post's abandonment seemed to portend.[9]

In late December, McKee reported on the diplomatic activities taking place between the Ohio tribes and the British government's native allies to the east. It was clear from the tone, if not the content, of the communication that the withdrawal of imperial support from the region was making it increasingly difficult for McKee to effectively manage the region's affairs on the Crown's behalf. The British Indian Department was not alone in manipulating native diplomacy along the Great Lakes frontier. Since 1768, the Six Nations had grown increasingly troubled as the Ohio tribes resisted the obligations imposed upon them under the Fort Stanwix agreement. The eastern Iroquois had a vested interest in seeing that the terms of the treaty were upheld. In addition to the considerable political leverage the pact conferred upon the league and the gifts and tokens given the confederacy outright when the treaty was signed, the agreement also directed white expansion away from the Six Nations' traditional land in western New York and into the Ohio Valley, territory in which further white settlement would cause little concern to the Iroquois.[10]

Acting in concert with Sir William Johnson, the Iroquois league had sent Kayashuta, a well-known and highly esteemed Seneca statesman, throughout the West to assure that the interests of the Six Nations in the region were respected. Kayashuta was no stranger to McKee. Born about 1725 on the Genesee River in New York, the Seneca diplomat had accompanied George Washington when the young Virginian demanded the French withdraw from Fort Duquesne in 1753. Remaining active in western affairs, he became one of Pontiac's most able lieutenants during the Ottawa chief's insurrection in 1763. Kayashuta took part in the attacks against Fort Pitt and the British post at Venango, and after the conflict served as a spokesman for the Ohio Senecas, Delawares, and Shawnees when Bouquet's expedition penetrated to the Tuscarawas. In the intervening years, he had continued to meet with native and Crown officials at Fort Pitt to discuss the many issues that confronted both parties.

The Seneca diplomat passed through Pittsburgh in December and used the opportunity to meet with McKee. Kayashuta reported that he had recently sent messengers to the western tribes, urging the Delawares and Shawnees to act with the utmost restraint. Further, he had issued an invitation to the western tribes to meet with representatives of the Six Nations in Onondaga, New York, to discuss their grievances. But the Ohio tribes were reluctant to continue their deliberations with the Iroquois Confederacy. They had, they claimed, grown weary of the "Contempt and Neglect" shown them in the past by their eastern allies and could see little purpose in further councils.

Kayashuta also shared his concerns about the Ohio tribes' diplomatic initiatives. Like McKee, he had heard rumors that the Ohio tribes were attempting to forge a new, hostile alliance with tribes to the west. But the reports were vague and contradictory. Though troubled, the Senecas remained uncertain about the true status of the region's diplomatic maneuvering.

As McKee reported his conversation with Kayashuta to Johnson, he also admitted he was having great trouble acquiring the provisions and gifts required for the meeting with the Ohio Shawnees, planned for the following spring. The British had completed their withdrawal from Fort Pitt in mid-December. When the garrison departed, the military authorities gave McKee over 930 pounds of flour left in the post's commissary. McKee subsequently discovered that none of it was fit for consumption. McKee's business partner, Alexander Ross, advised the agent that flour and beef were available through one of the army's private contractors. Complaining that he had been given only the "Sweepings of the King's Store" with which to work, McKee urged Johnson to ask General Gage for permission to use the newly found source of provisions.[11]

At about the time of Kayashuta's visit, Croghan informed McKee of his intention to establish a new colony, Vandalia, west of Pittsburgh along the Ohio River. Croghan requested that McKee travel to the tribes in the region at his earliest opportunity to inform them of the Crown's plans for the area. Vandalia represented the culmination of years of maneuvering and planning on Croghan's part. Backed by men of substantial wealth and influence, including Croghan and his old associates William Trent and Samuel Wharton, the proposed colony was to consist of over twenty million acres located south of the Ohio River, opposite its confluence with the Scioto. After years of negotiation in Great Britain, the colony's backers had finally received permission from England's Board of Trade to proceed with their project. The Board had acted favorably after long delay, hoping in part to fill the political void caused after the withdrawal of Crown forces from the region. Vandalia, the Board anticipated, would restore a sense of stability to the region by replacing the imperial bureaucracy with a new colonial government.[12]

Considering the continuing problems that afflicted relations between natives and whites in the region, McKee was perhaps overly optimistic about the reaction of the area's Indians toward the new colony. "There is not any Doubt but they will receive . . . a Civil Government with great Satisfaction," he predicted to Croghan in December 1772. Removal of the garrison at Fort Pitt had calmed many of the suspicions the area tribes harbored, and McKee reported that "they seem quite easy in their Minds & all their Jealousies on that account removed."[13]

McKee traveled to the Scioto in early spring 1773 to meet with representatives of the Ohio Country nations. His meetings were cordial, and eventually he was able to persuade the Scioto tribes to agree with Croghan's plans. Though McKee's earlier confidence was not misplaced, his success with the Ohio Valley tribes resulted more from his ability as a negotiator than any enthusiasm among the region's Indians for further white settlement in the area. Meeting with the nations living along the Scioto in early April, McKee again stressed that the Crown intended to live peaceably with the region's tribes, and he portrayed the abandonment of Fort Pitt as evidence of the British government's good intentions. Yet he could not deny that unrestricted settlement and unsupervised trade were causing many problems. The new colony, he told the assembled tribes, would provide the opportunity to reassert governmental control over the troublesome whites who were encroaching into the area. The new government, he hinted, would be guided by persons like Trent and Croghan, men who were well known and trusted by the Indians and sympathetic to their needs. By using his intimate knowledge of the Ohio tribes and capitalizing upon the high personal esteem in which he and Croghan were held, McKee was able to frame his arguments in terms of the Indian's hopes as well as their fears. It was true, the Indians admitted, that they were alarmed at the great number of whites who had already settled in the area. "The Irregularity of their Conduct," they confided, "has made us judge That for the Peace of this Country, it [is] necessary for Prudent people to Govern them." Swayed by McKee's skillful diplomacy and carefully worded pledges, the tribes agreed to the new colony's formation, hoping the person appointed to lead the settlement would prove to be "a wise man, and restrain the abuses in Trade and irregularities by the Frontier Inhabitants."[14]

McKee's promises were easy in the making, but the lack of meaningful government authority rendered them impossible to honor. At the time McKee was meeting with the western tribes, a long-standing border dispute between Pennsylvania and Virginia further disrupted the region's political stability. The disagreement, centering on a region that stretched southward from Pittsburgh to the Ohio Valley, had originated years before as a result of the ambiguous and seemingly overlapping descriptions of each colony's western borders contained in their colonial charters. The disposition of the controversy would determine the area's future economic development as well as its political configuration. Pittsburgh was the heart of the Ohio Valley fur trade. The few residents clustered around the western outpost saw their continued prosperity in terms of a continuation of Pennsylvania's traditional support for the fur trade. Generally, they supported the colony's policy of limited settlement and conscious conciliation and cooperation with the western tribes. Virginia, on the other hand, sought to extract wealth from the region by selling the land. It wished to extinguish native title to the region and open the area to speculation, sale, and settlement as rapidly as possible.[15]

In 1773, John Murray, the fourth earl of Dunmore and the royal governor of Virginia, moved to exploit the Crown's abandonment of Fort Pitt by asserting Virginia's authority in the region. Partly in response to the deepening rift between the two colonies, Pennsylvania had incorporated Pittsburgh and the immediate vicinity into newly formed Westmoreland County. Lord Dunmore wished to legitimize Virginia's claim to the area by fiat. Such a move would frustrate the consolidation of Pennsylvanian authority in the region and preempt the title of the Vandalia proprietors.[16]

In early summer, a group of surveyors opened Virginia's campaign for the Ohio Valley by trespassing into Shawnee territory and plotting sites as far west as the Falls of the Ohio (present-day Louisville, Kentucky). Led by land speculator Thomas Bullitt, the party had brazenly entered Chillicothe, a Shawnee village along the Scioto, unannounced; they informed the tribe that the Indians no longer held claim to any land south of the Ohio. Enraged at the affront, the Shawnee band determined to kill Bullitt and his party; however, Richard Butler, a Pittsburgh trader living among the tribe, interceded and saved their lives. Bullitt and his group were permitted to continue their journey, but Cornstalk, one of the village chiefs, immediately sent a delegation to Pittsburgh to complain of the incident to McKee and Kayashuta. Clearly, events in the Ohio Country were increasingly beyond the deputy agent's ability to control. Although McKee dutifully reported the incident to Johnson, there was little he could do to reassure the western nations.

Tensions remained high throughout the west during the summer and into early autumn of 1773. During the first week of October, McKee received another message from Cornstalk and several other Ohio Valley chiefs claiming that Mingos living within the region seemed determined to instigate trouble between the English and the Ohio tribes. Cornstalk urged Croghan and Kayashuta (though living in Ohio, the Mingo were still loosely affiliated with the Iroquois Confederacy) to appeal to the "Heads of their Nation" to prevent a general outbreak of violence.[17]

Calling a hastily organized conference in Pittsburgh, McKee and the Seneca diplomat met with Cornstalk on October 9. The meeting began with angry accusations and countercharges from both the eastern and western tribes. When he was finally given the opportunity to speak, Kayashuta indignantly denied knowing anything concerning the alleged mischief perpetrated by the Ohio Mingos, and he blamed the Shawnees for permitting the tribe to act in such an unruly manner. A Huron chief who had accompanied Cornstalk to the meeting quickly put an end to the heated exchange. This was not an Indian problem, he pointed out. Rather, the English were responsible for the continuing conflict in the west. Whites, he stated, were openly selling liquor, "the Source of many Evils and Cause of a great deal of our Unhappyness." They were flagrantly dishonest in their trading practices and unrelenting in their unauthorized penetration far into Indian territory. "We have told you now the Cause of the imprudent Behavior of our foolish Young Men," he claimed, "and we desire you to be strong who is appointed to take Care of the Indians in removing every Obstacle that stands in the way of our future Peace and Tranquility." At the conclusion of his speech, the meeting abruptly closed.[18]

McKee was sympathetic toward the plight of the western tribes, but he was powerless to act on their behalf. In reporting the meeting to

Johnson, he admitted that most of the traders held little regard for the welfare of their clients, "For nothing but their private Interest actuates their Proceedings." In addition, he observed that although many of the Indians who lived in the region sincerely desired good relations with the English, even the most well disposed among them deeply resented the increasing number of whites who now regularly trespassed onto their land. Virginia's aggressive attempt to settle the region, he warned, was only aggravating the already troublesome situation.[19]

The October 1773 meeting between Kayashuta and Cornstalk marked the opening of a series of talks between the western tribes, imperial officials, and the eastern confederacy that would last throughout the winter and into the following year. The meetings, originally scheduled to begin in the spring of 1773, had been postponed, in part due to McKee's failure to find provisions and gifts for the visiting tribes. But as tensions mounted along the frontier, it was no longer possible to delay the long-overdue assembly. By November 1773, nearly four hundred Indians were gathered in Pittsburgh. Presents and provisions for the visiting representatives were supplied by Croghan, who personally bore their cost.[20]

Throughout November and December, the assembled nations voiced their dissatisfaction with the actions of the British. The western tribes again centered their complaints on unregulated white settlement beyond Pittsburgh, unrestricted trading practices, and liquor sales by the area's fur traders. As the conference continued into January, Croghan attempted to calm the Indian's fears. Once more he claimed that the region's troubles were the consequence of Virginia's adventuring in the area and that the establishment of Vandalia would bring order to the Ohio Valley. The Indians, though, would have none of Croghan's finger pointing. "You Pennsylvanians," they said, "will endeavor to exculpate yourselves, and throw this Charge on the Virginians, but we are convinced you are equally culpable." The result, they predicted, would be a "general Quarrell which will not easily be made up afterwards."[21]

Although Croghan did not yet realize it, the Vandalia project had already been terminated. Increasingly apprehensive over the threat of domestic violence along the eastern seaboard, Crown officials had withdrawn their permission for the new colony in late December. In January 1774, Lord Dunmore's agent, John Connolly, took advantage of the region's political vacuum and physically took possession of Fort Pitt on Virginia's behalf. Connolly had been born either in 1743 or 1744 at Wright's Ferry, York County, Pennsylvania. Although he studied medicine as a youth, he joined the British army as a young man, serving first in Martinique and later in North America during the Seven Years War. Following the conflict, he entered the fur trade and by the early 1770s was a familiar figure along the Ohio River, all the way from Pittsburgh to Kaskaskia deep within the Illinois Country. Although he had become fluent in several Indian languages and was recognized for his knowledge of native custom and protocol, he had never been able to make a profit in the fur trade. In early 1770, deeply in debt, he returned to live in Pittsburgh, where he practiced medicine and dabbled in land speculation. In 1773, when Lord Dunmore visited Pittsburgh, he appointed Connolly as his western agent. Connolly renamed the facility Fort Dunmore and announced that the surrounding area was under Virginia's jurisdiction; he established a court system and organized the militia under the authority of Virginia's colonial charter.[22]

The bold move caused an uproar in the small community. Long acquainted with living their lives with little regard for the political ambiguity generated by the border dispute, the town's residents were confronted with a situation that demanded a clear articulation of loyalty to one faction or the other. Croghan, who viewed the rapid settlement of the Ohio Valley as necessary to his continued financial well being, sided with the Virginians. McKee, who rarely took sides on any issue, allied himself with Pennsylvania. Dunmore's actions also disturbed the western tribes as much as they had Pittsburgh's residents. Already suspicious of the British in general, they had learned to be particularly wary of the Virginians, whom they regarded as openly avaricious and dishonest.[23]

The local tribes had every reason to be distrustful of Connolly and his associates. On January 25, 1774, the local militia gathered at Connolly's request and drilled at Fort Dunmore. Following their exercises, a few members fired their arms into the huts of several Indians who lived across the river from the Virginians' fort. Though no one was injured, the needless provocation alarmed members of the band, and they complained to McKee about the incident a few days later.[24]

The Virginia initiative also took away from McKee and the imperial government what little authority remained for administration of Indian affairs and placed it in the hands of Virginia authorities. The disruption and tension that Connolly's actions brought to the surface in Pittsburgh were also felt throughout the Indian department. The bureaucracy's frustration at being summarily dismissed from its important role in the region was immediately apparent. In late January 1774, McKee drew a severe rebuke from Johnson, who reprimanded the assistant agent for his slow and incomplete reports. The following month Alexander Ross sent a bitter complaint to McKee, demanding payment for provisions delivered to the agent long before. The normally deferential McKee responded with an impertinent letter to Johnson, complaining of Sir William's seeming lack of interest in western affairs in general and asking in regard to Alexander Ross's complaint, that the superintendent "may be pleased to point out such Method as Your Honor may think most expedient for having the same adjusted." By early spring, Croghan was openly describing McKee as "indolent" and claiming that the agent was not looking after his duties in a manner consistent with "the honner of the Department and . . . the generall good of his Country."[25]

The open feuding between McKee, the Indian department, and his Pittsburgh business associates, overtly indicated that the imperial government was ill prepared to stem the rising tide of violence along the frontier. By early spring the Shawnees were threatening to raid the settlements that continued to appear along the Ohio River Valley. McKee warned the nation that "they must not expect That the White People wou'd long lett their Conduct in this manner pass with Impunity." But despite his harsh tone, McKee's sympathies still lay with the western tribes. As he explained to Sir William, "The Expeditious Settlement of this Country gives all the Indian Nations this way Uneasiness and is the Subject of their constant Complaints."[26]

On February 27, McKee learned that a party of Shawnees had returned to the Shawnee towns after a raid in which a number of horses were taken and six whites and two Africans were killed. Furthermore, the report suggested that the raid was simply a preliminary to an extended period of violence. On March 1, the deputy agent met with several Shawnee headmen, along with a delegation from the Six Nations and the Delawares. McKee again expressed his concern about the continuing violence and requested they investigate the report. Asking the Shawnees to return home quickly and use their "utmost strength and Influence to put a stop to such Flagrant Outrages," McKee warned that the "numerous White people settled now upon this River . . . once prejudiced against you, will not be easily restrained from taking ample Vengence." The Indians, though, were in no mood to be either lectured or threatened. They waited seven days to reply, then the delegation advised McKee not to believe the report until they had inquired further into the matter. Neither denying guilt nor protesting innocence, the delegation promised only to communicate with McKee after they had completed their investigation.[27]

In mid-April 1774, an unidentified Shawnee told McKee that the western tribes, exasperated at the continuing unauthorized settlement of their lands, had already determined to strike at the British. The attack would come, claimed the informant, once the Mingos and Delawares living in the Pittsburgh vicinity had moved their families to the safety of the Shawnee villages located in the Scioto Valley. McKee was unable to substantiate the report, but it clearly reflected the continuing deterioration of affairs in the region.[28]

The Ohio tribes had good reason to protest. Not only were Virginia authorities doing little to control the illegal migration, they also appeared to be encouraging a flagrant disregard for Indian claims to the land. Despite the strenuous objections of the Shawnees living in the area, Dunmore authorized the Virginia surveyor, John Floyd, to conduct an expedition into the Ohio Country in the spring of 1774. Fearing armed resistance, Connolly sent a letter to Michael Creasap, a trader and land speculator from western Maryland who lived at Wheeling, urging the frontiersman to organize a party of men and hold them in readiness to strike at the western tribes should open hostilities erupt. Much later, John Minor, an officer in the local militia, recalled that Connolly's warning was accompanied by another from McKee and Croghan, telling Creasap that the Indians were ready to strike. Unfortunately, at about the same time, about forty miles from Pittsburgh, four Cherokees ambushed a canoe carrying three traders and their goods. The incident was apparently unconnected to the wider discontent that afflicted the region. But Connolly overreacted to the violence and rashly followed his first communication to Creasap with an open letter, probably written on April 21, to the residents of Wheeling, claiming that the Shawnees were "ill disposed" toward the area's white settlers and urging the town's residents to be prepared to "repel any insults" that might be offered. To Creasap and his followers, all of whom were eager to extinguish native title to the western lands, Connolly's message was an open declaration of war. By the evening following the reading of Connolly's message, Creasap's men had attacked and killed a Shawnee and a Delaware traveling down the Ohio River from Pittsburgh. The following day, the Virginia irregulars also engaged fourteen Shawnees returning from a conference at McKee's, killing one and plundering their goods.[29]

The violence unleashed by Creasap's men spread unabated across the region, culminating in an incident that, even by frontier standards, was distinguished by its cold-blooded brutality. In 1773, a Mingo headman named Johnny Logan and a small band of followers had established a village thirty miles north of Wheeling, near the mouth of Yellow Creek (close to present-day Wellsville, Ohio). Logan was the oldest son of Johnny Shikellamy, and both father and son were well known along the western border for their steadfast loyalty to the British. During the Seven Years War, Shikellamy and his family had sought refuge at Thomas McKee's trading post. There can be little doubt that Logan and Alexander McKee knew one another well, but the extent of their contact during the spring of 1774 is unknown.[30]

Logan's home lay opposite the site of Joshua Baker's Virginia homestead and trading post. Baker and the Mingos had lived peacefully ever since Logan's arrival. But in early May, a group of Virginians, led by Daniel Greathouse, methodically lured ten members of the Mingo village to Baker's trading post where, over the course of the afternoon, they were murdered. Among the dead were several members of Logan's immediate family, including his mother and brother. Greathouse and his companions also killed Logan's sister as she carried her newborn infant on her back.[31]

The incident began on May 1, when two men asked Capt. Michael Myers of Washington County, Pennsylvania, to guide them over to the west side of the Ohio River where they wished to travel up Yellow Creek and examine some land a few miles from the stream's confluence with the Ohio. Myers's party did not have permission to be in Indian territory and crossed the Ohio at dusk to avoid detection. Camping for the night a short distance from their destination, Myers and the two men were wakened later that evening by the loud rattling of a bell attached to one of their horses. Investigating, they discovered an Indian apparently in the act of stealing the animal. Myers shot and killed the Indian.

A short while later, a second Indian, drawn to the site by the report of Myers's rifle, also was executed. Frightened, Myers and his two companions fled back to Virginia and Baker's trading post. Worried that their actions would prompt a retaliatory raid from the Yellow Creek Indians, Myers sent word to Greathouse and other neighbors within the vicinity to assemble at Baker's and prepare an ambush. Although Baker was not present, by dawn, thirty-two men were lying in wait.[32]

The following morning, unaware that the perpetrators of the previous evening's violence awaited them, eight members of Logan's band crossed the river to Baker's. Among the group were four men and three women, including Logan's brother, mother, and sister who carried her two-month-old infant on her back. Logan's band had frequently visited Baker's post and usually spent their time buying liquor, milk, and other small items. Today, Nathaniel Tomlinson, Baker's brother-in-law, was more generous than usual with his liquor and eventually invited the Indians to take part in a shooting match. As the contest began, one of the Indians, John Petty, who was somewhat intoxicated, wandered through the trading post. Coming upon Tomlinson's regimental coat and hat, he put them on and swaggered through the house claiming, "I am a White Man." The action insulted Tomlinson, and when the Indians discharged their weapons at a target, he grabbed his rifle and shot Petty as he stood in the doorway. The shot was a signal for Greathouse and the others to come out of hiding and kill the remainder of the Mingos.

The attack was swift and brutal. John Sappington, one of the Virginians, shot and killed Logan's brother and then scalped him. For years after, Sappington took particular delight in boasting of the feat and described the trophy, which still was adorned with trade silver, as a "very fine one." Logan's sister was panic stricken; she ran across the courtyard in front of the trading post and stopped six feet in front of one of Greathouse's men. In the split second that their eyes met, he put a bullet into her forehead. Grabbing the infant from her cradleboard, he took hold of its ankles and was about to dash its brains out when one of his companions intervened to save the child's life. The remaining Indians also were shot or tomahawked. Within seconds, all the Mingos were dead. The savagery of the attack was astounding, and even James Chambers, a neighbor of Baker's who was not present, declared that the murderers "appeared to have lost, in a great degree, all sentiments of humanity as well as the effects of civilization."[33]

Alarmed by the gunfire from across the river, seven other members of Logan's camp started across the Ohio in two canoes to investigate. Greathouse and his men spread out in the underbrush on the eastern shore and fired on the Mingos as they neared land, killing two and sending the others back in retreat. A second group of Mingos attempted another landing, but like the first, was turned away by Greathouse and his companions.[34]

McKee learned of the Yellow Creek murders on May 3, and he immediately called Connolly, Kayashuta, a deputation from the Six Nations, and members of the local militia together for a meeting at Croghan's home, where he informed them of the Mingos' deaths. McKee assured his guests that the incident was the act of "a few rash and inconsiderate White People, and not by the Intention or Knowledge of any of our Wise People"; he promised them that Dunmore, after he learned of the murders, would surely take every step to rectify the situation. In the meantime, McKee urged all parties to remain calm and to keep the peace. Two days later, on May 5, McKee met again with many of the same representatives. He performed the condolence ceremony, "covering the Bones of their deceas'd Friends with some Goods suitable to the Occasion and agreeable to their Custom," and he dispatched several messages to the western tribes "to convince those People to whom they were to be delivered, of our Sincerity, And That We did not countenance these Misdemeanors."[35]

McKee had responded appropriately and energetically to the dangerous situation. But the viciousness of the murders that had precipitated the crisis, when combined with the long-standing grievances of the western tribes, meant that a peaceful resolution would be difficult to obtain. Word of the murders raced through the western border settlements and with it the fear of Indian retaliation. Many fled, abandoning their homes and their possessions. "The panic becoming universal, claimed Connolly, "nothing but confusion, Distress and Flight was conspicuous."[36]

The frightened settlers were more than warranted in their apprehension. The Shawnees and Mingos had often disagreed over policy in the Ohio Country, yet Michael Creasap's adventuring and the Yellow Creek murders had been enough to bring the two tribes together for a council along the Scioto River. The two nations listened to the message sent from McKee on May 5. While dismissing McKee's words as lies, the

Shawnees refused for the moment to go to war with the Virginians. But fifteen to twenty Mingos under Logan set off for the Ohio Valley to seek retribution for the loss of their family and friends.[37]

By late May, only Logan's Mingos were at war. McKee, with Croghan's assistance, had fashioned a fragile peace that greatly restricted the scope of open warfare along the Ohio frontier. As the month drew to a close, Connolly, who had seemed to support McKee's efforts up to that time, began to take a much harder diplomatic stance, possibly at Dunmore's instruction. He called out the local militia, ordered needed repairs to Fort Dunmore, and sent a party of soldiers to patrol the Ohio River below Pittsburgh, hoping to engage and defeat one of the hostile bands that roamed the area. Clearly, Virginia sought to widen the conflict, hoping that a victory over the western tribes would legitimize Virginia's claims to the region.[38]

On June 10, realizing that the local situation was well beyond his ability to influence, McKee wrote to Johnson and advised the superintendent that only the reimposition of imperial or Pennsylvanian control could halt the violence. It was impossible to predict, wrote McKee, whether the worsening situation around Pittsburgh would result in a general Indian war. But despite the violence perpetrated by natives and whites alike, there seemed to be a temporary lull in the hostilities. Now was the time that "some wise interposition of Government is truly necessary, and would undoubtedly restore peace," claimed the agent. "Without it it is impossible, and thousands of the inhabitants must be involved in misery and distress." Speaking of the Indians living in the Ohio Country, McKee wrote that "they have given great proofs of their pacific disposition, and have acted with more moderation than those who ought to have been more rational." A war to chastise them would be ineffective and would inevitably lead to the "destruction of this country."[39]

McKee's efforts, along with those of Croghan and Kayashuta, brought a tenuous peace to the Pittsburgh region. Although tensions remained high, the Shawnees were inclined to remain at peace despite the violence that had been directed toward them. The Delaware and Iroquois who had also suffered from the Virginians' attacks seemed content to let matters rest for the moment. Even Logan's band had returned to camp with scalps and prisoners and declared that their retaliatory raids were completed. But Sir William's self-interested indifference and the Virginians' unwillingness to halt their aggression doomed McKee's attempts to find a peaceful settlement. On June 14, several Virginians fired upon a Delaware walking the woods with McKee. A few days later, Shawnee envoys sent to the Ohio Shawnee villages where they had been negotiating for McKee, returned to Pittsburgh escorting several English traders whom the tribe had been protecting. Despite their obviously peaceful intentions, Connolly ordered the militia to either seize or kill the Indians. The Shawnees escaped after being hidden by McKee and Croghan at Croghan's residence, but as they returned to their homes, they were found and ambushed by a party sent out by Connolly. One of the Shawnees, Silver Heels, was seriously wounded during the episode.[40]

The treachery enraged the Shawnees. As news of the incident spread throughout the Ohio backwoods, small groups of the tribe fanned out across the frontier, deploying toward the Upper Ohio Valley. One group moved directly toward Pittsburgh, where they hoped to assassinate McKee, Croghan, and Kayashuta, the three that they held most responsible for their present difficulties. Within a short time, the entire border was in a state of near panic as the tribe carried out retaliatory raids throughout the frontier region.[41]

The outbreak of open warfare did not signal either the end or the failure of McKee's diplomatic efforts. Throughout the summer, he and his envoys continued to negotiate with the western tribes, attempting to limit the size of the Shawnees' military alliance and thereby contain the scope of the violence. Although the Wyandots, Hurons, and Ottawas threatened to join the Shawnees, by August Croghan and McKee had succeeded in diplomatically isolating the warring tribe from its western neighbors. Further, McKee had also convinced a number of Delawares and eastern Iroquois to take an active role in the contest by scouting and supplying intelligence to the Virginians. To the east, Guy Johnson, Sir William's nephew, had likewise intervened to prevent the Shawnees from forming a military pact with the Six Nations. By fall, the Shawnees were facing their Virginia adversaries virtually alone.[42]

In late August, wanton violence, again perpetrated by the region's settlers, threatened Virginia's tenuous alliance. On August 29, a party of Delawares had come to Croghan's to trade. As they returned home, the party was ambushed, and two were killed. Croghan and McKee both persuaded Maj. Angus McDonald, a prominent Pittsburgh resident, to offer a reward of fifty pounds for the identities of the murderers. The following day, McKee met with a delegation of Delaware headmen. Calling the murders a "Barbarous Act," perpetrated by those who had committed a "flagrant offense against all Laws both Human and divine," the deputy agent claimed that the Virginia governor was on his way to Fort Pitt and promised that when Lord Dunmore arrived, he would personally administer justice to the guilty. Once again, promises, gifts, and diplomacy conducted at the personal level calmed a potentially calamitous situation.[43]

Dunmore arrived in Pittsburgh in September to personally chastise the belligerent Shawnees. The increasing tempo of violence had had an impact on the small community. When the missionaries David Jones and David McClure visited the village in the summer of 1772, they had found a community of about forty hewed-log dwellings, the homes to "Indian traders and some mechanicks." A good orchard of apple and peach trees and well-tended gardens stretched along the river banks. The fort itself was a "handsome & strong fortification" that contained "comfortable" buildings and a barracks housing eighty soldiers with one commanding officer. McClure noted that "a few fearers of God and friends of religion" lived in the town, and Jones agreed, claiming that some the residents were "agreeable and worthy of regard." Others, though, were "lamentably dissolute in their morals." Now the fort was abandoned, the gardens overgrown, and the buildings in the fort nearly in ruins. Because many residents had fled as the violence increased, only thirty of the homes in the village remained occupied. Dunmore strengthened the fort materially by facing the walls in brick and by rebuilding several of the bastions. In early summer, he also directed the local militia to fortify both Baker's settlement at Yellow Creek and the mouth of the Kanawha River (near present-day Point Pleasant, West Virginia). Maj. William Crawford, a "prudent, resolute officer," began construction of Fort Fincastle (present-day Wheeling, West Virginia) in early June, while the following month, Col. Andrew Lewis advanced with about fifteen hundred members of the Augusta, Fincastle, and Botetourt County militias to the Kanawha.[44]

Lewis and his troops arrived at the mouth of the Kanawha River on October 6, 1774, and encamped on its east bank at the confluence with the Ohio. Early on the morning of October 9, scouts from the camp discovered several parties of Indians in the vicinity and raised the alarm.

The Indians were part of a large force made up mostly of Shawnees and Mingos. Individuals from the Delaware, Ottawa, and Wyandot tribes had also joined the expedition, estimated to be more than one thousand strong. Led by several Shawnee chiefs, including Blue Jacket, Black Hoof, and Red Hawk, the group had crossed the Ohio River the previous night and was now moving into position to attack the awakening Americans. The assault came quickly. The army's second in command, William Fleming, and Lewis's brother, Charles, were wounded in the first volleys, Lewis mortally. Nonetheless, the Virginians held their ground and repelled the Indians' repeated assaults. By noon, the Indians began to give ground, and at dusk the ferociously contested battle drew slowly to a close as the Shawnee chiefs and the surviving members of their army withdrew across the Ohio. Both sides were exhausted, neither was defeated. But the Virginians claimed the field and the victory.[45]

On October 11, Lord Dunmore, unaware that the Battle of Point Pleasant had taken place, began his own advance against the Ohio tribes. Moving down the Ohio to the mouth of the Hockhocking River (the present-day Hocking River at Hockingport, Ohio), the Virginia governor proceeded upstream to the Ohio Country, stopping at the Pickaway Plains where he built a makeshift encampment, Camp Charlotte. Having heard at last of Lewis's victory, Dunmore was ready when Cornstalk, acting on behalf of the warring tribes, approached the American camp to negotiate a peace. Virginia's terms were simple and straightforward. The Indians would return all the prisoners, horses, and valuables taken over the course of the previous hostilities; they would promise not to attack boats traveling along the Ohio; and they would promise not to cross the river to hunt in Kentucky. Lastly, they would adhere to the King's future regulations governing the region's trade. The agreement marked the conclusion of Dunmore's War, the first colonial-era confrontation fought exclusively within the Ohio Country and the first in which the Ohio tribes were required to make a significant cession of land. Though the terms of the treaty seemed lenient, the Shawnees had been dealt a severe blow. Not until the Revolutionary War was well under way would the tribe be prepared to renew its challenge to American expansion.[46]

McKee's role in the western campaign is unclear and his activities during the period poorly documented. Following the battle, the Virginian army marched north into Ohio to rendezvous with Dunmore, leaving the sick, injured, and other invalids at the Kanawha under the protection of a small detachment of able-bodied men commanded by the wounded William Fleming. James Newell, an injured soldier who served with Capt. William Herbert's company of the Fincastle Militia, was one of those left to recuperate along the Ohio. On October 21, Newell recorded in his diary that Alexander McKee had gone fishing along the Ohio River and had returned to camp carrying a catfish that weighed over fifty-seven and one-half pounds. There seems to be no other record describing McKee's participation in the military action or its immediate aftermath.[47]

McKee's official silence during this critical campaign is difficult to understand. Perhaps McKee had simply reverted to the poor communication habits he had displayed over the course of the preceding few years, those that repeatedly had evoked Sir William's displeasure. A second explanation might lie with the fact that Sir William had died in August. The administration of the Indian department, already haphazard at best when dealing with western affairs, particularly after 1772, was thrown into further confusion after the superintendent's unexpected death. McKee's silence might simply be a reflection of uncertain and changing chains of command.[48]

McKee's behavior was no doubt also influenced by the steady decline in his ability to function effectively as a mediator for the Crown. McKee worked best when he occupied the cultural middle ground, the volatile intersections where the differing interests of the British government and the western nations could be negotiated and reconciled. As Great Britain became increasingly diverted by eastern affairs, the corresponding reduction of imperial interest in the Ohio region deprived McKee of the basic resources, such as provisions and gifts, required to conduct negotiations with the Ohio tribes. More importantly, the British abandonment of Fort Pitt in 1772 fundamentally altered the political dynamic that McKee had become particularly adept at manipulating. Although Crown and native issues still intersected with the same regularity as they had in the past, the familiar avenues for addressing and reconciling these issues were no longer present. Where McKee had once stood in the center of two interacting parties, only one—the western tribes—now remained within the agent's practical reach. The British had, in a sense, carried McKee's middle ground with them when they abandoned the Pittsburgh vicinity. Their departure took away the intimate social arena used by the agent to explore issues of mutual concern and in which a resolution acceptable to both parties could be fashioned. Distanced from the seat of meaningful imperial influence, he could represent neither party with the authority or immediacy that had been central to his earlier effectiveness.

Virginia's readiness to exploit the political void caused by the British departure only hastened the rapid erosion of McKee's tenuous hold on the political middle ground. Dunmore's occupation of the Ohio Country was not negotiated. The royal governor had little need for or appreciation of the skills reflected in persons like McKee. Dunmore's campaign was also one that elicited explicit declarations of allegiance from its participants. The overtly anti-Indian nature of Virginia's adventuring and McKee's open alignment with the Pennsylvania faction stripped the agent of much of the political and ethnic ambiguity he needed to function successfully as an intermediary between the Crown and the western tribes.

Ironically, the British withdrawal from Fort Pitt came when McKee's importance as a mediator was growing along the western border. The events that led to Dunmore's War marked McKee's first significant interaction as a Crown official with the Iroquois Confederacy. McKee worked well with Kayashuta throughout the crisis. Because the eastern league's and the Crown's diplomatic interests in the west were compatible, and because McKee's relationship with the Seneca chief was in many respects similar to that which he had previously enjoyed with the region's imperial officials, their efforts were generally successful. This bilateral expansion of McKee's role from one who mediated exclusively between the Ohio tribes and the Crown to one who mediated all native interests that affected the Great Lakes region reflected both the deepening complexity of the area's native diplomacy and McKee's growing skill as an intermediary. His demonstrated ability to reconcile eastern Iroquois and Great Lakes Algonquin interests would become a defining characteristic of his career after the outbreak of the Revolution.

Lastly, that the Shawnees were the targets of Dunmore's aggression also affected the agent's performance during the crisis. There is no reason to think that McKee's ties to the central Ohio tribe had weakened. But the crisis of 1774 had also deepened McKee's appreciation of the Crown and its potential ability to impose stability and act as a peacekeeper within the region. It was true that he had worked energetically to isolate the tribe from potential allies during the crisis. In so doing, he had promoted the Crown's as well as Virginia's interests, for it was clear that with the increasing political instability along the East Coast, Great Britain was ill prepared to become involved in a general Indian uprising along the western border. But in McKee's view, the reimposition of governmental authority would serve the Shawnee's long-term interests as well. The agent was all too well acquainted with the lack of governmental or social control exhibited by the throngs of Virginians eager to gain admittance to the Ohio Country. He also saw that without the reestablishment of imperial authority, nothing was going to stop the rising tide of white immigration into the region. In August 1774, Pennsylvania's governor, John Penn, alarmed at the impending violence, had sent a letter to the Ohio Shawnees warning that "the people of *Virginia* are like the leaves upon the trees, very numerous, and you are but few, and . . . they will at last wear you out and destroy you." McKee felt that a quick resolution to the conflict, followed by some sort of negotiated settlement and the reestablishment of orderly government, would limit the violence and bring some sense of stability to the chaotic situation.[49]

Although the Shawnees bore a disproportionate share of the misfortune unleashed by the Virginian expedition, few of those involved in Dunmore's enterprise gained from the experience. The outbreak of the Revolution negated Virginia's claim to the Ohio Country and caused Dunmore to take refuge in England. Johnson had died during the crisis, and the remainder of the Indian department was forced to flee to Montreal to prosecute the war with the Americans. Croghan and the other Vandalia proprietors never profited from the venture, and he and McKee remained estranged despite their brief period of cooperation during Dunmore's military preparations. The Great Lakes tribes were divided, suspicious, and reeling from the defeat inflicted by Lewis's army at Point Pleasant.

At least one person, though, benefited significantly from Dunmore's foray into the Upper Ohio Valley. In late 1774 or early 1775, the Virginia governor presented McKee with a warrant for three thousand acres of land south of the Ohio River. McKee quickly sold the parcel to his business associate, Alexander Ross. It seems likely that Dunmore granted the land to the agent in recognition of his efforts on the Governor's behalf during the summer and fall of 1774. In addition, Dunmore also named McKee a justice of the peace for Augusta County, Virginia (Pittsburgh), on February 23, 1775.[50]

Dunmore's excursion into the Ohio Valley was openly self-interested, a rapacious and vulgar grab for land and wealth. His actions were, in fact, so contrary to imperial policy that one recent historian has speculated that the governor was dangerously close to being recalled. Yet Dunmore must also have seen his quest for the Ohio Country, however peripherally, within the broader context of international imperial affairs. At the time Dunmore sought to assert his colony's claim to the Ohio Country, he also was growing angry at the increasingly defiant nature of the colony's politics. The Virginia governor undoubtedly realized that McKee was the only Crown official who remained west of the Allegheny Mountains and east of Detroit. Dunmore's actions in Ohio represented much that McKee found distasteful, but as a member of the peerage, Dunmore embodied the Crown and its importance to the continued well-being of the Ohio Country tribes. Dunmore's grant to McKee and McKee's appointment to the bench signified an attempt to openly recognize his importance to the Crown's continuing efforts in the West. McKee's acceptance of both reflected a reaffirmation of the agent's ideological affinity to the British government and an understanding that his own interests and those of the Ohio tribes would be best served by allegiance to the Crown.[51]

The conclusion of Dunmore's War was a defining moment in McKee's life. McKee's loyalty to the British government would prove an important element in the contest for the Ohio Country during the Revolution. The Virginia governor's instincts were correct. Dunmore's War represented the prologue to nearly eight years of bitter conflict throughout the Great Lakes region. McKee had emerged from Dunmore's campaign unscathed, recognized as one of the region's most important links between the Ohio nations and the Crown. The British government would find ready use for McKee's talents in the days ahead.

CHAPTER FIVE

— 🐉 —

The Revolutionary War,
1775–1778

———

The Revolutionary War years were a period of transition for McKee, a time when his sympathies for the Crown matured into an overtly Loyalist self-identity. By the end of the conflict, settlers throughout the Ohio Valley regarded McKee as one of the most able and notorious of the British agents who worked among the Ohio tribes. But such was not the case in 1775. As the war began, McKee's loyalties were divided. British officials had rewarded his ideological commitment to the Crown with steady advancement within the Indian department, political appointments, and modest land grants. His commercial attachment to the Pittsburgh fur trade establishment, dominated for the most part by men sympathetic to the Patriot cause, had also brought him wealth, status, and prestige.

McKee's activities during the war fell into two distinct phases. From the beginning of the war until the early spring of 1778, McKee publicly disavowed his affiliation with the Crown in an attempt to protect his substantial economic assets in the Upper Ohio Valley and to provide a measure of personal protection in what was becoming an increasingly hostile environment. After events forced him to flee to Detroit in March 1778, McKee became a willing, active, and energetic participant in the war effort, using the full measure of his talents to further the British cause. Both strategies were equally self-serving and both were driven by the pragmatic cultural ambivalence that defined the Ohio frontier.

News of the April 19, 1775, fighting between colonials and British regulars at Lexington and Concord reached Pittsburgh soon after the first of May. Almost at once McKee and nineteen other leading citizens of Pittsburgh, along with several hundred other residents of the area, wrote an open letter to Dunmore commending him for his actions on their behalf and applauding him for fulfilling his "duty as a faithful officer of the Crown." But at a meeting held at Fort Dunmore on May 16 to discuss the New England violence, the community appointed twenty-nine men to act as a committee of correspondence on behalf of Augusta County, Virginia. Many of its members, including George Croghan, John Campbell, Edward Ward, Thomas Smallman, and John Anderson, had worked with McKee either as Indian department employees or as members of Pittsburgh's large fur-trading community.[1]

The committee unanimously approved of the "spirited behavior of their brethren in *New England*," and they "encouraged their neighborhood to follow the brave example." Great Britain's actions during the April confrontation were "open acts of unprovoked hostilities," said the commission, "prompted by the wicked minions of power to execute our ruin." The delegation then called out the militia, directed a subcommittee to secure arms and ammunition, and recommended that the town's residents make every effort to cultivate friendship with the region's Indians.[2]

Despite its apparent commitment to the Patriot cause, the committee's response was a poor gauge of the region's political allegiances. Loyalties along the western Pennsylvania frontier were varied and fluid, defined more by self-interest than by ideology. At the same time Pittsburgh's Committee of Safety was meeting at Fort Dunmore, a similar committee gathered at Hanna's Town in Westmoreland County, only thirty-two miles away. The Hanna's Town delegation, while also decrying the British actions in Massachusetts, declared they were "possessed with the most unshaken loyalty and fidelity to His Majesty, King *George* the Third . . . who we wish may long be the beloved Sovereign of a free and happy people throughout the whole British Empire." Even in Pittsburgh, support for the Patriot cause was weaker than the Commit-

Clinch River

Niagara

Detroit•

Roche de Bout •

•Sandusky

• Fort Laurens
•Moravian Missions

Logan's Camp   • Fort Pitt

•Battle of Point Pleasant

•Vincennes

Blue Licks•
Martin's Station •   •Ruddle's Station
•Bryan's Station

THE OHIO COUNTRY FRONTIER
1773–1783

tee of Safety's actions indicated. Less than two weeks earlier, six members of the Augusta County committee, including John Campbell, John Cannon, Edward Ward, Thomas Smallman, John Gibson, and William Crawford, were among those who had joined McKee in expressing their appreciation to Lord Dunmore for his actions as a Crown official. Beneath the bombast, personal political loyalties remained ambiguous and, perhaps purposely, opaque.[3]

Lingering animosity stemming from the Virginia-Pennsylvania border dispute influenced the region's unsteady political allegiances fully as much as did international affairs. Virginia supporters dominated Augusta County, while Westmoreland County had generally remained loyal to Pennsylvania. Throughout the latter part of 1774 and into 1775, agents from both camps waged campaigns of intimidation and harassment against each other. Early in the spring of 1775, Lord Dunmore further complicated matters by secretly directing John Connolly to forge a military alliance between the region's Indians and the Crown. As one of the leading antagonists against Pennsylvania, Connolly was already held in low regard by the Westmoreland faction, who quickly became suspicious of his motives. The Virginia supporters sitting on the Augusta committee also soon suspected that his Indian diplomacy was a Loyalist ploy. By early summer, both factions openly distrusted the governor's agent. On July 25, 1775, Connolly fled Pittsburgh, never to return; he sought refuge with Dunmore aboard the governor's ship, the *Royal William*, at anchor along the Virginia coast.[4]

Connolly had begun his negotiations with the western tribes in the early spring by calling on the nations to meet in Pittsburgh in mid-May. The purpose of the council, he claimed, was to formalize the provisional agreement negotiated by Dunmore at Camp Charlotte the previous autumn. The western nations were slow to assemble. But once they had gathered, Dunmore's assistant began the proceedings under the watchful eyes of the Augusta committee. McKee, though present, played only a secondary role in the negotiations, interpreting and supplying small quantities of wampum, rum, and provisions. The Shawnees arrived too late to take part in the deliberations, but Connolly concluded an agreement by early July that served to reduce tensions between the Ohio tribes and the Crown.[5]

The representatives of the Virginia colonial assembly and the Continental Congress wisely placed little trust in Connolly's efforts. By midsummer 1775, both bodies had sent their own delegates to Pittsburgh to negotiate with the western nations. Though McKee's role in the subsequent proceedings was muted, he was still recognized by all parties as a figure of considerable influence. When the Shawnee contingent arrived in Pittsburgh, their leader, Cornstalk, reminded the Virginians that "Captain McKee was many Years ago Placed by our Wise People at this Council fire to have the Care of it and all our Young people look on him in that light." The Shawnees hoped that "he will still have an ear to our Mutual Interest as we think he ought to have as great a regard for ours as yours and hope he will have an Ear Open to Each of us." Andrew Lewis, who headed the Virginia commissioners, was forced to admit that "we have the same respect for Captain McKee you have." But privately he was wary of McKee's close association with the Crown and Connolly, and he prevented the agent from any meaningful participation in the negotiations that followed. Eventually, Lewis secured a declaration of neutrality from the western tribes.[6]

Before he departed from Pittsburgh, Connolly made a determined effort to engage as many "gentlemen of consequence" as possible into the Crown's service. These men were either officers in the militia or county magistrates and were, therefore, those whose wealth and influence could most effectively aid the British government. Just before his departure, Connolly met privately with those men he trusted the most; he informed them that he planned to flee the area and initiate some sort of military campaign against the Patriots who lived within the region. The clandestine Loyalists approved of the plot, and according to Connolly, they immediately entered into a solemn compact, promising that if Connolly could obtain the necessary authority to raise men, they would "at the risk of life and property, most willingly engage to restore the constitutional authority . . . after which the strictest secrecy was enjoined, and the company separated." Although Connolly's recollection of the meeting makes no mention of McKee, it is difficult, especially in light of Connolly's subsequent actions and the central place McKee occupied in Connolly's plans, to believe he was not present.[7]

When Connolly met with Dunmore following his escape from Pittsburgh, he proposed raising two companies of Loyalists from along the western frontier. The two forces, when combined with a small detachment of the Eighteenth Regiment of infantry already in the West and with the western tribes, would attack rebel settlements along the Ohio Valley, destroy Fort Pitt, and drive across Virginia, eventually linking up with troops commanded by Dunmore along the East Coast. Dunmore approved of the plan and sent Connolly to Boston to meet with Thomas Gage, the commander of British forces in North America. Gage endorsed the scheme. Claiming that the operation would "be of great use," he promised to do "all I can to promote its Success." He sent letters to several Crown officials, including McKee, advising them of the plan and ordering them to take the preliminary measures necessary to implement it. McKee was specifically advised to gather as many

Indians as possible for the expedition and to defer to Dunmore's orders regarding the enterprise. With Gage's support secured, Connolly returned to Virginia, hoping to find a way to travel to Detroit where he could put his plan into action.[8]

Connolly left for the western post in mid-November 1775. Earlier in the month, Dunmore had commissioned him a lieutenant colonel of the Queen's Royal Rangers and authorized the same rank for McKee. He traveled with three others, John Smyth, Smyth's servant, and a third Loyalist named Cameron. Connolly suggested that the party split in two; Smyth and his servant would go to Pittsburgh to deliver the dispatches to McKee, travel down the Ohio to the Scioto, and then go north up that river to the Shawnee towns. From there, they would travel overland to Lake Erie, and then to Detroit. Connolly and Cameron were to travel directly to Detroit. Unfortunately for Smyth and Connolly, they had traveled only as far as Hagerstown, Maryland, when members of the local militia recognized Connolly and detained the entire party for questioning. A search revealed a written draft of Connolly's proposal to Gage sewed in the lining of a portmanteau owned by Smyth's servant. The Patriot patrol placed the group under arrest. Smyth, pleading ignorance, was questioned and released, but Connolly, who was well known for his Loyalist sympathies, was escorted to Philadelphia where he remained imprisoned until his parole in July 1780.[9]

While in prison, Connolly secretly managed to pass two letters to Smyth. The first, addressed to his wife Susanna, claimed he had been in contact with McKee, and the agent, using Indian department funds, was to provide for her well-being. The second, addressed personally to McKee, advised that "I mentioned you in proper terms to General Gage," and it instructed the deputy agent to assist Smyth in procuring a canoe and a gun so he could complete his journey to Detroit. But once again Smyth and his dispatches were apprehended by a rebel patrol in mid-January 1776. Able to offer no plausible defense, Smyth was incarcerated at Fredericktown, Maryland. As a result, the revolutionary authorities in both Pennsylvania and Maryland quickly moved against McKee, who now seemed openly implicated in the Crown's activities along the western border. The Lancaster, Pennsylvania, Committee of Safety sent an agent to arrest McKee, but before the order could be put into effect, far more damaging evidence against McKee surfaced at Pittsburgh.[10]

On February 29, 1776, Col. John Butler, the British Indian Department official in charge of affairs along the Niagara frontier, wrote McKee, ordering the western agent to meet with him at Fort Niagara. "Your knowledge in Indian affairs, your hitherto undoubted zeal for his Majesty's service, and the duty you owe to your government," claimed Butler, made McKee's attendance "absolutely necessary." Further, Butler asked that McKee report "anything worth notice that you may know respecting the proceedings of the Rebels your way," and he ended by admitting, "I have much more to say to you than the compass of this paper will admit of; but must defer it on account of the precariousness of the times."[11]

Richard Butler (no relation to John), who had been appointed Indian agent at Pittsburgh by the Continental Congress, learned of the confidential communication shortly before it arrived. He and several members of the West Augusta Committee of Safety called on McKee when the message was delivered and demanded to see the letter. McKee promptly complied and denied knowing anything of Butler's intentions. The American agent then put McKee on parole, taking McKee's promise that he would send no dispatches nor conduct any business with the western tribes without the committee's knowledge. Committee member John Campbell remained dissatisfied with the arrangement and the following day demanded that Butler put McKee's parole in writing. McKee complained that the request was unnecessarily offensive and that the committee had overstepped its authority. Eventually he agreed to the demand, but he told Campbell and Butler that he had business to attend to at his farm in Lancaster and expected to be allowed to come and go to the estate as he pleased. McKee had reason to protest, for the parole was highly restrictive. Nonetheless, he promised not to transact any business with the Indians on behalf of the Crown, not to directly or indirectly correspond with any British official, and not to leave the immediate vicinity without approval of the Committee of Safety. The action also troubled Butler who, along with "several respectable inhabitants of this country," could find no fault with McKee's deportment. In fact, he found the committee's actions quite unnecessary. "I must say in justice to Mr. McKee," reported Butler, "that I have not seen one act that discovered an inimical intention to this country."[12]

For the moment, Butler's endorsement helped dissipate the community's fears, and on April 29 the Continental Congress, "Relying on the integrity and honour of Captain A. McGee," amended the parole to allow him to go at large after giving his promise that he would not engage in any activity that might harm the Patriot cause. But it was impossible for McKee to completely escape the web of suspicion that began to surround him. On May 10, 1776, George Morgan, a Pittsburgh fur trader and land speculator who had replaced Richard Butler as the region's congressionally appointed Indian agent, announced that a man named Molloy had arrived at the post with another message from Connolly for McKee to forward to Detroit. The rumor was apparently unfounded. On May 21, when members of the Committee of Safety intercepted Molloy and questioned him, they discovered he carried no contraband, and he professed to have no knowledge of either Connolly or McKee. The committee sent him on his way following the interrogation, warning him not to come to Pittsburgh again.[13]

The following month, John Neville, the newly appointed Virginia commander of Fort Pitt, reported that an agent sent to Sandusky to purchase gunpowder returned with the information that "some of our leading men in this Quarter are strongly suspected of Disaffection to the common Cause." In particular, Paul Long, "Who hath been long connected with Colo. Croghan and Capt. Alex'r McKee," had been discovered carrying correspondence to British officials in New York. Neville remained uncertain about the letter's contents and Long's intentions, but he vowed to "intercept him on his return and by his answers find out his business."[14]

Morgan, though, already knew all about Paul Long. Morgan, whose private sympathies for the Patriot cause may not have been as staunch as his outward actions indicated, had secretly sent Long to British-held Fort Niagara in early May, later claiming that Long was a "spy" in the Patriot service. When he arrived, Long met with Colonel Butler, the British Indian agent at the post, who was very eager to learn of developments in Pittsburgh and seemed especially concerned that he had not received correspondence that he apparently expected from McKee. Later in their conversation, Butler allowed Long to read a lengthy and detailed letter, dated April 22, in which the writer sent intelligence concerning the Pittsburgh vicinity and expressed "great sorrow for the mad proceedings of the people which the Writer said his influence could not prevent." The writer's name was defaced, and although Long claimed he recognized the handwriting, he did not identify the author in his report to Morgan. Clearly, though, Long's description of the author and the letter's contents are consistent with McKee's sympathies and position at the time.[15]

Despite the mounting body of circumstantial evidence that linked McKee to the Loyalist cause, Morgan permitted the British official to accompany him on a journey throughout the Ohio Country during June and the first weeks of July. Morgan was attempting to counter growing Crown influence among the western tribes by personally courting the Ohio nations, many of whom still wished to maintain peaceful relations with both the British and the Americans. McKee's long personal affiliation with the Ohio tribes and his ability as a translator undoubtedly served Morgan well during the expedition. Morgan and McKee traveled directly to the Indian villages along the Muskingum and Scioto Rivers where the American agent urged the western nations to remain neutral. Incredibly, on June 22, Morgan permitted McKee to leave him and travel unsupervised to Chillicothe. Morgan saw no more of the British agent until July 5. Morgan's decision was remarkable, considering McKee's past affiliation with the British government, the mounting body of circumstantial evidence that linked him to British intrigue within the region, and the fact that he still remained on parole because of his suspected Loyalist activities.[16]

There is no record of McKee's activities during his nearly two-week separation from Morgan. Undoubtedly, he used the time to rejoin his family and renew his many friendships within the tribe. There is no evidence to suggest that McKee used the opportunity to pass intelligence to Detroit or to sway the nations from their neutral stance. And yet, given the many rumors swirling about him that placed him in league with the British, it is nearly impossible to think he did not do so. Morgan, though, apparently remained satisfied that McKee had done nothing to further the British cause during his stay with the Shawnees. Once again, McKee had been able to negotiate a particularly delicate situation without openly indicating his political leanings. The journey may also have reflected a certain degree of personal ambivalence regarding McKee's relationship to the Crown. McKee may have used his time with Morgan during the trip to open a preliminary link to the region's Patriot authorities, reasoning that the gesture would counteract some of the accusations that had been directed against him. An alliance with revolutionary officials, he may have concluded, might also prove useful should the Crown's fortunes suffer a drastic reversal in the West. Ironically, as a result of his western mission, Morgan became the target of several rumors that accused him of spying for the British, but McKee's open cooperation with Morgan apparently quieted those Patriot voices that had been raised against him personally. Dunmore listed McKee and seven other Pittsburgh residents as "well disposed to His Majesty's Government" in a February 1777 letter to Lord Dartmouth, but no further accusations were leveled against the British agent throughout the remainder of 1776 or the first months of 1777.[17]

Changes in British policy in the spring of 1777 rekindled Patriot fears of Crown intrigue along the western border. In mid-June, Henry Hamilton, the British lieutenant governor of Detroit, received orders from Whitehall, directing him to enlist the western tribes in a general Indian offensive against American settlers who lived within the Ohio Valley. Hamilton coupled his negotiations with the Ohio nations with a widely distributed appeal to the region's white inhabitants to join the British war effort. The initiative, especially after the discovery of organized Loyalist activity at Redstone, a few miles from Fort Pitt, and an increase in sporadic violence within the region, fanned the lingering embers of suspicion at Pittsburgh into an open conflagration of rumor, innuendo, and accusation.[18]

Few in the community escaped the near paranoia that characterized the frontier outpost. In July, Cornstalk's sister, the Grenadier Squaw, a Shawnee woman "known to have an implacable hatred to the woman who lived with McKee," reported that McKee was secretly communicating with British officials in Detroit. For the moment Gen. Edward Hand, the new commander at Fort Pitt, commented that the report had "come from a bad author" and dismissed it as untrue. Hand also demonstrated his full confidence in McKee by issuing him ten muskets from the public stores for self-defense. But McKee was too closely associated with the British for the rumors to be easily quelled.[19]

In late summer, Patriot authorities learned that a substantial number of settlers in the Redstone area, about twelve miles south of Pittsburgh, had taken an oath of allegiance to the British Crown and were plotting on Great Britain's behalf. Col. Thomas Gaddis and Col. Zackwell Morgan led a detachment of soldiers from Fort Pitt to Redstone and arrested those implicated in the activity. When questioned, the Redstone Loyalists also accused McKee, George Morgan, John Campbell, and Simon Girty of taking part in the scheme. Alarmed, Hand incarcerated the accused and questioned all four men. McKee was placed under house arrest, not only to monitor his whereabouts, but also to protect him from armed colonials who were convinced of his collusion with the British.[20]

Hand's fears of vigilante violence were well founded. In September, Virginia irregulars had murdered the Shawnee diplomat Cornstalk and his son, Elinipsico, while they were being held at Fort Randolph at the mouth of the Kanawha River. The following month, Pennsylvania militia men arrested and then summarily executed a local Tory named Hickson (Higgison). The party had apprehended and handcuffed Hickson and then placed him in a wagon with his legs in chains. As the wagon crossed the Cheat River, Hickson fell into the water and drowned. "Whether he tumbled out or was thrown out, is uncertain," testified one of the guards at a subsequent inquest, but others swore that the patrol's leader, Col. Zachwell Morgan, had flung the Tory to his death.[21]

The results of Hand's inquisition were inconclusive. A few of the prisoners continued to implicate Morgan in the affair; a small number also mentioned Girty. But none identified either Campbell or McKee as co-conspirators. Concluding once again that the "clamor against . . . McKee was wrong-founded," Hand released all four men, but not before he reported the incident to Congress and received a second written parole for McKee. Although the lack of corroborating testimony won McKee his acquittal at Hand's inquest, John Green, an informer writing in a deposition some six months later, was positive that McKee was taking a leading role in coordinating Loyalist activities during the autumn and winter of 1777 and 1778. According to Green, six prominent men within the community regularly met at McKee's farm to exchange intelligence and to plot against the Patriots. Further, they appeared to be in regular correspondence with British officials in Detroit, who gave them their orders and who directed their preparations. Moreover, the Loyalists openly flew the British flag to announce their gatherings. The ringleaders had gathered an additional corps of about 150 men who planned to seize Hand and other Pittsburgh officials and put them in irons. When the local authorities were detained, the force would then take over Fort Pitt using scaling ladders that were already prepared and hidden in the woods nearby. Once the plot was put into action, claimed Green, McKee was to supply British uniforms "to cloath the people of this County, Town, and Garrison that would join them."[22]

Once informed of the state of affairs at Pittsburgh, the Continental Congress moved quickly, appointing a committee chaired by Richard Lee of Virginia to investigate both Morgan's and McKee's activities. Contacting the authorities at Fort Pitt, Lee requested that through the "fair and uninfluenced testimony of disinterested persons" the committee be informed of the "political character of Mr. McGee, whether he is considered as an Agent, or Friend of G.B. and whether he does not profess himself a Subject of the British King."[23]

Lee's committee quickly found itself confronting the same tangle of confused and conflicting testimony that Hand had encountered. One correspondent reported that the local Indians had brutally attacked a number of the region's settlers. The survivors were now "driven from their homes and reduced to great distress." The Indians had been encouraged, claimed the writer, by "British agents and emissaries," undoubtedly a reference to McKee and Morgan. These Loyalist sympathizers had also excited "a dangerous spirit of disaffection" among "some worthless and evil-disposed persons . . . who, lost to all sentiments of virtue, honor, or regard for their country have been induced to aid our remorseless enemy." On the other hand, Joseph Nicholson, a Pittsburgh resident unquestionably committed to the rebellion, reported that he had "not the least reason to believe" that McKee "has even in a single instance said or done anything to injure the American cause." Indeed, Nicholson claimed that McKee was an open advocate for the colonials, frequently recommending to the Indians that their true interests lay in "Peace and Friendship with the frontier inhabitants, for that Contrary conduct would end in their ruin."[24]

At the same time Lee's committee was meeting in York, Pennsylvania, to investigate McKee's activities, the emotionally charged atmosphere at Pittsburgh contributed to the spread of further allegations. In late December 1777, a widely circulated report alleged that McKee's wife was in Detroit purchasing supplies for the agent and that McKee had promised to come personally to the British outpost to pay for the materials. McKee was clearly in a position to do so. Unbeknownst to the local authorities, he had discreetly begun to liquidate his property within the area earlier in the year and to convert some of his substantial holdings to cash. In mid-June McKee transferred three parcels of land amounting to 6,102 acres and including buildings, contents, tools, and livestock to his younger brother James for fifteen hundred pounds, Pennsylvania currency. Previously, General Hand had been willing to place a great deal of faith in McKee's trustworthiness. But he and the other Patriot officials in Pittsburgh could not continue to overlook the mounting testimony that seemed to place McKee in league with the British. Maj. Jasper Ewing fully appreciated the enormous danger posed by McKee should he openly ally himself with the British. "A man of his capacity . . . so well acquainted with the situation of our affairs," he predicted, would "be no unwelcome guest at Detroit." On December 29, Hand ordered McKee to present himself before the Continental Congress's Board of War in York to give an account of his activities.[25]

The request angered McKee who curtly told Hand's courier that the order "required no answer." Receiving no response, Hand repeated his instructions on February 7, 1778. This time an apparently contrite McKee personally reported to Hand at Fort Pitt, apologizing for his actions and promising his prompt compliance. Hand, though, was too preoccupied planning a punitive expedition against the Ohio tribes, located near a British storehouse at the mouth of the Cuyahoga River, to ensure that McKee lived up to his word. Once again, McKee ignored the ultimatum.[26]

Hand's attention was being diverted by a scheme born more of frustration than of military pragmatism. In spite of Hand's careful preparation, the American commander's expedition against the Ohio tribes was an unmitigated failure. Leading five hundred raw Westmoreland County militia from Fort Pitt in mid-February, Hand traveled only as far as the Mahoning River, in eastern Ohio, before swollen streams and thick mud caused by an early thaw forced the army to turn back. On its return, the force encountered two small bands of Delawares. The army attacked both groups, killing an elderly man, a small boy, and four women and taking two other women prisoners before it completed its journey to Pittsburgh in early March.[27]

When he returned, Hand was chagrined to find that McKee was still in town and had not reported to York as ordered. McKee explained that a lingering illness had forced him to postpone his trip, but Hand suspected that he was only "pretending indisposition" in order to delay his appearance before Congress. In truth, McKee had no intention of ever keeping the appointment. During Hand's absence, Matthew Elliott,

McKee's close friend and confidant, had arrived in Pittsburgh from Detroit. Elliott's and McKee's lives had intertwined for much of the agent's career at Fort Pitt. From County Donegal, Ireland, Elliott had come to America in 1761 and had begun to trade with the western nations in 1763. Like McKee, he was married to a Shawnee woman and was raising his son with the tribe. Elliott set out on a trading expedition to the western tribes in the fall of 1776. Much later, both he and McKee would claim that when he left, McKee explicitly understood that Elliott was carrying intelligence about the rebel forces at Fort Pitt and that he planned to give this information to the British authorities at Detroit. Whether or not McKee's and Elliott's recollections were correct, it is certain that shortly after he left Pittsburgh, Elliott's goods were plundered by a party of hostile Senecas. Afterwards, the trader proceeded on to Detroit where he attempted to obtain compensation for his loss from British authorities at the garrison. The British officials, however, were suspicious of his motives, and Elliott endured a stern inquiry before he was permitted to return to Pittsburgh. Elliott warned McKee that local Patriots planned to ambush and kill him when the agent traveled east to testify before the Board of War. Indeed, Elliott may not have been the first to inform McKee of the plan. George Morgan later claimed that the plot against McKee's life was an open secret in Pittsburgh and that he had learned of the plan from several persons earlier in the month. Taking Elliott's warning to heart, McKee was already planning his escape.[28]

On March 28, Hand's patience came to an end. The commander sent a detachment of soldiers to McKee's home to arrest the agent, but the squad found that McKee, Elliott, Simon Girty, McKee's cousin Robert Surphlitt, McKee's servant John Higgins, and two of McKee's African servants had fled to the British the previous night.

McKee's flight surprised many of his Pittsburgh associates. Hand, caught completely by surprise, was "mortified" by the escape, and George Morgan considered McKee's flight both "dishonourable" and "inexcusable." But McKee's departure was noteworthy not so much for its occurrence as for the fact that it had taken place nearly three years after the outbreak of hostilities.[29]

McKee had good reason to remain in Pittsburgh. As a man of influence and position, he was involved in a successful business partnership, held public office, and had acquired large landholdings throughout the region. Although sympathetic with Crown aims, he was also pragmatic and self-interested. McKee's decision to flee, while seemingly made in haste, was the result of a long and complex series of events, each requiring McKee to weigh his personal and financial interests against those of the realm. The murder of Cornstalk, a man with whom McKee was well acquainted, and the desultory nature of Hand's spring campaign against the Ohio tribes undoubtedly contributed to his determination to leave, as did anger over his past arrests and continued harassment by colonial officials. The threat of immediate incarceration, coupled with the probability of physical injury or death at the hands of his captors, were only the immediate factors that influenced his decision.

The depth of his complicity against the Patriot cause is difficult to ascertain. His long affiliation with the British Indian Department, close association with Crown officials, and overt sympathies for the Ohio Country tribes were well known throughout the region. Yet from 1775 to 1778 McKee was able to exploit his personal cultural ambiguity, his ability to reconcile diverse political interests, and the skill in interpersonal relationships that he had used successfully with the Ohio tribes to mask his allegiances. McKee's actions from 1775 through March 1778 were predicated on a cautiously crafted and carefully maintained ambiguity designed to deflect suspicion and to protect his financial holdings. It is only through the actions of those who knew him best and those who worked closely with him during the period that McKee's political loyalties become defined. Colonial officials on several levels, including John Butler, John Connolly, Lord Dunmore, and Thomas Gage, explicitly understood that McKee remained a loyal servant of the King and assumed that he was actively working on the Crown's behalf. Further, other observers in Pittsburgh reported with some consistency that McKee was fomenting discontent, gathering intelligence, and passing information to the British authorities. It seems likely that McKee was working for the British to the extent that his circumstances allowed.

McKee's relations with the region's Indians during the period are difficult to piece together. Except during his trip with Morgan in the spring and early summer of 1776, McKee had little opportunity for direct contact with the Ohio nations after Connolly's departure. Informal contact in and around Pittsburgh, however, permitted McKee to remain in communication with them. Given the close scrutiny that his actions received, it seems likely that any attempt by McKee to incite the tribes to violence would have been immediately reported to American officials. It is probable that Joseph Nicholson's 1778 report, indicating that McKee urged the tribes to adopt a policy of peace and friendship toward the Americans, accurately reflected his actions during the period. McKee was aware that military assistance from Detroit would be difficult to provide to the tribes along the eastern Ohio border and that the frontiersmen living along the Ohio Valley would be quick to respond to any perceived threat to their homes. McKee's policy of friendship appears to be an extension of the one he was following in Pittsburgh. Amiable relations with the region's whites would shield the Indians from American hostility and permit them to protect their resources until circumstances changed.

The plot against McKee's life demolished these carefully constructed stratagems. His open alliance with the British ushered a period of renewed violence along the Ohio frontier. After learning of McKee's escape, troubled settlers throughout the Ohio Valley turned a frightened eye to the west and prepared for the worst.

CHAPTER SIX

The Revolutionary War, 1778–1783

McKee's flight created an uproar along the western border. Many of the settlers who lived in the Pittsburgh vicinity assumed that now McKee had fled, he would immediately encourage the Indians to attack the settlements along the frontier. Patriot officials agreed. "From his knowledge of Indian affairs and Influence among the different tribes, we fear [he] is capable of doing us extensive mischief," reported the commission sent to Pittsburgh by the Continental Congress to investigate McKee. "There is no doubt but this affair will excite alarms throughout the country." As word of the Loyalist's escape spread throughout the region, many residents abandoned their homes and sought safety to the east. The Moravian missionary, John Heckewelder, noted that during the first week of April, the road to Pittsburgh was lined with empty houses deserted by their frightened owners. "Good people, avoid this road," chalked one terrified Pittsburgh resident on the door of his now-vacant house, "for the Indians are out murdering us." Other residents, though, were encouraged by McKee's example. Those within the community who still clung, however clandestinely, to their Loyalist sympathies had watched the episode with great interest. McKee's party was not the first to leave Pittsburgh for the British outpost at Detroit. From January through March, nearly twenty other individuals also had fled the American garrison, and even Hand complained that "desertion prevails here to a great degree." Fourteen more, mostly from a single company of soldiers led by Sgt. Alexander Chambers, fled from the post on April 23. The group had been organized by a local resident, a known Loyalist named Eleazor Davis who, emboldened by McKee's and Girty's success, had secretly worked throughout the spring planning the escape. Hand immediately dispatched a forty-man squad to pursue the deserters, and although eight of the fugitives managed to elude the trackers, the rest eventually were caught and returned to Pittsburgh where three were executed and two publicly whipped. But even after their capture and punishment, some of the traitors remained unrepentant. Patriot informants reported that the Loyalists continued to believe McKee would return to free them and put Fort Pitt to the torch. While Hand responded promptly to this latest crisis, Patriot officials understood that he had done too little, too late. Facing a congressional investigation of his actions, which had led to McKee's departure, the American commander resigned on May 2.[1]

McKee and his party traveled directly to Coshocton, the Delaware town on the lower Tuscarawas River. There he had the good fortune to meet Edward Hazle, a member of the British Indian Department, who was delivering a message from Henry Hamilton to the Moravian minister at the village. McKee gave Hazle a letter that advised Hamilton of his escape and told what he knew of the Americans' immediate military plans, namely that the Virginians were unprepared to launch any expedition of consequence against Detroit. But McKee also told the Delawares that the Americans were assembling a large army at Pittsburgh with which to invade the Ohio Country. Any Indian they met, friend or foe, would be killed. The Delawares "no longer had a single friend among the American people," claimed McKee, who advised the band either to prepare to fight the Americans or flee for their lives. McKee was persuasive, and before his departure, several warriors had shaved their heads and "turned out to war."[2]

McKee spent only a short time among the Delawares. Soon the fugitives moved on to the Shawnee villages along the Scioto River where they met Simon Girty's brother, James, who promptly agreed to join the defectors. Both Girtys shared much with McKee. Like the McKees, the Girtys had come to Pennsylvania from Ireland in the 1730s. The family had moved to the Susquehanna River when Simon was a youngster, and Simon's father, Simon Girty, Sr., and Thomas McKee, Alexander's father, knew one another well. Simon's father died in 1751, and his mother quickly remarried, but tragedy and violence seemed to dog the family. In 1755 an expedition of French soldiers and their Indian allies swept through western Pennsylvania, capturing Girty's stepfather, John Turner, his wife, and their five sons. Turner was tortured and burned to death in front of his horrified family. As the war party prepared to return home, they divided the remaining captives. Simon's mother, his stepbrother (a newborn infant named John), and his youngest brother, George, were taken by the Delawares. James, two years younger than Simon, was taken by the Shawnees, while the western Senecas claimed Simon. His older brother, Thomas, managed to escape. The Girtys continued to live with the Indians until they were returned to white society and reunited in 1759. During their captivity, each of the three brothers had been adopted into his captor's nation, and each deeply absorbed their tribe's customs and language. In fact, George's assimilation was so complete that even after his release he preferred to live among the Delaware, and little is known of his subsequent life. James entered the fur trade, while Simon moved to Fort Pitt where he frequently aided British officials by acting as a scout and translator during their many meetings with the Ohio nations.[3]

Girty had served the Crown well. Recognized as a skilled interpreter and a sensitive, effective intermediary, he had worked particularly closely with Kayashuta in the days before Dunmore's War and had formed a strong and abiding friendship with McKee. But he also became known for his enjoyment of strong drink and a violent temper that could erupt with little provocation. As the Revolution began, Girty worked for Pittsburgh's Patriot officials, but his drunkenness, unpredictable behavior, and a series of heated squabbles with persons in authority at the American outpost eventually diminished his usefulness to the point that by late 1777 he was regarded as unfit for any type of military service. Bitter, holding many personal grudges, and at the bottom of a self-destructive cycle that had cost him his employment, many of his friends, and his standing within the community, it took Girty little time to decide to join McKee and Elliott as they planned their escape. Now, reunited with James and relatively safe from pursuit, Girty and the remaining escapees lingered at the central Ohio settlement for several weeks, waiting for instructions from Hamilton and allowing McKee to visit his family. White-Eyes, a Delaware headman in

Coshocton who had long been a friend to the Americans, had not believed McKee when the escaped agent attempted to turn the band against the soldiers at Fort Pitt, and he sent a warning to the Scioto Valley Shawnees. "Some days ago, a flock of birds that have come on from the East lit at Goshochking (Coshocton)," claimed the Delaware leader, "imposing a song of theirs upon us, which song has nigh proved our ruin." "Should these birds . . . impose a song on you likewise, do not listen to them, for they lie." But White-Eyes's warning was ignored by the Shawnees who, since the conclusion of Dunmore's War, harbored little love toward either the Pennsylvanians or the Virginians. Indeed, the central Ohio villages were extremely pleased to see McKee and more than willing to help him on his way to the British post at Detroit.

Hamilton was delighted to learn of McKee's defection. He was "a man of good character," reported the lieutenant governor, who "has great influence with the Shawanese, is well acquainted with the country & can probably give some useful intelligence." Hamilton and Jehu Hay, the deputy agent for Indian affairs at Detroit, both sent their congratulations to McKee. Hamilton ordered the group on to Detroit, and Hay advised that provisions and other supplies would be waiting along their route at the Sandusky and Maumee Rivers. With Edward Hazle as their guide, McKee and his companions left the Shawnee villages in late May and traveled up the Scioto Valley to Snipe's Town near present-day Wyandot, Ohio, and then to Sandusky and Detroit. They reached the British stronghold in early June 1778.[4]

McKee's defection came at an opportune time. Military planners on both sides of the contest had realized that the war would neither be won nor lost in the west. Separated from supplies and manpower by the Appalachian Mountains, British officials at Detroit and their counterparts at Pittsburgh watched as the war turned into an unending series of raids and counterraids. These marauds, any one of which could be brutal in the extreme, were never strong enough nor sustained for a sufficient period of time to inflict a fatal blow to the enemy. But while McKee made his way to Detroit, Hamilton was growing increasingly concerned about the rebels' ability to penetrate the Ohio Country. These raids, he felt, might eventually pose a threat to Detroit, and the lieutenant governor was eager to challenge the brash Americans. To Hamilton, McKee seemed perfectly qualified to rally the western tribes against the rebelling colonists. The lieutenant governor predicted that he would use McKee to raid the Kentucky settlements with Indians and irregulars from Detroit. "I shall place great dependencies on his knowledge of the Country," he wrote to Lord George Germain a few days after McKee's escape, "and of these people employed for its defense." Hamilton commissioned McKee a captain in the Indian department immediately upon his arrival and, within a few days, introduced him to representatives from the Great Lakes tribes who had come to Detroit at the Indian department's invitation.[5]

The council, begun on June 14, lasted nearly three weeks and brought more than 1,680 Indians to Detroit. Throughout the proceedings, Hamilton distributed gifts, gave thanks for the tribes' past allegiance, and urged them to take up the hatchet against the rebels. The Americans who fought the king were also the ones who fought against the western nations and attempted to take their land, said Hamilton. Now, the king had ordered "the axe to be put into the hands of his Indian children in order to drive the Rebels from their Land, while his ships of war & armys clear'd them from the seas." In response, the assembled nations claimed they would take hold of their father's hatchet and promised not to bury it until the king, their father, ordered peace. From June 29 through July 3, McKee also attended a secret meeting with Hamilton and a small group of tribal leaders from the western nations. McKee detailed the weaknesses he knew to exist at Pittsburgh, and as a result the assembly determined to move against the American garrison. Hamilton sent the plan to Sir Guy Carleton for approval, but on August 8, Hamilton learned that the Kentucky frontiersman, George Rogers Clark, and a small force of frontiersmen had crossed deep into the Illinois Country and had taken possession of Vincennes. Clark's advance put an end to the planned action against Fort Pitt. In September, the British commander sent McKee to live with the Scioto Valley Shawnees to gather intelligence, distribute ammunition, and enlist their support in a strike against Clark.[6]

As Hamilton prepared to move against Clark along the Wabash, McKee worked to counter growing Patriot influence among the nations within the Tuscarawas and Muskingum Valleys. In early September, Continental officials had persuaded the Delawares to permit construction of two military posts within their territory. The garrisons, Fort McIntosh on Beaver Creek north of Pittsburgh, and Fort Laurens on the lower Tuscarawas, were to be the first in a series of outposts that would stretch across the Ohio Country from Pittsburgh to Detroit. By mid-October, McKee had convinced the Shawnees and a few Delawares to oppose the American advance in northeast Ohio and had sent a party of Shawnee warriors to join Hamilton who had begun his own expedition against Clark on October 7. Leaving the Shawnee towns late in the month, McKee caught up with Hamilton during the second week of November 1778. For the next three weeks, McKee helped orchestrate the lieutenant governor's final, successful thrust into Vincennes in mid-December.[7]

Hamilton began his advance to Vincennes on September 24 by sending an advance guard, commanded by Capt. Normand MacLeod, down the Detroit River and across the western basin of Lake Erie. Following MacLeod, the main force, with Hamilton in command, traveled up the Maumee River to its headwaters at present-day Fort Wayne, Indiana, and across the portage to the Wabash. McKee joined Hamilton's expedition at the forks of the Wabash, near present-day Huntington, Indiana, on November 11. By then, Hamilton's force had grown to a considerable size. In addition to 3 officers and 30 regulars, the expedition also included members of several volunteer militia units, a sizable contingent from the Indian department, and over 550 Indians. McKee remained with Hamilton throughout December and January, helping the British commander negotiate with the numerous tribes that had been attracted to the expedition and accompanying Hamilton as he repatriated Vincennes on December 17. On February 7, 1779, he returned to the Shawnee villages on the Scioto to monitor native actions directed against Forts McIntosh and Laurens. Earlier, on December 9, McKee had been traveling in a boat with White Fish, a Shawnee headman from Ohio. A large flock of wild turkeys had flown over the river and several Indians shot at the fowl. One of their spent balls glanced off the river's surface and struck White Fish in the face, knocking one of his eyes out. McKee was also returning to central Ohio to escort the aged warrior home and carry several dispatches destined for Detroit. His early departure spared him from being in Vincennes when Clark retook the western settlement on February 25. Clark's bold initiative resulted not only in the recapture of the town, but the capture of Hamilton and Hay as well. As Clark's mission drew to a close, the Virginia militia escorted both men to Williamsburg where they remained imprisoned until the end of the war.[8]

Hamilton's and Hay's capture was a serious but not catastrophic blow to the western counterinsurgency. The Shawnees and their allies, assisted by Simon Girty, had halted the American advance from Pittsburgh and forced the meager garrison at Fort Laurens to undergo a season of deprivation and harassment. Clark's dramatic reemergence on the Wabash, though, rekindled British fears of an American offensive against Detroit and hampered their efforts to forge a unified military alliance with the western nations. The Ottawas, Chippewas, and tribes living along the Wabash in particular were reluctant to continue their alliance with the British, and McKee reported they had "determined to set still" (remain neutral) and had advised the Shawnees to be wise and do the same. Hoping to reinvigorate the western war effort, McKee gathered nearly two hundred Shawnee to renew the attack against Fort Laurens in the early spring, but a May 1779 expedition, led by John Bowman of Kentucky, against the Shawnee villages clustered along the Little Miami River forced the warriors already assembled by McKee to return to western Ohio to defend their homes. The nearly three hundred men in Bowman's expedition had crossed the Ohio River a few miles below its confluence with the Licking and had then been able to approach the Shawnee villages undetected; however, a poorly executed attack and volunteers more interested in acquiring plunder than in fighting rendered the campaign a tactical failure. Bowman's men put the Shawnee town to the torch and accumulated more than 180 horses, silver valued at over thirty-two thousand pounds sterling, and what was claimed to be Simon Girty's scarlet regimental coat and double-barreled rifle, but at the cost of nine dead and several wounded. Several Indians were killed, but most escaped and were able to harass Bowmen's retreat most of the way back to the Ohio River. While doing little lasting damage, the raid pointed out the Ohio nations' vulnerability to retaliatory expeditions from Kentucky and ended all hopes for McKee's planned expedition against Fort Laurens. Stymied for the moment from taking action against the Americans, McKee spent the remainder of the year dividing his time between the Scioto Valley Shawnee villages and Detroit. In July he met with Crown officials at Fort Lernoult to ask for troops to be sent to the Shawnee villages along the Scioto. Bowman's advance against the Shawnees had greatly frightened the Shawnees, Delawares, and Wyandots who lived near Sandusky. "This unlucky event has not only discouraged many tribes well disposed," McKee reported, "but inclined others who were wavering to stand neuter." The governor general of Canada, Frederick Haldimand, was unable to supply the troops McKee requested, but he did authorize clothing, ammunition, and other supplies for the Indians. Haldimand also appointed McKee to the post of deputy agent to replace Jehu Hay, but for the moment the Crown had only limited means at its disposal. In November 1779, McKee reported that the Americans and some Delawares loyal to the Patriot cause planned to attack the Ohio Shawnees the following spring. The new commander at Detroit, Maj. Arent DePeyster, urged McKee to use his meager resources to "baffle the designs of the enemy on all occasions," but the lack of supplies forced McKee to spend the remainder of the year quietly watching and waiting.[9]

During the spring of 1780, McKee survived a serious challenge to his authority, instigated by John Connolly, the still-imprisoned former agent for Lord Dunmore. Stymied in all his attempts to secure his freedom, Connolly had contacted Haldimand and suggested that British officials secure his release, then place him on parole. Claiming that his influence with the western Indian nations was unrivaled, particularly among the Shawnees, Connolly urged Haldimand to see his release as an opportunity to replace McKee, whose actions along the western theater, Connolly suggested, were less than satisfactory. McKee, though, had many friends within the Indian department and had repeatedly demonstrated his loyalty and usefulness. Responding to an inquiry from Haldimand, Sir Guy Johnson reported that McKee was a "good and attentive officer & I believe that he is at present very usefully employed with Indians over whom he has influence." Likewise, John Butler stated that he was not acquainted with Connolly (hardly likely given Connolly and Butler's extensive correspondence prior to the outbreak of hostilities) and that "Mr. McGee is the only man I know of that has the most influence on the Shawnees & etc. to the Southward, nor do I know of man more beloved than he is." Given the strength of these testimonials and his own assessment of McKee's strengths and abilities, Haldimand failed to act on Connolly's request.[10]

In the early spring of 1780, DePeyster proposed an offensive strike against Kentucky. Several targets seemed to present themselves. The Americans had just completed Fort Nelson, at the Falls of the Ohio near present-day Louisville, while the Kentuckians had built a string of stations, stockaded civilian settlements, along the northern border of

Kentucky. These fortified settlements served as a type of fence that made penetration into the territory difficult for the many war parties that originated with the Ohio tribes. Further, these stations were also used as staging areas for offensive actions taken against British forces and their allies and as a supply and communication line to service garrisons far to the west. On March 8, McKee traveled to Detroit with a large delegation of Shawnees, Delawares, and Wyandots who urged the British commander to join them in a strike against the Kentucky outposts. DePeyster was easily swayed and promised to supply fifty men, officers, and two artillery pieces to be used against the Americans. DePeyster hoped the raid would divert American attention from Detroit, demoralize the western settlements, and encourage the Ohio tribes to renew their allegiance to the British cause.[11]

DePeyster's plan met with quick approval, and the British commander ordered Capt. Henry Bird to lead the expedition. An engineer with the Eighth or King's Regiment, Bird had been serving at Detroit since 1778. Known as an able and energetic officer, he had supervised the construction of Fort Lernoult, the new British military installation at the city, shortly after his arrival. In 1779 he had spent about six months living with the Wyandots near Sandusky. His experience with the Indians, however, was not altogether successful. During his stay with the tribe, he witnessed the torture and burning of a prisoner; afterwards he raged at the Indians, calling them "cowards and rascals." The episode, claimed John Heckewelder, brought the "ill will of [the] Indians upon him." Perhaps as a consequence of this incident, McKee was ordered to go on the mission also, to coordinate the actions of the large contingent of Indians that DePeyster hoped would be drawn to the expedition. Moreover, DePeyster also ordered that should Bird be incapacitated during the raid, his successor was to take no action without first consulting the deputy agent.[12]

DePeyster also appointed McKee to lead the expedition's Indians so that the agent would restrain the tribes from wanton acts of violence against prisoners and civilians. British officials realized from the first that unrestrained Indian warfare marked by depredation and atrocity could be the agent of a powerful propaganda campaign directed against the Crown, one that would both hinder British efforts to recruit western frontiersmen into the British alliance and stiffen American resolve against England and her native allies. McKee's key responsibilities were to forge a military alliance with the western tribes and to ensure that native military participation in the war adhered to British notions of "civilized" conduct. In particular, McKee was to instruct the Indians in the type of behavior the Crown considered acceptable and to intervene, if necessary, to protect the lives of prisoners and unarmed civilians.

Hamilton had developed the policy, and it was reaffirmed by DePeyster and acknowledged by McKee throughout the war. In June 1778, in McKee's presence, Hamilton had instructed a large delegation of Potawatomis to spare the blood of the aged, women, and children, and "as they shewed a firm attachment to His Majesty and Government in taking up the axe at his request, it was hoped & expected they would lay it down, when required in the same obedient manner." Only a few days later, again with McKee in attendance, Hamilton told a large delegation of Great Lakes Indians, "I cannot but praise the behavior of the Indian nations who have taken hold of their Father's axe and who have acted as men. I hope you'll act the same part and not redden your axe with the blood of Women and Children or innocent men. I know that men kill men and not children. I speak to you who are men." McKee also was expected to intervene on the part of civilian prisoners. In November 1779, DePeyster sent McKee among the Munsee and Delaware tribes to retrieve Peggy West and her daughter, Nancy, who had been taken with Nancy's sister the previous year near Pittsburgh. Promising that if the two were located, he would spare no expense to secure their release, DePeyster ordered McKee to "go in search of them, assuring the Indians of a good Price, and my grateful acknowledgement." McKee continued to seek the safe release of American prisoners until the end of the conflict. In September 1780, he negotiated the return of C. Riddle's wife and children, and in 1783 he attempted to aid Captain Polke, an American officer posted at Fort Nelson, find his missing family. As Bird's expedition was being organized in February 1780, DePeyster reminded McKee that his influence with the western tribes was to be "a means of furthering His Majesty's Service and preventing Cruelty to Prisoners, many instances of which you have already given, much to your honor."[13]

Bird began the expedition on May 25, leaving Detroit with 150 soldiers and Indian department officials, including Simon, George, and James Girty and Matthew Elliott; two small-caliber artillery pieces (a three-pounder and a six-pounder, both on wheeled carriages) and a detachment from the Royal Regiment of Artillery to man them; and nearly 100 Indians from the upper lakes region. The party, traveling by boat, advanced along the Warriors Trail from Detroit, moving along the western basin of Lake Erie and up the Maumee River to the river's confluence with the Auglaize River, then south along the Auglaize to the Miami Valley and from there to its confluence with the Ohio. McKee joined the expedition on May 31 with about 300 Indians from Ohio. Within a few days, nearly 400 others also came into the British camp. Eventually, Bird's native allies numbered in excess of 850, with representatives from the Mingoes, Delawares, Shawnees, Hurons, Ottawas, Potawatomis, and Chippewas within the group.[14]

McKee and Bird lingered along the Great Miami to consolidate their forces. On June 3, they learned that several American prisoners held by the Hurons had escaped, carrying a warning of McKee's and Bird's advance to Clark at Fort Nelson. Bird feared that with this knowledge, Clark might be able to assemble anywhere from 400 to 800 men to oppose the invasion. Bird urged the force to move against Fort Nelson as quickly as possible, before Clark could organize his defense. Once Fort Nelson was destroyed, claimed Bird, the Kentucky stations would be defenseless and could be taken easily. McKee agreed, but he warned Bird that the Indians would also consider these new developments and arrive at their own conclusion. The Indians debated for nearly two days; eventually they rejected Bird's call to attack Fort Nelson and insisted that the party attack the Kentucky stations. An attack against the American garrison, they claimed, would leave their villages vulnerable to a counterattack from Kentucky. With nearly 85 percent of their force demanding to abandon the attack against Clark, McKee and Bird reluctantly began to move their army toward Martin's and Ruddell's Stations on the Licking River, the two closest Kentucky settlements, on June 12. The unexpected wait, though, was taking an emotional toll on Bird who complained, "It is now sixteen days since I arrived at the Forks, [the place] appointed by the Indians to meet, and by one ridiculous delay & the other, they have prolonged or retarded [the expedition] to this day."[15]

Ruddell's Station had been founded in 1775. In 1780 the small community was home to about twenty families who lived within the stockaded enclosure, protected by picketing and a blockhouse. Martin's Station, established the same year, was similar in size and defenses. Bird's force approached the two villages by traveling up the Licking River. Low water forced the expedition to stop at the Forks of the Licking, near present-day Falmouth, Kentucky, and construct a temporary depot for their boats and supplies. Continuing overland, the army advanced the final forty-five miles to Ruddell's Station, arriving undetected at the settlement before dawn on June 24. McKee took two hundred warriors and surrounded the post, while the remainder of Bird's army brought up the rear with the artillery. At dawn, an Irishman named Mc-Carty disobeyed orders and shot into the stockade, beginning a general engagement that lasted until noon. At midday Bird arrived with the remainder of his force. Deploying his three-pounder, Bird fired two artillery rounds into the pioneer stockade, with little effect. But when he brought his larger, more powerful six-pounder into view, the Kentuckians realized they had little chance of withstanding the siege and immediately surrendered. While McKee and Bird entered the fort to finalize the capitulation, several Indians "rush'd in, tore the pore children from their mother's breasts" and killed a number of the defenders. One American survivor later recalled that "the picketts were cut down like cornstalks," and "twenty persons were tomahawked in cold blood." Neither Bird nor McKee could stop the slaughter. The following day, the force moved on to Martin's Station. While on the march, Bird demanded that the Indian headmen restrain their warriors and promise that any prisoners they took would be placed directly under Bird's personal protection. The Indians agreed, but when the station surrendered without firing a shot, Bird noted, "The same promises were made & broke in the same manner." Once again the Indians killed some prisoners and slaughtered the livestock.[16]

Lacking the provisions and supplies to continue and burdened with captives and plunder, Bird withdrew from Kentucky and safely returned to Detroit in early August. The mission had not accomplished all that it could have, but neither was it a failure. Fort Nelson remained untested, and the Kentucky stations had, for the most part, escaped destruction. Nonetheless, Bird was justifiably pleased with the results. He and McKee had returned with nearly three hundred prisoners and a great deal of personal property, including a number of slaves. Further, the expedition proved that British forces could attack the settlements deep within Kentucky virtually unmolested. The English captain also came away from the expedition with great admiration for McKee. "I confess to you," he reported, that "my patience . . . would have been long ago exhausted had I not so excellent an example before me as the one Capt. McKee sets, indeed he manages the Indians to a charm." De-Peyster shared Bird's pleasure in the expedition's outcome, but he was disturbed by the violence perpetrated on the Kentuckians after their surrender. McKee had been sent on the raid in part to prevent such atrocities. DePeyster had told the agent as the mission began that "taking a few scalps is not the object of the present enterprise," and he ordered McKee to "loose no opportunity" in directing the Indians to treat prisoners with humanity. While not apologizing for the Indian's actions, McKee claimed that the bloodshed resulted when the Lake Indians (those from the Upper Great Lakes region) rushed into the enemy compound and seized their prisoners "contrary to previous agreement," throwing everything "into confusion." His explanation was weak, but McKee escaped reprimand.[17]

The sortie against Kentucky defined McKee's role with the Indian department for the remainder of the war. He spent his time living among the Ohio tribes, gathering intelligence, exchanging captives, and persuading the Indians to remain loyal to the British. As opportunity arose or circumstance dictated, he organized raids against military and civilian targets in the Ohio Valley and assembled the nations to defend their homes against American invasion. American officials in Pittsburgh fully appreciated McKee's importance to the western war effort. McKee spent the summer and fall of 1780 organizing raids against the Americans and building a large storehouse close to Roche de Bout, along the Maumee River near present-day Waterville, Ohio. In December, Col. Daniel Brodhead, the commander at Fort Pitt, warned the Ohio Delaware that McKee and the other officers in the Indian department were doing "great harm to your Grand Children [the Shawnees] by the Lies they tell them." He urged the Delaware to make war on the British and offered a reward of "sixty Bucks" for the capture of McKee and "twenty Bucks" for that of any of the Girtys.[18]

Brodhead's concern also reflected the American commander's frustration over his inability to take effective military action against the British and their Ohio allies. Clark's victory at Vincennes in 1779 had been the last American success of note in the West. Raids led by Continental troops and Ohio Valley militia had inflicted casualties, taken prisoners, destroyed villages, and acquired plunder. In August 1780, Clark undertook a punitive raid against the Shawnee towns of Piqua and Chillicothe on the Great Miami River, in part as retaliation for Bird's expedition earlier in the year. Clark burned and looted both towns, and McKee reported that he also killed six Indians and wounded three others in the attack. But the expedition, and others like it, did little to destroy the Ohio tribes' ability or willingness to wage war. Within two weeks after the attack against Piqua and Chillicothe, McKee was able to organize the Ohio nations to oppose a reported Patriot offensive aimed at the Wyandot villages at Sandusky.[19]

In December 1780, Thomas Jefferson proposed that Clark raise two thousand men for another attempt against Detroit. Clark rose to the challenge, but the traditional factionalism between Virginia and Pennsylvania denied him the troops necessary for the mission. By August 1781, Clark had managed to assemble only four hundred volunteers, divided between Pittsburgh and Wheeling. Unwilling to delay, Clark departed Wheeling for the falls in early August and sent word to his second in command at Fort Pitt, Capt. Archibald Lochry, to follow immediately with the troops under his command. Plagued by desertions as he floated down the Ohio, Clark quickened his descent. Lochry, unaware of Clark's actions, never managed to overtake the senior officer.[20]

Indian spies along the Ohio River monitored Clark's efforts from the outset. As early as February 1781, McKee was receiving fairly accurate intelligence concerning Clark's intentions. On February 27, three prisoners brought to McKee by Simon Girty reported that the garrison at the falls was employed in curing buffalo meat to supply Clark's expedition. "This will be their last effort," claimed McKee. "Should they be unsuccessful, their settlements on the South side of the Ohio must undoubtedly fall. But on the contrary, their intention is to clear the Indian Country and penetrate as far as Detroit." In April, he traveled to Detroit and met with the western nations. Despite the destruction of Piqua and Chillicothe, the Ohio tribes were not discouraged and told McKee they were "determined to revenge themselves upon the Enemy." Later in the month, McKee and the Ohio nations were joined by a large delegation from the eastern Iroquois Confederacy who had traveled to Detroit to offer their services to the Ohio Valley tribes. DePeyster, who had been too preoccupied with strengthening Fort Lernoult to take offensive action against the Americans, was impressed by this substantial show of force. By mid-July he and McKee had organized a party to intercept Clark as he made his way to Fort Nelson. A second Indian party of thirty warriors, led by the Mohawk chief, Joseph Brant, already lay in ambush as Clark's men passed the mouth of the Great Miami River on August 18. Clark's men drifted past the ambush unaware, but their passage took place at night, and they took the precaution of firing a light artillery piece blindly into the woods as they moved through the confluence. Brant's party, unable to determine the strength of Clark's force, let him pass, but shortly after captured an officer and seven men.[21]

The prisoners were an advance guard sent by Lochry to convince Clark to stop and consolidate his forces, now separated by a considerable distance along the river. Using the prisoners as decoys, Brant lured the main body of Lochry's troops ashore on August 24. The Indians destroyed the detachment, killing Lochry and 37 others and capturing every other member of the 101-man expedition.[22]

McKee, with nearly three hundred Indians and a hundred-man detachment of Butler's Rangers, joined Brant on the Great Miami two days later. Brant's Indians felt their victory over Lochry had weakened the Americans enough that they posed no immediate danger to the Ohio tribes. McKee convinced them, though, that with the large number of Indians on hand they should follow Clark for a few days to determine his intentions. McKee and Brant pursued Clark to within fifteen miles of the falls; but when they captured two of Clark's men and brought them into camp a few days later, the captives informed the Indians that Clark was unable to mount an expedition into Ohio that winter. The threat to Ohio was over, and many of McKee's Indians left the party and returned home.[23]

With his numbers depleted, McKee was unable to attack Clark directly. But he was able to convince those who remained to cross into Kentucky and attack the stations that lay along the Ohio Valley. Within a few days, the party encountered and defeated a Virginia cavalry patrol led by Captain Cloyd, "Killing a number and dispersing the rest." But three Hurons, including the band's principal warrior, died in the attack. The fatalities discouraged the Indians who decided to end the expedition and return to Ohio. McKee tried to tempt the Indians further by suggesting an attack against nearby Boone's Station, but the Indians would not be swayed. Quickly the expedition broke apart.[24]

McKee returned to the Shawnee villages on the Mad River on September 26. Overall, he considered the excursion a success. He complained that the Indian force was burdened by several "small parties who's View was only to plunder," but he also calculated that nearly two hundred Americans had been killed during the campaign, "Amongst whom are near thirty officers some of considerable Rank." Furthermore, the mission had also advanced the Crown's diplomatic initiatives within the region. The offensive nature of the raid, as well as the participation of the eastern Iroquois, had favorably impressed the Ohio Country nations. As the expedition broke apart at Kispoko, a delegation of Shawnees, Mingos, and Delawares informed McKee that the Americans had invited them to a council, but they had determined not to go. Instead, they promised to continue to fight alongside the British. "We mean to defend ourselves to the last man," they claimed, "before we give up our Lands & we will spare none, if they begin with us." DePeyster was generally pleased with McKee's leadership during the raid and was disappointed only that the Indians had not been more aggressive in pursuing Clark. Congratulating McKee on his achievements, the commander forwarded a vessel of supplies to Roche de Bout and asked McKee to try to keep the Indians in the field until he was positive Clark posed no threat to Detroit.[25]

Both men were correct in their assessments. The mission had been fraught with difficulties, and McKee had successfully encountered and dealt with several problems that, in the hands of a less capable officer, could have spelled disaster. One such problem was the long-standing animosity that existed between the Iroquois League and the western nations. Relations between the eastern Iroquois and the Ohio Country tribes had been strained for some time. Guy Johnson suggested that he was sending Brant to Ohio, in part, to mend the rift. But Brant's appearance on the Ohio in the midst of loosely controlled, heavily armed members of the Ohio nations could have set the stage for a violent confrontation between the two groups. Adding to the danger, rumors from Niagara hinted that Brant had been sent to the west because his behavior was becoming increasingly erratic and unpredictable. One unconfirmed report stated that a short time before his departure, Brant had been involved in a particularly nasty brawl with an Indian department officer.[26]

The accounts proved all too true. At one of the camps along the Ohio River, after his victory over Lochry, a drunken Brant began to boast of his prowess as a warrior, loudly recounting the number of Americans he had killed and captured. Simon Girty, also drunk, called Brant a liar. In the heated exchange that followed, the enraged Mohawk drew his sword and brought it down across Girty's forehead, rendering the Indian department interpreter senseless and giving him a scar he would carry for the rest of his life. A later account of this incident told how a distraught Brant, thinking he had killed Girty, fled from the camp. A few miles away he encountered McKee who calmed him down and urged the Mohawk to return. When Brant came back, he was surprised to find Girty alive and made "offers of money and services to his family if he would make up with him." Girty, never one to forgive easily, refused, but he did agree to continue on the mission. Within a few days he was on the march, picking bone fragments out of the open wound. The details of this version, told to Lyman Draper sixty-six years after the fact, are suspect. But the story speaks to a deeper historical reality. The expedition had been successful in spite of the incident because McKee was able to mollify the volatile Brant, control tensions between the eastern and western nations, and focus the expedition, more or less, on military objectives significant to the western war effort.[27]

With the campaign ended, DePeyster ordered McKee to turn his attention to troublesome Moravian missionaries who lived with the Delawares along the Muskingum River. The Moravians maintained three missions in eastern Ohio under the leadership of six missionaries, the most prominent of whom were John Heckewelder and David Zeisberger. The Moravian clergy publicly professed a policy of neutrality but privately supported the Patriot cause. Zeisberger, in particular, was in close contact with American officials in Pennsylvania, and his correspondence frequently included references to British troop movements and other intelligence that American officials undoubtedly found useful.[28]

British officials had suspected the Moravians' duplicity for some time. As early as July 1779, McKee had intercepted correspondence that suggested the evangelists' activities on behalf of the Americans. Further, native leaders of considerable stature, including the Wyandot half king (Pomoacan or Sweet House) and Captain Pipe (Hopocan), a Delaware war captain, had frequently complained to British officials about the Moravians' aid to the American authorities. By mid-1781, Crown officials were convinced of the Moravians' collusion and determined to remove the Moravians from the vicinity. In August, Matthew Elliott traveled to the Ohio mission towns, accompanied by a delegation of over three hundred Ohio Indians and Indian department employees. Meeting with the Moravian Indians throughout August, Elliott and Pomoacan urged the Christians to abandon their towns and move with them to near Upper Sandusky for their own protection. The Moravians agreed to consider the offer and promised to return a reply the following spring. But Elliott refused to go along with the delay. On September 3, the half king again demanded that the Christian Delawares leave their missions and move to the interior of Ohio. After that, claimed Heckewelder, the Ohio tribes sang their war song, then "killed our fowls, and hogs, and Cattle." In fear of their lives, the Moravians agreed to move. On September 11, they accompanied the Wyandots to the Sandusky River, near Upper Sandusky, where they established a new village that would be their home for the next fifteen months.[29]

Following the Moravians' removal, Elliott returned to Kispoko on September 25 and reported the incident to McKee the following day. McKee was in complete agreement with Elliott over his handling of the affair. "If the whole of these white people can be removed from the Indians," he claimed, "it will be so much the better for it is not likely they will be our friends whilst they have such teachers." The authorities in Detroit also agreed. In October, DePeyster requested that McKee arrange for Heckewelder, Zeisberger, and the other missionaries to be brought to Detroit for questioning. On October 4, McKee sent Captain Pipe and Wingenund, a Delaware shaman and inveterate enemy of the Moravians, to the Sandusky River with a message for the pro-British Wyandots and Delawares. Congratulating the two nations for the firmness they had shown in their earlier actions against the Moravians, McKee claimed that their "father over the lake" was "much pleased" and that now "the birds will no longer sing in the woods and tell you many lies." He then invited the two tribes to go to Roche de Bout to receive provisions for the winter and asked that the Wyandots and Delawares bring the missionaries to Detroit as quickly as possible. Captain Pipe and Wingenund arrived at the Wyandot town on October 14 and escorted the missionaries to the British stronghold on October 25. DePeyster questioned Zeisberger and the five other missionaries on several occasions during the autumn and winter. Each time the Moravians were able to acquit themselves. Unable to convict the missionaries of treason, DePeyster eventually required the Christian Delawares to move again, resettling them on the Huron (Clinch) River near present-day Mt. Clemens, Michigan. There, under the close supervision of the British and far from American influence, they remained throughout the war.[30]

The episode marked an important departure for McKee. On his diplomatic missions to the Ohio tribes and on his raids into Kentucky, McKee had often disagreed with his native allies, but he always sought to mediate a mutually satisfactory means of executing Crown policy. In his dealings with the Moravian Indians, loyalty to the Crown prevailed, and the will of the British government was forcefully imposed upon the Christian Delawares. To be sure, the Moravians were not his allies, and McKee held a very low personal opinion of Zeisberger, whom he referred to as a "Jesuitical old man." Nonetheless, the incident was the first time McKee worked to directly demand a course of action for any of the Ohio Country tribes that was explicitly against their wishes and contrary to their interests.[31]

Among the Americans, who showed little inclination to differentiate between the various political factions that made up the western nations, the Moravian relocation rekindled suspicions that the Delawares were responsible for a series of bloody raids along the Pennsylvania border during the winter and early spring of 1782. To many Patriots, the Delaware move seemed to be a voluntary migration that simply underscored both the tribe's allegiance to the British and their hostile intent. In March, a company of Pennsylvania irregulars led by Col. David Williamson, seeking to put an end to the attacks, organized an expedition against the offending nation. The captive Delawares at Upper Sandusky had suffered through a severe winter in which clothing and other necessities had been sorely lacking. In the same month that Williamson began his offensive, a large group of converts had returned to Gnadenhutten, one of the abandoned mission towns along the Tuscarawas, as soon as the weather permitted, to retrieve food and other provisions stored there at the time of their departure. While at the village, they were discovered by the Pennsylvanians who, feigning friendship, gathered nearly one hundred of the Indians into two cabins. The Moravians, not suspecting any danger, surrendered without a struggle.[32]

With the converts safely under lock and key, Williamson announced that he believed it had been this village that perpetrated that violence along the frontier the previous winter, and he intended to put all of the captives to death. The Indians protested their innocence, but to no avail. Williamson held a short meeting with his officers to determine how best to carry out his plan. But despite his eagerness to begin, a few of his men spoke out vehemently against the proposed deed, claiming, said Heckewelder, that they refused to take part in the murder of a people whose innocence was beyond question. But when they could not convince the Pennsylvanian to change his mind, "They wrung their hands—and calling God to witness that they were innocent of the blood of these harmless Christian Indians, they withdrew to some distance from the scene of slaughter." Facing no further opposition, Williamson and the remaining Americans entered the cabins and bludgeoned ninety-six men, women, and infants to death with a cooper's maul.

Outrage at the murders sped throughout the Ohio Country. Simon Girty reported the incident on April 8, while McKee did likewise two days later. Each agent realized that the murders had the potential to fuel retaliatory raids by their western allies of unprecedented brutality, raids that, despite their orders to the contrary, both men knew they could do little to control. Girty related that a party he had given ammunition to the previous fall had recently returned with fourteen adult male scalps and four adult male prisoners. "There have neither Woman or Child suffered this time," he observed, but clearly tensions throughout the western border were near the breaking point.[33]

Any opportunities for retaliatory raids by the western nations, however, were extinguished by continuing American military ambitions in the area. Even after the Williamson raid, American officials suspected that the Upper Sandusky Delawares and Wyandots were continuing their attacks to the east. In early spring, Congress authorized a second expedition against the tribe. On May 25, four hundred Washington and Westmoreland County troops, with Col. William Crawford at their head, left Mingo Bottom on the Ohio River for the Upper Sandusky village.[34]

Spies, deserters, and captives kept British officials and the Indians well informed of the army's advance. Indeed, Simon Girty, relying on the testimony of a captured American soldier, reported the planned expedition with considerable accuracy and in great detail on April 8. Ten days before the force left the Ohio River, DePeyster and McKee warned a council of Indians in Detroit that the Americans were planning an advance against Sandusky and urged them to "be ready to meet them in a great body and repulse them." Following the meeting, Capt. William Caldwell and Matthew Elliott led a company of Butler's Rangers and a contingent of Indians from Detroit to reinforce the waiting Delawares, while McKee returned to the Upper Miami valley to rally additional support against the invasion. British officials had little doubt that the Indian department and the western tribes would be well prepared when the Americans arrived. As Crawford and his force made their way toward the Wyandot villages, Haldimand wrote to DePeyster to express his pleasure at the Detroit commander's efforts to thwart the invasion. Hoping to exploit the animosity that had existed among the Delawares since the Gnadenhutten murders, he also commented, "I hope the melancholy Event at Muskingum will rouse the Indians to a firm and vigorous opposition and Resentment at St. Duskey."[35]

When Crawford arrived at the Upper Sandusky settlement on June 3, he found the village deserted. The following day, the army encountered the main body of Indians, lying in ambush a few miles from their home. The battle was sharply fought, and by nightfall Caldwell was wounded and Crawford still claimed the field. During the evening, McKee arrived with 150 additional Shawnees who took up positions to Crawford's south, across his line of retreat. At daybreak, the contest began again. Surrounded, outnumbered, and after sustaining numerous casualties during the day, Crawford decided to break off the engagement at dusk and escape under the cover of darkness. Many of his men did so successfully. Crawford evaded capture for two days, but he was finally apprehended after he was separated from the main body of his troops. Taken to the nearby Delaware town of Tymochetee (Crawford, Ohio), the American commander was tied to a stake and burned as retribution for the earlier murder of the Gnadenhutten converts.[36]

Crawford's death reverberated throughout the British military establishment, eliciting a sharp reprimand to the Indian department from Haldimand. McKee was present during the American commander's captivity, but not at his execution. The agent maintained a small log residence, probably built when he was active in the fur trade, a few miles from the village. John Slover, another American prisoner, remembered seeing McKee, dressed in gold-laced clothes, frequently about the camp, but "he spoke little, and did not ask any questions or speak to me at all." The Indians made it clear that Crawford was to die, and McKee realized that there was little he, or any other British official, could do to save the American. But in reporting the incident, McKee was less than candid when he explained that "it was done in my absence or before I could reach any of the places to interfere."[37]

"You must be sensible that I have lost no opportunity to request that you would recommend Humanity to the Indians," wrote an obviously angered DePeyster. "It has ever been the Principle that I Have acted upon, and I am convinced that no task is more agreeable to your wishes." McKee responded that "there is not a white person here wanting in their duty to represent to the Indians in the strongest terms the highest abhorrence of such conduct." DePeyster again urged McKee to "endeavor to convince those Nations that by persisting in acts of retaliation they will in the end draw Mischief upon themselves and upon their Posterity." "But," claimed the British officer, "if they make Warr agreeable to the Example set them by their Father & Brothers the English they will always find themselves supported against their enemy."[38]

British officials feared that Crawford's death would prompt an immediate retaliatory raid from the Americans. McKee was in central Ohio in early July when several scouts hurried into camp with reports of American expeditions aimed against the Ohio nations. The reports continued throughout the month, and by July 22, one spy informed McKee that the American force was "the most formidable Army that has yet come into their Country and from their appearance must intend more than attacking their Villages."[39]

McKee and a large party of warriors left at once to join Caldwell, Girty, and Elliott at Upper Sandusky to oppose the American invasion. The force, approximately eleven hundred strong, moved eastward in mid-August, intending to attack Fort Henry at Wheeling. The British and Indians were still buoyed by their victory over Crawford, and an obviously elated McKee wrote that the army represented the "greatest Body of Indians collected . . . that have been assembled in this Quarter since the commencement of the war, and perhaps may never be in higher spirits to engage the Enemy." DePeyster was quick to check McKee's enthusiasm. He had been informed that the Shawnees were still putting prisoners to death, and he demanded that McKee order the tribes to put an end to the practice. Threatening to pull all British troops out of Ohio if the executions continued, DePeyster warned McKee to "do all in your power to instill humane Principles into the Indians" during the excursion. News soon reached the expedition that Clark was prepared to launch an offensive against western Ohio, and the army redirected its course to Wapatomica, a Shawnee town on the Mad River, to await Clark's advance.[40]

The information regarding Clark was false. When it became apparent that no invasion was in progress, most of the Indians abandoned the campaign, leaving Caldwell and McKee with only three hundred warriors and about thirty rangers at their disposal. Caldwell decided to take the remaining force on a raid into Kentucky and led the expedition south along the Elkhorn River to Bryant's Station, a civilian outpost about five miles from present-day Lexington.[41]

The British siege began early on August 12, and continued throughout the next day. The Kentucky defenders had strengthened the outpost in anticipation of Caldwell's advance. Well armed and protected, the Americans easily repulsed the attack. The Indians "rushed up to the Fort and set several out Houses on fire," but to no avail. At the end of the second day, Caldwell destroyed the settlement's crops and livestock and withdrew to the Blue Licks on the Licking River, where he "encamp'd near an advantageous Hill & expecting the Enemy would pursue, determined here to wait for them."

Frightened messengers had escaped from the station during the battle and alerted the Kentucky militia. Soon, 182 backwoods irregulars, led by John Todd and including Daniel Boone and his son, Israel, were in pursuit. As the Kentuckians approached the Blue Licks, Boone, who was familiar with the region, immediately perceived that an ambush awaited the patrol. The group paused along the banks of the river and a heated argument ensued between Boone and several others who saw no danger. Eventually Maj. Hugh McGary, a reckless hothead from Harrodsburg, ran to his horse, spurred it into the river and called out, "Them that ain't cowards follow me!" Todd, embarrassed by this open challenge to his courage, ordered the rest of the expedition to follow.[42]

The party had moved only a short distance into the woods when McKee and the Indians unleashed a deadly volley. The Kentuckians briefly held their ground but soon were turned back by a ferocious fire from their front and flanks. Within minutes, the survivors began a disorganized retreat across the river and back to Lexington. Nearly seventy of the Americans were dead, including Israel Boone and Thomas

Boone, Daniel's nephew. Many others had been taken prisoner. Among the British, ten Indians had lost their lives, and one ranger was slightly wounded. Following the battle, Caldwell and McKee walked the battlefield, collecting more than one hundred rifles. Both men remained at the Blue Licks one more day, hoping to lure a second party of Kentuckians into the same ambush. When the Americans did not advance, Caldwell withdrew his force across the Ohio where the expedition broke apart. DePeyster's strict injunctions must have had effect. One of the American prisoners later recalled that McKee in particular had treated the captives very well.[43]

American officials would not allow the raid into Kentucky to go unanswered. At once, Patriot authorities ordered George Rogers Clark to organize a retaliatory raid against the Shawnee villages along the Upper Miami Valley. As before, the British were well informed of Clark's preparations long before the expedition was launched. But while the British knew a great deal of Clark's plans, they could not determine whether the American thrust would be directed toward the Miami Valley, the Wyandot villages at Sandusky, or Detroit itself. Further, Clark's invasion had come when British manpower, supplies, and morale were at the lowest point of the war. In late September, DePeyster cautioned McKee that he should be prepared to retreat if the American force proved too strong. The following month, the British commander wrote that the rangers under Caldwell's command were all ill and that regular soldiers garrisoned at Detroit were "ill equipped" and "little prepared with wood fighting." Although DePeyster urged McKee to encourage the Indians to strike at Clark at the first opportunity, he could send no soldiers and only a small amount of tobacco and ammunition to support their efforts.[44]

Clark began the offensive in late October. Detroit's inability to mount a defense permitted him to reach the upper Miami in early November. On November 3 or 4, after encountering virtually no opposition, the American expedition destroyed the Shawnee towns of Piqua and Chillicothe and the trading post of Louise Lorimeir, a known Loyalist sympathizer. McKee was at Pipe's Town, near the Wyandot villages at Sandusky, at the time of the attack. Able to gather fewer than seventy warriors with which to repel the invasion, he was still on his way to the western Ohio Shawnee villages when Clark abandoned the attack and withdrew to Kentucky. McKee and his force encountered a rear guard of Clark's cavalry, but they were too weak to inflict any damage on the retreating Americans.[45]

The victory at Blue Licks and the attempted relief of Piqua marked McKee's last campaigns during the Revolution. By the end of the war, the agent's stature had risen within the Indian department. According to most accounts, he was regarded by superiors and colleagues as a capable and energetic officer who displayed uncommon influence among the Crown's native allies.

The war years had been a period of both continuity and change for McKee. The bilateral focus of his Indian diplomacy, established during Dunmore's War, expanded and matured as a result of his leadership in the field. His exploits frequently brought him into contact with the Iroquois Confederacy and its leadership, particularly Joseph Brant. During his expeditions, McKee also worked closely with the Northern Lake tribes, nations such as the Hurons, Potawatomis, and Chippewas, that previously had been beyond his sphere of influence. In dealing with his native allies, McKee had negotiated and bargained, as he had during Bird's expedition; prodded and placated, as he had done with Brant; and demanded, as he did with the Moravian Delawares. By war's end he was a central figure in the process that mediated the divergent political and military aims of the eastern, Ohio Country, and northern tribes into a working accommodation with British strategic policy for the Great Lakes region.

The Revolution also precipitated a dramatic shift in how McKee viewed himself and his role within the British establishment. Throughout the opening years of the conflict, his personal political allegiances were defined by a cautious and calculated ambiguity motivated by financial self-interest and concern for his personal safety. After his escape to Detroit in 1778, his actions displayed an overt political loyalty to the Crown. To be sure, this loyalty at first was driven by circumstances not of his making. His choice to openly ally with the British was in large measure forced upon him, and self-interest was a factor that never entirely disappeared from his involvement with the Indian department. Yet McKee's activities in the late war years reflected an emerging personal identification with the British realm that went deeper than mere pragmatism.

McKee's duties during the war reflected not only a commitment to British military goals for the region, but an acceptance of British cultural values. His orders to protect prisoners and restrain his native allies are a clear articulation of those values. There are also indications that McKee began to internalize the broader set of British cultural norms reflected in the Crown's policy toward its native allies. Beginning in 1779 and lasting throughout the rest of the war, McKee engaged in a continuing correspondence with Haldimand and DePeyster in which he complained about the financial and personal burdens that his service in the Indian department forced him to endure. The letters demanded reimbursement for expenses spent on the government's behalf, complained that his rank (captain) was inadequate for the duties performed, revealed an uncharacteristically haughty attitude toward junior officers, and frequently threatened that should his demands go unmet, he would resign from the service and move to England. Although Haldimand could not comply with McKee's demand for rank, and DePeyster found it necessary to bluntly refuse the agent's request to go to Great Britain, eventually Haldimand was able to smooth McKee's ruffled feathers by giving him a house and lot in Detroit, "As a mark of my approbation."[46]

It would be easy to dismiss these episodes as thinly veiled, self-interested ploys by McKee to extract money and other concessions from his Indian department employers. But closer inspection shows that restitution was only a small part of McKee's demands. More importantly, the correspondence displays a preoccupation with status. Rank, passage to Britain, financial stability, and property were the outward signs of McKee's entry into Britain's military and, by extension, social elite. In sum, they reflect McKee's commitment to the values espoused by British North America's governing aristocracy. It would be fair to characterize McKee on the eve of the Revolution as one whose sympathies and loyalties were still divided between the Crown and the western Indian nations. Although McKee's participation in the conflict had permitted him to live among the tribes far more extensively and with a far greater degree of intimacy than had been possible for many years, he emerged from the war having unambiguously embraced the British.

Reports of the British defeat at Yorktown filtered back to Detroit during the late winter and early spring of 1782. Both the British and the Indians found the initial intelligence worrisome. The Ohio Country tribes feared that a cessation of hostilities would leave them militarily isolated and vulnerable to punitive raids launched from western Virginia and northern Kentucky. British officials realized that the defeat potentially represented a fatal blow to the war effort. Ordered to use his best judgment and not alarm the Indians, McKee spent the remainder of the year among the central Ohio Shawnee, working to counter the many rumors that hinted of peace negotiations between Great Britain and the colonies.[47]

Crown officials realized that unrestrained Indian violence could derail the sensitive talks now underway between Great Britain and America. McKee, therefore, spent considerable energy trying to limit all Indian military ventures to those that were strictly defensive in nature. In January 1783, DePeyster warned McKee to calm some dissident Wyandots bent on violence near Sandusky. In April, McKee traveled to Wapatomica on the Mad River to prevent a large party of Shawnee warriors from seeking revenge for the defeat they had suffered at Clark's hands the previous fall. On May 6, 1783, DePeyster learned of the proclamation of peace that ended the war. Although unaware of the specific terms of the peace agreement, he instructed McKee to restrain the Indians from all further violence.[48]

The Treaty of Paris presented the Indian department with a difficult problem. Under the terms of the pact, Great Britain ceded a huge western area that included present-day Ohio, Indiana, Illinois, Michigan, and Wisconsin to the United States. Britain's native allies had not been consulted during the treaty negotiations, had not given permission to the British to make territorial concessions on their behalf, and had not been informed of the document's contents. DePeyster's anxiety to pacify the western tribes sprang in part from the realization that continued violence might undo the tenuous peace. He also realized that should the tribes learn of the pact's full ramifications, they would correctly see it as an act of betrayal and possibly turn their weapons on the British posts along the Great Lakes frontier. Once fully informed of the terms of the treaty, DePeyster looked to McKee to protect the Crown's interests in the region. That DePeyster picked McKee to bring the terms of the agreement to the Ohio nations is a measure of McKee's influence among the western tribes and of how completely McKee was regarded by Crown officials as a member of the British governing elite.[49]

In late August and early September 1783, McKee assembled delegates from the Iroquois Confederacy, the Ohio Country tribes, and the Northern Lake tribes at Lower Sandusky. Throughout the two weeks of the conference, McKee told the nations that the treaty recognized

Indian sovereignty to the land north and west of the Ohio River, that the United States could not claim any Indian territory by right of conquest, and that the King still considered the western tribes "his faithful allies . . . & will continue to promote your happiness by his protection." He then urged the tribes to accept the peace, release their prisoners, and conclude the "long, bloody, expensive and unnatural war." The Indians were swayed. Although still apprehensive, they agreed to end the hostilities.[50]

The Revolution was over. McKee had survived with his reputation and influence among the Ohio tribes undiminished and his stature with the region's civil and military authorities widely recognized. Nearly without property after his flight from Pittsburgh, he was poised to recoup his loses and fully reestablish his fortunes as a member of the region's political and economic elite.

CHAPTER SEVEN

Land Acquisition, Public Affairs, and Politics, 1783–1799

Following the Revolution, McKee began the process through which he gained full membership as one of the region's social and civil elite. The transformation was deliberate and was accompanied by a self-conscious thirst for status, demonstrated in both his public and private affairs. Moreover, he brought about this transformation by employing the same skills he had used with the Ohio Country nations. He manipulated his control of resources and forged and then exploited ties based on family and trade. In 1783, British officials addressed the matter of rank that had so vexed McKee throughout the conflict, advancing him to the rank of colonel in the Indian department. The promotion was not the military rank that John Connolly had promised in 1777. Though organized along a military-like chain of command, the Indian department was a semiautonomous bureau that operated in cooperation with the British army. The military supplied the department with its budget, and both the army and the Indian department were under the direction of the commander in chief. The Indian department, however, was headed by its own superintendent general and operated outside the military's formal command structure.[1]

The promotion recognized McKee's contributions during the war and the increase in his responsibilities following the conflict. During the war, Indian department officials at Detroit had been directed by the post's commanding officers, Henry Hamilton and Arent DePeyster. In August 1783, DePeyster, recognizing the need to reestablish independent control of the Indian department, urged Sir John Johnson, the superintendent general, to appoint McKee as head of the department. Lieutenant governor Jehu Hay also supported McKee's appointment and wrote to Haldimand, describing McKee as "a very good man [who] understands the management of Indians as well as any officer in the Department." By mid-August, DePeyster delegated full responsibility for the management of Indian affairs to McKee, who had been acting deputy agent at Detroit ever since Hay's capture by George Rogers Clark in 1779. McKee retained this duty, greatly expanded and under a variety of administrative titles, until the end of his career. In March 1790, Lord Dorchester, describing McKee as "an old Servant universally spoken of for his merits," named him to be Indian agent at Detroit. In March 1794, McKee's duties were expanded to include supervision of the department at Michilimackinac. Later that year he was appointed deputy superintendent and inspector general for Indian affairs for Upper and Lower Canada, the position that he held at his death in January 1799.[2]

McKee's visibility within the Indian department, his demonstrated administrative strengths, and his familiarity with the region's military affairs prepared the way for his appointment to other posts within the colonial administration. In the 1790s, as increased tensions between Great Britain and the United States threatened to expand into open warfare, British officials, fearing for the safety of Detroit, attempted to strengthen the area's militia. As the Indian department's senior officer, McKee was named lieutenant colonel, commandant of the militia for the Detroit region in 1792. McKee played an active role in organizing, training, and equipping the district's irregular forces until relations with the United States were normalized in 1795.[3]

McKee's advancement within the colonial administration also paralleled his efforts to advance socially through private involvement in civic affairs. Following the Revolution, he became an active member of the Church of England, and in 1786 he persuaded the Rev. Mr. George Mitchell to serve the congregation at Detroit as its clergyman. Later,

McKee and two prominent members of the Detroit area fur-trade community, Jacques Baby and John Askin, helped establish a grammar school in Sandwich (present-day Windsor, Ontario).[4]

Yet no matter how rapid his advancement within the colonial administration or how laudable his involvement in community affairs, it was the acquisition of land that was the sine qua non for his entry into the region's gentry. The home that the Indian department had purchased for him in Detroit was modest, but it was comfortably furnished and staffed with servants and slaves. Capt. William Mayne, who briefly stayed at McKee's residence in October 1794, noted that he and his traveling companions were "happy enough to find ourselves so comfortably situated and once again in the style of gentlemen."[5]

Soon after the Revolution, McKee acquired other property on the Canadian side of the Detroit River. At the conclusion of the war, the Crown wished to recognize the contributions of American Loyalists who had lost their property during the conflict by opening to settlement land on the Canadian side of the Detroit River, south of Detroit. The land was to be occupied by Loyalists who sought refuge in Canada who were willing to take possession of their allotment and improve it within one year. This property was to be a gift from the Crown. Although Indian tribes held title to much of the land in the region, individuals were prohibited from treating with the nations by the terms of the Royal Proclamation of 1763, which stipulated that tribal lands could be ceded only to the British government, which, in turn, would pass it to others at its discretion.[6]

Nonetheless, Jacob Schieffelin, the secretary for the Indian department in Detroit, purchased nearly forty-nine square miles of this territory for himself by entering into a secret treaty with the Ottawa Indians on October 13, 1783. The purchase encompassed a seven-mile section of the Detroit River, opposite Bois Blanc Island (present-day Amherstburg, Ontario). Unfortunately for Schieffelin, McKee and three other Indian department employees, Matthew Elliott, Henry Bird, and William Caldwell, were also planning to acquire the land for themselves. McKee attempted to prevent Schieffelin's transaction by writing to Sir John Johnson two days before the treaty was signed, claiming that the agreement was negotiated in a "Clandestine manner" with "a few drunken Indians who are not the real owners." Within a few days, McKee's accusations were confirmed by Capt. Bird. Reaffirming that the treaty was signed by intoxicated chiefs "who really have not the power to grant the Land," Bird also claimed that Schieffelin, in an attempt to mask his duplicity, had attempted to keep the transaction secret from Bird and the other officers of the Indian department.[7]

The transfer also caused a general uneasiness among the Indian tribes within the region once the circumstances surrounding its negotiation became known. Throughout October and November, McKee met with several tribal officials and attempted to quash the deal. In late November, he reported that the treaty had excited "disturbances amongst them of a very serious nature" and that, subsequently, several of the chiefs who had signed the agreement publicly claimed they had done so only after Schieffelin lied to them. Although the commanding officer at Detroit refused to either repudiate the treaty or censor Schieffelin, McKee claimed that Schieffelin's actions were so disagreeable to the Indians that it had become "incumbent upon me to dismiss him from the office he held in the Department."[8]

McKee's energetic opposition successfully thwarted Schieffelin's scheme. In November, Frederick Haldimand ordered the governor of Detroit, Henry Hamilton, to disapprove the purchase should Schieffelin attempt to register the transaction, and Sir John Johnson, the Indian department's superintendent general, to express the Crown's displeasure with Schieffelin's conduct to the Indians in the area. To make sure there was no lingering misunderstanding, Haldimand sent a directive to Lieutenant Governor Jehu Hay in April 1784 that stated the claims of all individuals upon Indian lands near Detroit were "without distinction," invalid. "These instructions," claimed Haldimand, "lay totally aside the claim of Mr. Schieffelin to an Indian Grant of Land even had he obtained it by less unworthy means than He did."[9]

With Schieffelin's claim undone, McKee and his partners set out to acquire the land themselves. By early summer of 1784, Caldwell had written to Haldimand proposing that the disputed area be given to himself, Bird, Elliott, and McKee, to be reserved for Loyalists fleeing the United States. Caldwell was particularly interested in seeing that members of his old military unit, Butler's Rangers, found homes within the region. He also claimed that the Indians were "desirous with them for the speedy and effectual settling of the same." Haldimand, who wished to see the area populated by persons loyal to the Crown, was easily swayed. "I consider the intended Settlement as a matter that may prove of infinite utility to the Strength and Interest of this Province," he wrote, "and wish to give it every encouragement in my power." With Haldimand's approval, McKee began to negotiate with the resident tribes for transfer of the title, and by June, the area bands had given the land originally granted to Schieffelin to McKee and his partners.[10]

Yet the transfer was as legally flawed as the original grant, and for the same reason: the land had passed directly from the Indians to the Indian department employees and not the Crown. Even Schieffelin, now thoroughly discredited with Crown officials, complained. "It is not the value of the Land that I avoid to sacrifice," he wrote to Sir John Johnson, "but the consequent acknowledgement of having done wrong in accepting it when so many superior to me in Fortune and in power, have set the example." Nonetheless, Haldimand, in his haste to have the area quickly settled by Loyalists, was willing to overlook the irregularity. He instructed McKee to "explain to the Indians the nature and intention of the precautions the King has taken to prevent their being iniquitously deprived of their Lands," and then he named McKee as one of the settlement's proprietors.[11]

Before the Indian department employees could occupy their land, the grant needed to be surveyed and the new owners' lots laid out. The survey was completed by Philip Fry in March 1785. Acting in accordance with his instructions, Fry plotted lots six square acres wide for McKee, Bird, Elliott, and Caldwell and lots four square acres wide for all others who wished to settle there. Each of the lots extended back from the Detroit River nearly seven miles. But when the survey was audited a few years later, local officials discovered that the four Indian department employees actually occupied lots that measured ten square acres across. Because all four men had made extensive improvements to their holdings, Crown authorities permitted the "error" to stand.[12]

As McKee worked to improve his holdings opposite Bois Blanc Island, he also entered into negotiations with the Ottawas and Chippewas for a second parcel of land directly north of the grant given to the Indian department employees. Like the first, this parcel extended seven miles north, along the Detroit River to the River Canard, and approximately seven miles east. McKee's negotiating skill served him well, and on May 15, 1786, the Indians, "In consideration of the good will, friendship & affection which we have for Alexander McKee, who has served with us against the Enemy during the late War," gave up the land to

McKee to hold in trust for the Crown. Later, McKee also acquired other parcels within the region, including a large tract on the River Thames, one thousand acres near the mouth of the Detroit River, and several smaller parcels scattered about the settlement. These purchases represented the beginning of a significant improvement in McKee's personal finances. After the agent's flight to Detroit in 1778, Patriot officials had quickly moved to confiscate McKee's sizable land holdings within Pennsylvania and Kentucky. At war's end, McKee submitted a claim to the government, seeking restitution for his losses. He stated that his support of the Crown, while he was in Pittsburgh, had brought him "all the distresses of Confinement and every personal Insult that an opinion of . . . Loyalty could beget in the minds of a Frantic Republican Mob," and he sought reimbursement in the amount of 9,180 pounds sterling. Matthew Elliott also submitted an affidavit in support of his friend's claims, reaffirming that McKee had lost significant real and personal property as a result of his service to the Crown, including an estate in Lancaster County and several lots and two houses in Pittsburgh. Elliott described McKee's personal residence (one of the dwellings lost in Pittsburgh) as "the best House there." In December 1788, the government granted McKee three thousand pounds as compensation for his losses—less than McKee had requested but nonetheless a sizable settlement. With his newfound fortune, McKee invested in real estate. Within three years after the close of the Revolution, McKee personally held or played a significant role in the control of nearly one hundred square miles of the most economically and strategically important land along Canada's Detroit frontier, and he was well on his way to becoming a major landholder elsewhere in the region.[13]

With the status that accompanied land ownership came opportunities to serve the Crown in a political capacity. In 1785, Hamilton proposed McKee for the post of governor of Detroit, pointing to the agent's closeness with the region's Indians and his demonstrated "firmness and moderation." Hamilton observed that McKee had served the Crown ably during the Revolution, was a respected and landed member of the community in Pittsburgh before his escape to Detroit, and enjoyed the support of most of the region's fur-trading community. Nonetheless, colonial officials refused to consider McKee for the office, citing his lack of military (i.e., army) experience. Hamilton responded by defending McKee's qualifications, arguing that "if Mr. McKee has not had a military education and a Commission from his Majesty, he has acted with approbation in a military capacity." Further, the governor observed that the increasing likelihood of an Indian war along the Detroit frontier required the "cool, moderate measures [and] experience" McKee demonstrated. Despite Hamilton's support, McKee was passed over for the appointment.[14]

Other opportunities, however, quickly presented themselves. In July of 1788, Lord Dorchester created four judicial districts, including the District of Hesse. The district comprised all land west of Lake Erie's Long Point to Detroit, and then northward to the unsurveyed and undefined northern limits of the colony. The proclamation that created the district also appointed McKee a judge of the court of common pleas.[15]

The following year, McKee was also named to the Land Board of Hesse. Land boards were appointed in each judicial district to ensure that the Crown's interests were respected and its policies followed as the district developed and to settle disputes regarding land disposition that might arise among the region's residents. Before the land board was established in Hesse, colonial officials had allowed Indian department officers to occupy property ceded directly to them by the Indians. Because Crown policy now strictly prohibited such transfers, the board found that it had no land at its disposal for which native claims had been completely extinguished. Settlement in the region halted as the board attempted to obtain clear title to the land. Dorchester directed the panel to "call Mr. McKee . . . to your assistance . . . that you may have the advantage of his knowledge of the temper and disposition of the Indians," and upon his recommendations permit him to begin the steps needed to secure the Indians' "clear and complete cession to the Crown."[16]

McKee met with tribal officials throughout the winter and spring. By May 1790, he had concluded an agreement that would give the Crown nearly 1,344,000 acres comprising most of the southern peninsula of Ontario and including most of present-day Essex, Kent, Elgin, and Middlesex counties. The tract was bounded on the east by a line running north from Lake Erie to a point a few miles east of present-day London, Ontario. The Thames River bounded the grant on the north, Lake St. Clair and the Detroit River on the west, and Lake Erie on the south. Two tracts, a small parcel near the Huron mission opposite Detroit and a seven-mile-square parcel south of the River Canard, were reserved from the grant.[17]

The board questioned both the necessity and the motives behind the large reservation below the Canard. The parcel was the one granted to McKee a few years earlier. McKee argued that he had agreed to the reservation merely to accommodate a few Indian families already living on the tract, who because of their "attachment to the Government have been drove from their antient settlements." In reality, McKee had petitioned Dorchester in 1789, asking the Crown to ratify the grant so he "might have it in his power to place such loyal subjects upon it as he might conceive worthy of such an indulgence." Possibly because of the objections raised by his colleagues on the board, McKee formally withdrew his request on May 14. On May 19, the treaty permitting the purchase was ratified.[18]

The agreement was a complex document that reflected both McKee's skill as a negotiator and his commitment to Crown interests. Four Indian nations, the Ottawas, Chippewas, Potawatomis, and Hurons, relinquished their titles to the land under the treaty, which was signed by thirty-five tribal leaders. In return, the Indians divided "valuable wares and merchandise" consisting of 1,680 blankets, combs, looking glasses, penknives, ribbons, silk handkerchiefs, hats, tobacco, and rum, valued at twelve hundred pounds, Quebec currency. One recent historian has calculated that the Indians received 0.214 pence per acre in consideration of the transfer.[19]

The transfer, known as the McKee Purchase, was the largest but not the last land cession that McKee would negotiate for the Crown. In September 1796, the agent acquired two other parcels of land from the Chippewas, amounting to two hundred twenty-four thousand acres. The government's desire to provide for expatriate Loyalists after the Revolution had shaped the Crown's earlier quest for land. Now, Canadian authorities feared that the provisions of the 1795 Treaty of Greenville might prompt a second wave of refugees from America made up of displaced native peoples fleeing the United States in the wake of Anthony Wayne's victory over the Ohio Country tribes at Fallen Timbers. The government acquired the first parcel, ninety-two thousand acres bordering the St. Clair River in present-day Lambton County, as a reserve for members of the Ottawa nation who faced forced removal from the United States. A second treaty with the United States, Jay's Treaty, ratified in 1796, prompted the second purchase as well. Jay's Treaty required the Crown to abandon Detroit, the seat of British government in the Great Lakes region. John Graves Simcoe, the newly appointed lieutenant governor of Upper Canada felt that an area along the Thames River, located adjacent to the area purchased by McKee in 1790, held the key both for the region's defense and for continuing control of the Great Lakes fur trade after the Crown's eviction from Detroit. Simcoe had viewed the area during February and March of 1793 when he walked from Niagara to Detroit, and his appreciation for the location had not wavered in the intervening years. The lieutenant governor envisioned a large governmental complex for the region that would include a naval shipyard, the new provincial capital, and a second large town to be named Oxford. The second parcel, a tract of 132,000 acres near present-day London, Ontario, was originally purchased to supply the site for the proposed capital of Upper Canada, but when the overly ambitious plan fell through, Crown officials opened the parcel to white settlement. Claiming that the land to be purchased by the king "is not for settling his own people, but for the comfort and satisfaction of yourselves and all his Indian Children," and the merchandise to be exchanged for the parcels was "of greater value than you have been ever accustomed to receive," McKee acquired both sections for eight hundred pounds worth of trade goods.[20]

McKee also used his seat on the land board to enforce the Crown's policies regarding land transfer and distribution, even if those policies seemed at times contrary to the interests or wishes of the region's Indians. For many years McKee led the board in a bitter dispute with Sarah (Sally) Ainse, an Indian and trader who claimed to own a substantial parcel of land along the Thames River. Ainse was an Oneida who had grown up (possibly knowing McKee) along the Susquehanna River during the 1730s and 1740s. In 1743 she married Andrew Montour, an acquaintance of McKee during his days in Pittsburgh. After the union dissolved in the 1750s, she went on to establish herself as a trader near Fort Stanwix, New York, where her business flourished and expanded. By the late 1760s, she had established several posts along the Great Lakes frontier. At the outbreak of the Revolution, she moved to Detroit and continued her trading activities. By the war's end, she was one of the region's leading merchants.[21]

In May 1787, Ainse acquired a small plot of land near the Thames River. The following year, she enlarged her holding by purchasing nearly 150 square miles of surrounding land from the local Indians.

Eventually, her property extended from the mouth of the Thames, on Lake St. Clair, to the river's forks at present-day Chatham, Ontario. Ainse's land was part of the tract that McKee acquired for the Crown in 1790. Ainse claimed, however, that her land had been specifically exempted from the purchase, and her assertion was supported by nearly twenty Indian chiefs and Jean-Baptiste-Pierre Testard Louvigny de Montigny, another member of the land board who had been present during McKee's negotiations with the Indians. As early as 1789, Ainse had petitioned the government to acknowledge her title to the parcel, but she had repeatedly met with stiff opposition from McKee, who now claimed that her purchase was illegal and that she was entitled to neither title nor compensation. According to McKee, Ainse's purchase was not unlike many others that "usurped Titles under Indian Deeds." Further, he warned that if Ainse's claim were recognized, Loyalists who had already moved onto the land would be undeservedly inconvenienced. Simcoe felt the land board's decision was wrong. Attempting to overrule the panel, he urged the board to "satisfy the poor woman that we have done her justice." The board refused to be swayed, and the lieutenant governor was later obliged to announce "with real regret" that he would enforce the land board's decision. Ainse continued to press her claim, and on March 7, 1794, eight Chippewa chiefs testified before the land board, asserting that McKee recognized Ainse's claim at the time of the purchase and had also accepted a string of wampum to that effect during the negotiations. By late 1794 and early 1795, both Sir John Johnson and Joseph Brant openly supported her efforts. Writing to David Smith, an influential Detroit-area politician, on April 3, Brant complained, "You very well know that Sally Ainse's land was her right, before the purchase was made by the Government, and that the land board cut it in pieces afterward." But despite the pressure created by Ainse and her allies, McKee remained unmoved and refused to concede any legitimacy to the trader's claims. Speaking before the county executive council in 1795, McKee reported, "The Indians have . . . spoken to me since [the 1790 purchase] and have expressed a wish that she should hold her possessions. My only answer to them was, that in the distribution of lands, the King's Government would no doubt consider the claims of His Majesty's subjects, but how far Mrs. Ainse came within that description was not to be decided by me." McKee knew, he said, that many people had acquired Indian deeds to the land within the same region claimed by Ainse prior to the cession of 1790, but "no reservation was made by the Indians for any of these lands at the time of the purchase." Ainse continued to press her right to recompense, and Simcoe eventually awarded her 1,673 acres as partial compensation for her earlier loss, but the county's executive council prohibited any further settlement in the matter in 1798.[22]

McKee's commitment to the Crown and what he viewed as its prerogatives likely shaped much of the confrontation with Ainse. Ainse's Oneida affiliation may also have influenced McKee's actions. Long-standing friction had marred relations between the eastern Iroquois Confederacy and the western Ohio Valley tribes ever since the conclusion of the French and Indian War. Both parties had placed this animosity aside during the Revolution, except for a faction of the Oneida and their allies, the Tuscaroras, who supported the Americans. After the war, the traditional hostility began to reassert itself. By the early 1790s, McKee and the Iroquois league's principal spokesman, Joseph Brant, were openly feuding over the diplomatic and military measures necessary to oppose United States expansion into the Ohio Country. It may have been that McKee focused some of his personal enmity toward the Iroquois Confederacy at Ainse, an Oneida and a league member. If this was the case, it may explain why later in life Ainse preferred to refer to herself as a Shawnee and not an Oneida.[23]

McKee also was influenced by local politicians, representing the region's land speculators, who saw Ainse's holdings as a barrier to further development, and by representatives of the area's fur-trade community, who may have viewed her as a competitor. Patrick McNiff, the king's surveyor, complained in 1790 that the land board was "composed of so many individuals whose views can only be extended to the increase of their private interests." John Clarke, a modern-day Essex County geographer, agrees. Citing the board's actions against Ainse and a host of other would-be landowners whose claims were summarily dismissed, Clarke claims, "It is indeed hard to resist the conclusion that anything that stood in the way of the local elite's designs on land was to be cast aside."[24]

McKee's affiliation with the land board and his continuing involvement with Indian affairs also placed him in the middle of Crown efforts to normalize its relations with the Moravian Delawares who had been brought to the Detroit vicinity in 1782. At the end of the Revolution, David Zeisberger hoped that British officials would permit him and his assistants to move the Delaware congregation back to Ohio. The unsettled nature of diplomatic relations between the United States and Great Britain, though, had thwarted those plans. Although he would not admit it to the Moravian missionaries, McKee actively opposed the relocation in the years immediately following the war. His sympathies were well known, however, and as late as 1785 Zeisberger noted, "We see that we have a secret foe in him. . . . He can do what he will, without giving account to anyone."[25]

By 1786, the political situation within the region had stabilized, and Crown officials, including McKee, granted the Moravians permission to take their congregation back to the United States. Leaving Detroit in April, Zeisberger established a new mission community, Pilgerruh, on the Cuyahoga River near its confluence with Tinker's Creek. The Moravians remained at Pilgerruh only one year before they relocated to a different site, New Salem, on the Pettquotting (present-day Huron) River in April 1787. For the next four years Zeisberger's work at New Salem was productive, but by 1790, because of increasing violence between Indians and whites along the Ohio River Valley, the missionary was concerned for the safety of the settlement. Zeisberger was worried not only about the possibility of violence perpetrated by whites against the mission. He also was alarmed over the growing number of Indians at war with the United States who passed through the village and who clearly were suspicious of the Moravians and their motives. The lesson of Gnadenhutten was not lost on Zeisberger. Unwilling to allow his mission to remain between belligerents a second time, he quietly contacted McKee in early 1790 and asked him to allow the Moravians to return to Canada.[26]

Despite McKee's earlier animosity toward the Moravians, he immediately understood that Zeisberger's request provided an opportunity to bring a sizable native community back under British influence. He quickly dispatched Matthew Elliott to New Salem in January 1791 to assess the mission's needs. Finding a new home in Canada would take some time, McKee told the Ohio Christian Delawares, but if they were forced to move before summer, then they were welcome to make a temporary camp at his and Elliott's adjoining farms opposite Bois Blanc Island. To Zeisberger, McKee's unexpected offer seemed providential. He accepted the proposal on March 10, and by early April he and his congregation, using boats supplied by Elliott and McKee, were making their way to Detroit.[27]

Zeisberger and his congregation stayed at the Indian department employees' estates for nearly fourteen months. Zeisberger was McKee's personal guest and resided at the agent's home the entire time. Eventually, McKee was able to acquire a tract of land for the congregation on the Thames River, near present-day Fairfield, Ontario. In early spring 1792, again with assistance provided by Elliott and McKee, the Moravians moved to their new and permanent home on the Thames. McKee's dealings with the Moravians had been extraordinarily successful. The agent's ability to manipulate the region's land policy for the Crown's benefit, coupled with his personal generosity and skilled diplomacy, had converted enemies to friends, denied the Americans a potentially powerful ally, and by its example gave British officials much-needed leverage in their struggle to create a Native American diplomatic and military response to American expansion.[28]

McKee's actions on the land board in dealing with Sally Ainse and the Moravians demonstrated his continuing influence among the region's Indian nations and a growing affiliation with local economic interests. His activities during the same period also revealed a growing alliance with the region's political interests. The Constitutional Act of 1791, which created Upper Canada, called for each county to elect representatives to the sixteen member House of Assembly. During the colony's first election, held in August 1792, McKee supported the candidacy of David W. Smith, a captain in the Fifth Regiment of Foot and the son of Maj. John Smith, the commandant of Detroit. Smith was elected and took his seat at the first parliament of Upper Canada in September.[29]

Simcoe was particularly anxious to see Smith elected. Intensely distrustful of republicanism, he feared that "the prejudice ran in favor of Men of a Lower Order, who kept but one Table, that is who dined in Common with their Servants." Grateful for McKee's help in securing Smith's election, Simcoe appointed the Indian agent to the office of Essex County lieutenant. The office was a minor one that required

McKee to recommend persons to serve as magistrates and militia officers. But Simcoe saw the position as an important way to "promote an aristocracy so necessary in this country."[30]

In addition to an elected legislative assembly, the 1791 Constitutional Act also called for the creation of an appointed executive council to serve as an upper house within the colony's parliament. The council was to represent aristocratic interests in the colony and balance the democratic elements represented in the lower house. As early as 1790, McKee had been recommended for a seat on the council of the proposed province. In 1794 Simcoe wrote, "I wish to see Colonel McKee, a man of real ability and sound Loyalty, at the Board of the Executive Council of the Country," and he again suggested that the Crown offer McKee a position with the group. Once McKee was appointed, Simcoe also hoped to have him named chairman of a policy-making committee to oversee Indian affairs for the colony. Simcoe's recommendations went unheeded, and Crown officials never offered McKee a position with the assembly. Nonetheless, the episode clearly demonstrated McKee's emergence as a full member of the region's landed gentry.[31]

McKee also used his newfound status, wealth, and influence to indulge in the personal prerogatives of his class. In June 1793, McKee wrote to Crown officials in Great Britain to inquire about purchasing an officer's commission for his son, Thomas, in the Sixtieth Regiment of Foot. In August, he learned that a vacancy existed, and the money he had sent to England in anticipation of the promotion had been given to the proper authorities. By year's end, Thomas had received the rank of lieutenant and had begun his career with the military.[32]

As such episodes demonstrate, Alexander McKee was a man transformed. Within fifteen years following the Revolution, he had acquired riches, land, position, and power. He was, without question, one of the most influential men living along Canada's western border. McKee's rise to the gentry had been driven by his unflagging support of the Crown; his willingness to work at first for, and later with, the leaders of the colonial administration; and his ready acceptance of British upper-class values. Moreover, the insights McKee began to grasp in the wake of Dunmore's War had come to full fruition. McKee now believed that the western nations were incapable of protecting themselves, and only the Crown could look after their interests. As a result, when Crown and native interests differed, he energetically promoted the Crown's, understanding that even if it appeared in the short term as if native interests were weakened, their long-term well being would be preserved. McKee continued to use his position to mediate issues between the Crown and the Indians and settlers within the region. But his objective was no longer to resolve differences between the parties that might prevent a mutually acceptable policy implementation. Rather, he now simply worked to secure the execution of the colonial government's wishes.

Before the Revolution, McKee had gained wealth by successfully exploiting his economic and cultural ties to both whites and Indians along the Pittsburgh frontier, but the war had destroyed the fragile economic and personal links that McKee had so adeptly manipulated before the conflict. The widespread devastation caused by the war had either crippled or eradicated many, if not most, of the economic opportunities open to those who sought to exploit the resources controlled by the Ohio tribes. Cultural disruption hindered the fur trade, and the Treaty of Paris, although actively contested by the Ohio nations, ceded the land to the United States. At the war's end, only the Crown retained the political power and could impose the social stability necessary to acquire land and to dictate the distribution of resources and wealth that would flow from it. While McKee remained active in the fur trade throughout the mid-1780s, he understood that if wealth was to be obtained, it would come through the agency of the British government and not that of the Ohio Country tribes. As a result, McKee had spent much of the post-Revolutionary period creating new links to Upper Canada's landed elite, based on finance and family.

Two loosely knit family groups dominated much of Upper Canada's economic life during the years that followed the Revolution. The first revolved around the Detroit land speculator and fur magnate John Askin. The second, somewhat smaller than the first, consisted of those in the orbit of Jacques Duperron Baby who, like Askin, had made a fortune trading in land and pelts. McKee was closely affiliated with both cliques. Askin and Baby were both involved with the region's militia, and each worked closely with McKee during the crisis of 1790–94. Askin had invested heavily in the lower Maumee Valley fur trade, creating the Miami Company in the late 1780s to exploit the area's rich fur resources, and he was the largest contractor to supply goods and provisions for the Maumee Valley tribes during their conflict with the United States. McKee watched over Askin's interests in the region and directed Miami

Company employees from his post at the Maumee Rapids during the 1790s. Further, McKee's son, Thomas, married Askin's daughter, Theresa, in April 1797. Among those involved with Jacques Baby were William Caldwell and Matthew Elliott, two of McKee's closest friends and joint proprietors in his land holdings opposite Bois Blanc Island. McKee had prospered following the Revolution because he had been able to fashion the same type of personal network of family, business partners, and acquaintances with the Detroit region's aristocracy that he had previously enjoyed with the Ohio Country Indian nations. As economic opportunities disappeared in Ohio and reemerged in Canada, he had wholeheartedly embraced the British and the values they articulated, and he had profited enormously as a result.[33]

CHAPTER EIGHT

Indian Affairs,
1783–1794

British Indian policy was poorly defined along the Great Lakes frontier following the Revolution. In the conflict's immediate aftermath, Crown officials attempted to maintain the outward signs of their alliance with the Ohio Country tribes, hoping to avoid an armed confrontation over the terms of the peace accord. British policy gained focus during the mid-1780s when growing Indian dissatisfaction over their treatment at the hands of the United States presented the British with an opportunity to reestablish a unified native resistance against American expansion into the Ohio Country. Crown authorities encouraged Indian diplomatic opposition and began to supply covert military aid to the western nations. John Graves Simcoe's appointment as lieutenant governor of Upper Canada in 1792 led to increased military support for the Ohio tribes. Simcoe, a man of strong anti-American prejudices, committed his administration to regaining the territory ceded to the United States in 1783 through the agency of the Ohio tribes. British Indian policy in the period between the 1783 Treaty of Paris and the 1795 Treaty of Greenville, while fluid and evolving, was defined by the Crown's use of the western nations to protect and expand Britain's interests in the region.[1]

"I have now the pleasure to inform you that the business which called me to this place is finished and has ended to the General Satisfaction of the Indians," wrote McKee following the September 1783 conference at Sandusky that ended the Revolution in the Northwest. The Iroquois, Ohio Country, and Lake tribes had agreed to return their prisoners and respect the peace. Further, claimed the agent, the Indians were satisfied that the British had "fulfill'd on our parts the promises made them to their utmost expectations."[2]

But McKee's optimistic tone masked a deep-seated sense of uncertainty that pervaded the council and its aftermath. Mutual animosity had defined relations between the western tribes and the United States during the war years, and the poorly defined terms of the peace agreement exaggerated the suspicion both parties felt. During the council, an Indian from Fort Pitt reported that numerous boats carrying settlers were passing down the Ohio River, that surveyors were already plotting town lots along the Muskingum Valley, and that Virginia squatters were preempting Indian land all along the Ohio River. McKee warned that although the Indians appeared to accept the peace, "They are not without apprehensions of the designs of the Americans upon their country which by their Accounts they have just reason."[3]

The American delegation also left the council fire feeling apprehensive. The Americans harbored a profound mistrust of the British and believed the ceremony cloaked carefully laid intrigue planned by the Indian department. Ephraim Douglass, one of the American commissioners at the Sandusky meeting, said that while the British claimed to have taken the tomahawk out of the Indians' hands, they had not placed it "out of sight or far from the Indians, but [had laid] it down carefully by their side, that they might have it convenient to use in defense of their rights and property."[4]

McKee also was worried as he left the council. A degree of mutual distrust had always characterized the British-Indian military alliance. A sense of urgency as both sides worked to defeat the Americans had reduced much of this mistrust. But British officials reasoned that with the alliance's raison d'etre ended, the old suspicions might reassert themselves. They also feared that once the more onerous terms of the peace accord became widely known, Indian resentment might fuel a general uprising directed against their former allies. McKee spent the winter and spring of 1783–84 monitoring the region's tribes, meeting with them in person, sending spies to live among them, and remaining in close con-

THE OHIO COUNTRY FRONTIER
1784–1799

tact with Indian department and military officials throughout the area. In June Capt. Daniel Robertson, the commandant of Michilimackinac, warned that he had heard rumors of a plot, directed by the Ottawa, to strike at the British. McKee's network of informers confirmed the intrigue, and once exposed, it collapsed. Further, they also reported an attempt by the Shawnees to establish a military alliance with the Potawatomis and claimed that some of the Ohio Country Delawares were negotiating for land with tribes west of the Mississippi. McKee's covert intelligence operation against the Great Lakes tribes was widespread and effective. "I have had people constantly amongst the Indians to the Southward during the Spring and winter," he reported to Sir John Johnson. "I am in hopes we shall be always able to discover in time their General Design (should there be any against us) in time to prevent its effects."[5]

The Indian policy established by the new American government did little to calm native uneasiness. The United States based its policy on the claim that the Ohio tribes had forfeited possession of the Ohio Valley frontier because they had allied themselves with Great Britain during the war. The 1768 Treaty of Fort Stanwix had designated the Ohio River as a permanent boundary between Indians and whites. The boundary had been observed throughout the colonial era and acknowledged by the Continental Congress in 1775. Moreover, British officials, including McKee, had claimed that the peace accord between the United States and Great Britain continued to respect the border. But now, America claimed the land north of the Ohio River by right of conquest and held that all right to the soil and all territorial sovereignty once asserted by the Ohio Country tribes were extinguished. Between 1784 and 1789, the United States codified its policy by entering into a series of agreements with the Iroquois Confederacy and the Ohio nations. The first three of these treaties, the 1784 Treaty of Fort Stanwix, the 1785 Treaty of Fort McIntosh, and the 1786 Treaty of Fort Finney, reaffirmed that the Ohio tribes ceded the land north of the Ohio River as a consequence of their alliance with the British during the war.[6]

The first treaty negotiated with the Ohio nations was signed at Fort McIntosh on January 21, 1785, by the Delawares, the Wyandots, and a few bands of Chippewas and Ottawas. The treaty ceded all of the northwest controlled by these tribes to the United States, except for a small reserve along the southern shore of Lake Erie, between the Cuyahoga and Maumee Rivers. The other Ohio tribes reacted sharply against the pact once its provisions were known. In March, four Shawnee chiefs wrote an angry letter to McKee that urged the agent to instruct the other Ohio nations to disavow the accord. The Delawares and Wyandots had "sold their Lands and themselves with it" claimed the Shawnees. Throughout the remainder of the year, McKee conferred with the Ohio tribes to rally support against the agreement. Hostility against the Americans was widespread, and by August, McKee reported that the

Ohio nations "will never tamely submit to be deprived of a Country on which they think their existence depends."[7]

American commissioners hoped to conclude a general agreement with the remainder of the Ohio nations in 1785 or 1786 and issued an invitation for the tribes to assemble for that purpose at Fort Finney, near the mouth of the Miami River. Widespread opposition to the American initiative prohibited all but a few bands of Shawnees from attending. The terms proposed by the American commissioners were similar to those contained in the Fort McIntosh agreement. The Shawnees were reluctant to agree, but eventually succumbed to thinly veiled threats by the American negotiators and signed the Treaty of Fort Finney in January 1786.[8]

The haughty demeanor, open intimidation, and demeaning insults of the American negotiators weighed heavily on the Shawnees. The tribe soon repudiated the pact and sent its warriors against settlers and surveying parties along the Ohio River. Kentucky officials reacted quickly to the violence. By early autumn, they had organized two punitive expeditions, one led by George Rogers Clark, the other headed by Benjamin Logan, to strike against the Shawnees. Poor logistical support thwarted Clark's effort from the start, but Logan's expedition was successful. The raiding party, made up of 790 mounted troops, including Daniel Boone, Simon Kenton, and James Trotter, left Limestone, Kentucky, on October 1. Crossing the Ohio River, the column moved directly up the Miami Valley to the Shawnee villages clustered on the upper Mad River near present-day Bellefontaine, Ohio.[9]

The Kentucky army reached the outskirts of the Shawnee settlement at noon, October 6. As Logan's force entered Mequashake, the first of the Shawnee towns that they encountered, they were met by Moluntha, an aged warrior and now the village headman. Carrying a peace pipe and flying an American flag above his lodge, Moluntha attempted to shake hands with the invaders as they entered the town. But Hugh McGary, one of Logan's soldiers and the man responsible for the debacle at the Blue Licks, roughly pushed his way through the crowd that surrounded the Shawnee leader and drove a tomahawk into his forehead. The murder signaled the beginning of the destruction and general plundering of the village. The Kentuckians quickly razed Mequashake and then advanced to Wapatomica and Blue Jacket's Town, dispersing the residents and burning the buildings. Logan also destroyed Kispoko, or McKee's Town, where McKee maintained a hewed-log house with a brick chimney and an orchard. While the Americans set fire to the village, Simon Kenton personally put McKee's house to the torch. Running from the burning building, he grabbed McKee's laced cocked hat and wore it throughout the remainder of the expedition. Within two days, the entire settlement lay in ashes.[10]

The destruction of McKee's home must have been a point of particular satisfaction for Logan. In early May 1786, American officials at Fort Finney had warned the Miami Valley tribes that they would not permit any white person to live among the Indians without a special permit. The warning clearly was about McKee and other Indian department employees who remained active in the area, for the Americans had also explained, "We mean those people who have been so active during the war to lead you astray and who we find are still endeavoring to continue their influence over You." In September 1785, Pacanne, a Miami spokesman, reported that William Caldwell and Simon Girty were living with the Ohio nations and using their influence to turn the tribes away from the Americans. Further, claiming that McKee and the Shawnees were "determined for mischief," he also said that the British agent was sending provocative speeches to the nations along the Miami Valley. Pacanne's report was verified by William Doleman, one of two American spies who had lived at McKee's Town during the previous winter and spring. According to Doleman, Girty, Caldwell, Matthew Elliott, and a host of other Indian department officials were encouraging the Indians to attack American settlers, plunder American traders, and defy American diplomatic initiatives. These British agents were people who "continue their intercourse with you, who have no right," claimed the Americans at Fort Finney, "and . . . even busy themselves with the affairs between you and us to the great detriment of both." Logan had destroyed the Shawnee settlement, in part, because of the Indians' open defiance of American authority in the area. McKee's home was one of nearly two hundred destroyed by the Kentuckians. For McKee, the loss had few lasting consequences. Likewise, Logan's raid was a serious, but only temporary, blow to the Shawnees. The destruction strengthened the tribe's resolve to oppose the Americans and enhanced their attachment to the British, to whom they now turned for provisions, shelter, and arms. By spring 1787, the tribe had increased the number of raids it launched against the Ohio River Valley.[11]

The Iroquois, Lake, and Ohio nations had attempted to unite politically in order to defend against American expansionism. As early as 1783, the tribes had vowed to form a confederation and to act in concert as they negotiated with the United States. America's insistence on treating with individual tribes or small groups of nations, as they had in the Fort Stanwix, McIntosh, and Finney accords, successfully frustrated this strategy. The Kentucky raids gave a new sense of urgency to the Indians' efforts to establish a meaningful union. In late December 1786, a deputation of the Six Nations, led by Brant, met at Detroit with McKee, other Indian department officials, and representatives from the other western tribes to reestablish the confederacy and to agree upon a course of action. The council was a success. At its conclusion, the reinvigorated league determined to write a letter to the American Congress, proposing a general conference between it and all the Indian nations to reconsider the Stanwix, McIntosh, and Finney agreements. At the proposed conference, the Indians would insist that both parties establish a permanent boundary between the United States and the Indian nations. McKee was pleased with the proposal and noted that he was happy with the "firmness" and "calmness" that the Indians had shown in their deliberations.[12]

American officials were slow to acknowledge the Indian proposal. Realizing that increased violence could abort the planned negotiations, McKee worked throughout the year to restrain the western tribes. "We earnestly recommend coolness and moderation in every part of your conduct," he told a visiting delegation of Miamis, Shawnees, and Delawares who had come to Detroit with complaints about the Americans. Once the conference began, he explained, "The wise men of all the Indian Nations will . . . determine upon such measures as Shall be most advantageous for [the] general interest." McKee was still attempting to restrain the western nations throughout the spring of the following year. On June 29, 1788, he attempted to stop a twenty-man war party of Ottawas and Chippewas from Mackinac from leaving Detroit. Unsuccessful, he sent warnings to travelers near Pittsburgh and at the mouth of the Cuyahoga River to be on their guard.[13]

Continued American reluctance to schedule the council caused McKee to change his tactics later in the year. In August 1788, the agent held a council at Roche de Bout. Jean Baptiste Constant, a French interpreter in the pay of the Americans, reported that every day prior to the meeting "five and six scalps were brought in," and "a number of our prisoners were burnt." During the council, McKee ridiculed the proposed meeting with the Americans and told the Shawnees not to go to the conference. The treaty would accomplish nothing, he claimed, for even if the tribes could negotiate a settlement with the federal government, the accord would quickly be broken by Kentucky irregulars.[14]

The shift in McKee's tactics reflected both the poorly developed, ad hoc nature of British diplomatic strategy within the region and a growing discord among the Indian ranks. A fundamental policy disagreement split the confederacy along clearly defined tribal lines. According to Brant, the Wyandots, Chippewas, Ottawas, Potawatomis, and Delawares favored negotiating with the Americans, even if it meant giving up a small amount of territory, provided the talks would avoid war and establish a well-defined, permanent boundary. But the Shawnees and Miamis preferred warfare to land cessions and refused to enter into talks with American officials. The Americans were quick to detect and then exploit the rift. The meeting the Indians had so long awaited was finally held at Fort Harmar, at the confluence of the Muskingum and Ohio Rivers, in January 1789. American Indian policy had also shifted in response to the continued violence along the Ohio River. In order to avoid a potentially expensive and lengthy Indian war, Congress had agreed to treat with the Indians on a footing of equality. This action, claimed the government, would convince the northwest tribes that the United States acted with justice and humanity. In practice, the new policy meant that the United States no longer claimed the Northwest by conquest and was prepared to purchase the territory from the Indians. However, realizing that the Indian nations were badly divided, the federal government refused to reconsider the amount of territory it sought. The American commissioners at Fort Harmar would not discuss the new boundary proposed by Brant and his supporters. The Treaty of Fort Harmar, signed on January 9, 1789, confirmed the cessions already given up under the Fort McIntosh agreement but provided a small sum as payment for the ceded land.[15]

The confederacy's political factionalism and the Shawnees' and Miamis' open hostility toward the Americans prevented most of the Ohio tribes from attending the Fort Harmar council. Only a few bands of Senecas, Wyandots, and Delawares, along with scattered Ottawas, Potawatomis, and Shawnees were signatories to the pact. Opposition to the agreement was widespread throughout the Ohio Country. The more warlike factions continued their raids against American settlements along the Ohio Valley, and in June 1789, Lord Dorchester, the governor general of Canada, reported that the Indians seemed determined to remove all American settlement northwest of the Ohio River. The warring tribes, he claimed, had sent war pipes to the differing Ohio nations and a large delegation to Detroit to demand supplies and ammunition. They had also come to Detroit "with an intention of presenting the war-pipe to the commanding officer of Detroit." Great Britain was willing to continue its clandestine support to the Indian nations, but it had no intention of entering into an open confrontation with the new republic. Just before the council, McKee held a private conversation with one of the tribal leaders and convinced him that such a move would be inappropriate. The war pipe was not offered to the British. McKee's quick intervention prevented the Crown from being maneuvered into a potentially embarrassing international incident, but it in no way reflected a lessening of his commitment to supply the tribes in their struggle against the United States.[16]

American officials were not fooled by McKee's machinations. "For whatever they may say (and I hope it is true that the British government does not countenance it), they [the Indians] are prompted to much of the mischief they do by the British traders," complained Arthur St. Clair in 1790. "Mr. McKee's being among them distributing ammunition and stores looks so like the support of the government that it is impossible they should view it in any other light."[17]

By early 1790, McKee was using two posts along the Maumee River, one at the foot of the rapids in present-day Perrysburg and the second at the Glaize in present-day Defiance, to distribute arms, ammunition, and provisions to the warring tribes. McKee's post at the rapids had been established on the site of Grant's Blockhouse, a small British fort built and then quickly abandoned during the final days of the Revolution. Thomas Rhea, an American prisoner brought to the rapids in 1791, noted that the post was a large complex that contained eleven storehouses filled with arms, ammunition, corn, pork, and peas. At the Glaize, McKee occupied one of two hewed-log cabins (the second was used by James Girty) that stood about fifty yards from the Maumee River, surrounded by a wooden stockade. Isaac Freeman, an American spy at the Glaize, reported that McKee would send supplies to the settlement by boat and packhorse and then personally deliver the goods, including powder, ball, and muskets, to each chief's home. The Indians acknowledged their gifts by flying the British flag from their house-tops. Freeman also reported that the tribes were determined to drive the American settlers from the Ohio Country. They had delayed doing so because they had not been supplied with adequate military stores. Now that the goods had arrived, "They only waited the return of Mr. Magee . . . and they would proceed without further delay down to the Ohio."[18]

The conference at Detroit was one of the last that McKee attended before he was appointed to the post of Indian agent in March 1790. The promotion changed the focus, but not the purpose, of his duties. Following the promotion, he still worked to maintain the British-Indian alliance and to promote the Indian confederacy opposing the United States. But his contacts with the western tribes became more formal and less intimate than before. Dividing his time between Detroit and the Maumee Rapids, McKee developed policies to guide the British government in its dealings with the Ohio nations, maintained diplomatic relations with the region's Indians, facilitated the flow of intelligence to Crown officials at Detroit, and worked to keep British supplies moving along the Maumee River. Although he regularly met with tribal officials at the rapids and elsewhere, his new obligations prevented him from traveling as extensively among the Ohio Country tribes as he had pre-vious to his promotion. This responsibility he delegated to other Indian Department subordinates, including his son Thomas, Matthew Elliott, and Simon Girty.

An American military expedition directed against the Maumee Valley tribes shortly after he accepted his new assignment provided McKee with his first major challenge. American officials had hoped that a quick, punitive raid against the Maumee Valley tribes would put a halt to the violence along the Ohio River. In 1790, Congress authorized Josiah Harmar to lead an army of regulars and militia against Kekionga, a large Miami settlement at the headwaters of the Maumee River (present-day Fort Wayne, Indiana). The American offensive began on Septem-ber 30. After traveling up the Miami Valley, Harmar arrived at the Miami villages on October 15. Well aware of the American advance, the Indians burned their homes and deserted the settlement before Harmar arrived. Assuming that the Indians would not fight, the Americans

Although frequently identified as a likeness of Alexander McKee, this portrait is probably that of his son, Thomas. The painting, which has a long and well-documented history of ownership in the McKee family, shows an officer of the 60th Regiment of Foot wearing the uniform of the 1790s era. *Community Museums of Windsor.*

remained at the site until two well-executed Indian counterattacks led by the Miami chief Little Turtle on October 19 and 21 forced the army to retreat.[19]

The Indian victory at Kekionga had been facilitated to a considerable degree by arms, ammunition, and intelligence supplied by the Indian department. British officials also understood that the American offensive represented a major escalation in the United States's conflict with the Northwestern tribes. Harmar's attack prompted McKee to make several policy recommendations designed to increase the efficiency of Britain's efforts to aid the warring nations. McKee felt that the lack of political unity among the western tribes had invited the American offensive. In early spring 1791, he proposed that a general conference be held at the rapids to strengthen the confederacy and to end the divisiveness that he held to be "the source of the present calamities." Moreover, in June he recommended that British troops fortify the rapids with a "small work of sod or Picketts" manned by at least one hundred regulars and fifty militia. Lastly, he urged Sir John Johnson, the superintendent general of Indian affairs, to take whatever measures were necessary to stop the uncontrolled flow of liquor to the Maumee Valley tribes. Alcohol was "the source of every mischief," the agent claimed. Strong regulations administered by the Indian department would "render the Indians happier among themselves and more powerful friends in case their assistance should ever be wanted."[20]

Continued American raids prevented many of the region's tribes from attending the proposed conference, but a small number of nations met with McKee at the rapids in early July. During the conference, the agent asked the tribes to define the terms upon which they would be prepared to negotiate a settlement with the Americans. The Indians repeated their demand for a firm, permanent boundary between the western nations and the United States and proposed that the boundary be drawn at the Muskingum River. White settlement was already entrenched in eastern Ohio and the suggestion indicated a willingness to cede land to the east of the Muskingum in exchange for undisputed native sovereignty to the west. When the meeting ended, Joseph Brant and a deputation from the Iroquois Confederacy carried the proposal to Lord Dorchester in Quebec. McKee called for a second council to discuss the proposal in depth and suggested it be held at the Maumee Rapids the following autumn.[21]

The conference never took place. A second American army, led by Arthur St. Clair, began an advance against the Maumee Valley tribes in early autumn. By November 1791, St. Clair had advanced to the headwaters of the Wabash River in west central Ohio (present-day Fort Recovery). Once again, Little Turtle and a large force of native warriors, organized in part by the Indian department and aided by arms and intelligence supplied by the British, crushed the American force.[22]

The Indian victory at the Wabash was a staggering blow to the Americans, costing the invaders more than nine hundred men either killed or wounded. Among the dead was Richard Butler, St. Clair's second in command, and thirty-six other officers. In addition, the army abandoned virtually all its supplies and equipment, including pack animals, arms, provisions, and artillery, in the frantic retreat following the engagement. The enormousness of the victory was not lost on McKee. In December, he predicted that the Americans would soon negotiate a settlement favorable to the western tribes. If the United States had treated with the Indian nations in good faith the previous year, he claimed, then "we should not now have occasion to deplore the effusion of so much blood." "I most sincerely wish that the Americans, now convinced of the difficulty of subduing a Brave & warlike race of People, may listen to the Voice of Equity and Reason."[23]

McKee was not alone in his assessment. Following the American defeat, British, American, and Indian officials alike began to explore diplomatic channels in an attempt to end the conflict. In March 1792, the British foreign secretary, Lord Grenville, instructed his minister in the United States, George Hammond, to propose the Muskingum River boundary suggested by the Indians in 1791 as the basis for a negotiated settlement. The American secretary of war, Henry Knox, also sought a diplomatic solution and invited Joseph Brant to a series of high-level talks in Philadelphia, the nation's capital. Brant was willing to open negotiations but was disturbed that British officials seemed unwilling to provide a definitive policy from which he could proceed. Writing to McKee in May 1792, he complained that while the Americans had "paved the way for Peace," his requests for instructions from the Indian department were repeatedly ignored. "If Great Britain wishes us to defend our Country, why not tell us so in plain language," he asked. "If the reverse, let it be mentioned, then we will know how to act, and be enabled to take such steps as will secure us and our posterity."[24]

Brant's comments were the first indication of what would become an ever-widening rift between the Mohawk leader and the British government. Slowly, Brant had begun to see the Indian nations as inextricably caught between a powerful enemy and an unsympathetic ally. His talks with the Americans proved unproductive. But following the meeting, fearing both American aggression and British duplicity, he became an increasingly vocal advocate for a negotiated peace that would protect "our own [Indian] Interests and the happiness of our Women and Children," regardless of how the settlement would effect British interests.[25]

Partly in response to Brant's criticisms, McKee traveled to Montreal in June 1792 to meet with John Graves Simcoe, the newly appointed lieutenant governor of Upper Canada. In the discussions that followed, Simcoe and McKee devised a policy that coupled the Indians' demands for a firm boundary with the creation of a permanent, neutral Indian buffer state that separated the United States from Canada. The plan called for the western nations to retain the land west of the Muskingum River. The British would also retain possession of Detroit and acquire a strip of land, six miles wide, that ran from east to west along the southern shore of Lake Erie to the Maumee Rapids. In return, the British would dismantle their military posts at Niagara, Oswego, and Detroit and abandon Fort Michilimackinac. The proposal seemed to be framed in terms of the diplomatic demands presented by the western nations. But it was not native interests that guided the plan's creation. Most importantly, Simcoe and McKee had created a strategic document that outlined the military defense of Detroit. The plan denied American access to Lake Erie, while the buffer state insulated Upper Canada against direct military action from the United States. The proposal also cemented native loyalty to the Crown and provided a dependable (and expendable) pool of military support should the Americans renew their aggression.[26]

McKee returned to Detroit in early summer to oversee the distribution of supplies to the Maumee Valley tribes and to organize Indian support for the buffer state. In August, Simcoe realized that if the United States and the western tribes agreed to a negotiated settlement, then direct British arbitration at the talks would be a powerful tool to protect the Crown's interests in the region. McKee had planned to hold a general conference at the Glaize to discuss the buffer state proposal, and Simcoe urged McKee to use the meeting to convince the Indians of the necessity of British participation at all future negotiations with the Americans. Simcoe knew that American officials would reject Crown mediation if it seemed the British were in collusion with the Indians. To avoid the appearance of intrigue, McKee was to see that the western tribes "*themselves* solicit the King's good Offices," as a "result of their own spontaneous Reflections."[27]

McKee met with twenty-eight of the eastern and western tribes at a grand council held at the Glaize from September 30 through October 9. The meeting demonstrated the continuing disagreements between the Iroquois and their Ohio Country allies. As the council began, Cow Killer, an Iroquois (Seneca) headman, stated that the Americans had always dealt justly with his nation, both at the Treaty of Fort Stanwix and the Fort Harmar accord. But Painted Pole, of the Shawnees, claimed that Cow Killer was a liar and that the Americans wanted to turn the Indians into farmers to supply their markets along the East Coast. If the Americans truly wished to achieve a lasting peace, he claimed, then they should destroy the forts they had built along the Ohio and Miami River Valleys and enter into serious negotiations with the assembled nations. The Shawnee's speech touched a responsive chord, and soon the meeting reached a consensus that called for a general council with the Americans at Sandusky the following year. Just as Simcoe had anticipated, McKee was persuasive. At the council's conclusion, the Indians, after consulting with representatives from the Six Nations, "spontaneously" requested British mediation on their behalf during the upcoming negotiations.[28]

Simcoe forwarded the tribes' wishes to Hammond, who had already discussed the possibility of British mediation with American officials. Secretary of State Thomas Jefferson opposed direct British mediation, but he was willing to allow British agents to attend the peace talks to translate and otherwise facilitate the negotiations. British officials reluctantly agreed, but they insisted that the agents would also be the sole providers of provisions at the conference. The terms were acceptable to the Americans, and in December 1792, both sides agreed to begin talks at Lower Sandusky in early 1793. Simcoe quickly appointed McKee and John Butler from Niagara to represent the Indian department at the meeting.[29]

McKee understood that British interests would be protected during the scheduled negotiations only if the Indians presented a strong, unified front. Simcoe agreed, claiming that "one general Union amongst the whole Nations can alone furnish the basis of a real Peace." But discord was already making itself felt among the western tribes. After their victory over St. Clair in 1791, the Maumee Valley tribes had reconsidered the terms upon which they would make peace with the Americans. The decisiveness of the Indian victory had convinced many of the tribes to increase their demands. By early 1793, most of the western nations were openly calling for the Americans to be expelled from Ohio and insisting that the Ohio River, not the Muskingum River, serve as the permanent boundary between the Indian nations and the United States.[30]

The western nations' demands disturbed Brant who, by the early spring of 1793, was firmly committed to a negotiated settlement based upon the Muskingum River compromise. Urging McKee to keep the young men of the Maumee nations "within bounds" so as not to endanger the planned negotiations, Brant confided that, in his opinion, the discussions scheduled for Lower Sandusky represented the western tribes' best means to obtain an equitable peace and were, moreover, an opportunity that "if lost may not be regained."[31]

But Brant's opinions no longer carried any influence with either Simcoe or McKee. Although the Mohawk chief did not fully realize it, both men had come to support the western tribes' demand for the Ohio River boundary. McKee and Simcoe were predisposed to be sympathetic with their Maumee Valley allies, McKee because of his long and intimate affiliation with the Ohio tribes and Simcoe by virtue of an open commitment to increase the Crown's influence within the region. Events in late 1792 and early 1793 strengthened the natural inclinations of both men. After St. Clair's defeat in 1791, the United States created a third expeditionary force, the Legion of the United States, and placed it under the command of Anthony Wayne. In 1792, Wayne's army traveled down the Ohio River from Pittsburgh, to Fort Washington, (Cincinnati) and then up the Miami Valley to Fort Jefferson (Fort Jefferson, Ohio), where it paused to await the outcome of the government's diplomatic overtures. In August 1792, McKee wrote to Simcoe, justifiably concerned that the army's advance indicated the United States was not prepared to bargain in good faith. By late spring 1793, Simcoe agreed, claiming that Wayne's actions "breath War." From that time forward, both men waged a deliberate campaign to discredit Brant, while they encouraged the Maumee tribes to press for the Ohio River boundary.[32]

McKee called for the tribes to meet at his post on the Maumee River in early summer, hoping to reach a general agreement among the various nations before their meeting with the United States commissioners at Lower Sandusky. On June 29, he reported that a large number of Indians, including nearly one thousand from "distant quarters" were gathered at the rapids. Among those who had traveled the furthest were representatives from the Creek, and Cherokee nations, southern tribes from as far away as Tennessee, Georgia, Alabama, and Mississippi. McKee's dealing with North American Indian nations had continued to expand in the post-Revolutionary era, and although his dealings with the southern tribes were never extensive, he had been in regular correspondence with British sympathizers who had lived with these nations since 1791. The southern nations had sent delegates to the rapids to seek British support for their own war against the Americans and to promote a general Indian confederacy between the southern and northern tribes. McKee was unable to comply, partly because both he and Simcoe understood that open aid to the southern nations might harden United States resolve against the Maumee Valley nations and partly because hostilities within the Great Lakes region had stretched Detroit's logistical capabilities to their limits. Nonetheless, delegates from the south continued to cooperate with the Ohio Country nations throughout 1794. McKee's role in the proceedings that were to follow was evident in the instructions Simcoe issued to Walter Sheehan and William Johnson, the two interpreters assigned by the Indian department to assist McKee during the deliberations. "In all points whatsoever," ordered Simcoe, they were to be directed by McKee, who had been invested "with all such civil and military authority as may be necessary to fulfill the object of his important trust, and is solely responsible to the due execution of the same."[33]

Brant arrived for the conference in late May, only to find he had become the target of numerous rumors spread by the Shawnees, alleging he was a traitor and in the pay of the Americans. Despite Brant's attempts to remove the cloud of suspicion, the allegations continued to circulate throughout the first two weeks of June. McKee's dispatches were silent regarding the discord, but one easily suspects the Indian department's involvement in the incident.[34]

As June drew to a close, the conference reached a general consensus to support the Ohio River boundary. On July 1, McKee held a private meeting with Brant and asked him to meet with the American peace delegation waiting at Niagara. Brant was to present the demand for the new boundary and to determine if the commissioners were authorized to act on it. McKee's request was a shrewd political maneuver. The mission was diplomatically important and highly visible, and McKee realized that Brant would not decline the invitation. At the same time, McKee also knew that Brant's acceptance would force the Iroquois leader to voluntarily leave the rapids and end his challenge to the Indian department as it continued to mold the western nations' diplomatic response. The mission allowed McKee to both flatter and neutralize his troublesome enemy. As McKee had anticipated, the Iroquois leader readily accepted, and the following day he and a small delegation from the Six Nations set out for New York.[35]

Brant met with the American commissioners on July 7. During the meeting, the Americans stated that they were empowered to negotiate a boundary. Despite his instructions from McKee, Brant equivocated and seemed to suggest that the Indians would still negotiate for the Muskingum line. Simcoe, who was also in attendance, was shocked by the Mohawk's conduct. The lieutenant governor immediately wrote to McKee, giving him the details of the conference and advising the agent to "more strongly fix upon Brant's mind the necessity of . . . Union."[36]

Brant returned to the rapids on July 21 to find his influence diminished and his pretensions to leadership challenged at every turn. Although he continued to lobby for the Muskingum boundary in open council, his overtures were thwarted in private meetings to which he was not invited. When Brant asked to know the cause of this flagrant insult, Buckongehelis, a Delaware chief, stood, pointed to McKee, and claimed, "That is the Person who advises us to insist on the Ohio River for the Line." Over Brant's strenuous objections, the council dispatched a second deputation, including the principal chiefs of the Maumee tribes, to the American negotiators on July 28. On July 30, the delegation presented its unambiguous demand for the Ohio River to the commissioners. The Americans replied that the Indian ultimatum was unacceptable. While they were prepared to make small concessions concerning the Muskingum River boundary, they were not empowered to negotiate away the land east of the river. The reply ended the meeting, and with it, any hope for a negotiated settlement.[37]

When the delegation returned to the rapids in early August, the split between Brant and McKee was open and bitter. An obviously offended Brant, after complaining about the secret meetings from which he had been excluded, claimed that "we came here not only to assist with our advice, but other ways if Just. But the unmerited Slight offered us is too apparent to be passed over in silence." Brant's remonstrance was in vain. McKee remained unapologetic. He described Brant's character as "problematical" and his conduct as "very unsatisfactory." "I expect from the malevolent, disappointed, & all ill disposed, to be blamed for the Opinions which the Indians have adopted," he wrote to Simcoe. "I shall not, however, lament on account of their Animadversions." Simcoe was in complete agreement. The following month he reassured McKee that his conduct throughout the deliberations appeared to be "perfectly proper in all respects."[38]

The failure of the peace negotiations ensured that hostilities would resume. When the discussions collapsed in August 1793, Wayne went on the offensive. By autumn, the Legion had advanced beyond Fort Jefferson and constructed Fort Greene Ville (Greenville, Ohio), where most of the army paused for the winter. In December 1793, a small detachment continued beyond Fort Green Ville to the site of St. Clair's defeat where they built Fort Recovery as a forward base. Aided by accurate intelligence supplied by spies, deserters, and prisoners, McKee was well informed of the legion's advance. McKee spent the autumn of 1793 and the winter and spring of 1794 procuring and distributing weapons, provisions, and supplies to the Maumee Valley tribes. Moreover, Simcoe acted upon McKee's recommendation to fortify the vulnerable southern overland approach to Detroit. By late spring 1794, the lieutenant governor had constructed Fort Miamis, a formidable fortification manned by militia, infantry, and royal artillerymen, at the foot of the Maumee Rapids, directly across from McKee's post. He also constructed and garrisoned two blockhouses, one north of the rapids at the River Raisin, the second on Turtle Island at the mouth of the Maumee River, and he placed a corporal's guard—about twenty men—at Roche de Bout.[39]

McKee's and Simcoe's actions reinvigorated the Indian alliance. Responding to a call from the confederacy's leadership, nearly twelve

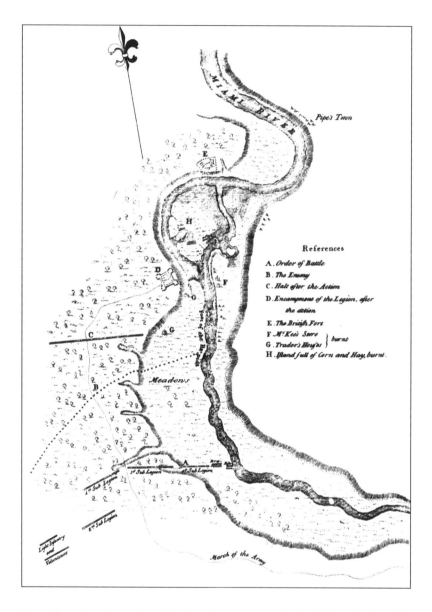

References

A. *Order of Battle*
B. *The Enemy*
C. *Halt after the Action*
D. *Encampment of the Legion, after the action*
E. *The British Fort*
F. *McKee's Store* } *burnt*
G. *Trader's Houses* } *burnt*
H. *Island full of Corn and Hay, burnt.*

Drawn by an American officer following the August 1794 Battle of Fallen Timbers, this map designates McKee's post (*F*) and notes that the facility was destroyed by the legion following the engagement. *Ohio Historical Society.*

hundred Indians, including Miamis, Shawnees, Delawares, Wyandots, Ottawas, Chippewas, and Potawatomis, met at the Glaize in June 1794. On June 16, Indian department officials proposed that the Indians sever the legion's supply line by attacking Wayne's lightly guarded convoys. The warriors agreed, and on June 17, the war party moved southward toward the Miami Valley.[40]

The expedition represented one of the largest hostile assemblages of native Americans ever brought together to oppose the United States military. Despite the group's numerical strength and apparent unanimity of purpose, powerful forces converged to disrupt the fragile Indian alliance. Poor logistical support plagued the mission from the beginning. Provisions were scarce, and Joseph Chew, an Indian department official who accompanied the party, reported that nearly 10 percent of the force was without weapons. Further, the expedition's leadership appeared undecided concerning the mission's objectives. Bowing to internal dissention, on June 27 they were persuaded to abandon the plan, which called for an attack on Wayne's supply lines. Instead they opted for an assault directly against Fort Recovery. Most importantly, twenty-seven Mackinaw and Saginaw Indians from the Upper Lakes region had joined the band on June 18. The Lake tribes and the Maumee Valley confederacy had disagreed over policy ever since conclusion of the 1793 council at McKee's post. Although relations between the two groups were noticeably cool, neither side had acted to overtly antagonize the other. But Chew reported that as the Lake warriors passed through several Maumee-area Indian villages from which the men were absent, they "committed depredations and ravished the women."[41]

The Indian party cautiously approached the American garrison during the early hours of June 30 and launched the attack shortly after dawn. Inadequately planned, recklessly executed, and ferociously contested by the Americans, the assault lasted for nearly two days before it ended in failure. During the battle, the Shawnees and Delawares shot into the attacking ranks of the Saginaws and Mackinaws, using the opportunity to take their retribution for the violations perpetrated against their homes and families. The lack of internal cohesion doomed the Indian effort. Unable to defeat the garrison, the Indians broke off the engagement and withdrew in midmorning, July 1.[42]

McKee had badly mismanaged the expedition against Fort Recovery. Charged with maintaining the Crown's relations with the western tribes and coordinating Indian affairs for the Crown's benefit, the Indian department was aware of long-standing antagonism between the Lake and Maumee Valley tribes. The nations were brought together at the Indian department's instigation, despite the volatility of their relationship. Moreover, as the confederacy unraveled before its eyes, the department seemed ill prepared to do little more than watch helplessly. Never again would the Indian confederacy regain the military potential represented by the invading force as it had left the Glaize in mid-June. Politically factionalized as a result of the undertaking, the league had become incapable of taking coordinated military action on its own behalf. Subjected to centrifugal forces that had been exacerbated by McKee and the Indian department, the alliance was pushed apart from within.[43]

Stunned by its defeat at Fort Recovery, the Indian alliance was dealt another blow when British officials, including Simcoe and McKee, deliberately misrepresented Great Britain's policy for the region to the warring tribes. The United States and England had disagreed over the implementation of the 1783 Treaty of Paris ever since the end of the Revolution. As a result, England continued to occupy military posts along the Canadian-United States border that were within American territory. These posts included Forts Niagara, Michilimackinac, and Detroit. The outbreak of war between France and Great Britain in 1793 convinced Whitehall to conclude an agreement with the United States that would reduce tensions in North America. By the summer of 1794, British negotiators had nearly completed a pact that called for the removal of British troops from the northern posts. Canadian officials along the Great Lakes frontier clearly understood that the treaty would specifically require the abandonment of Detroit and would end the Indian department's adventuring in the Ohio Country.[44]

Despite Whitehall's unambiguous intention to establish peace along the western border, Canadian authorities continued to urge the Maumee Valley tribes to resist by force American expansion into the region. British officials did not inform their native allies of the peace negotiations. Moreover, they redoubled their efforts to supply provisions and arms to the hostile nations and continued the military buildup along the Maumee River. On February 10, 1794, while meeting with a delegation from the Six Nations, Sir Guy Carleton, Lord Dorchester, unexpectedly announced that he felt open warfare with the United States was imminent, and in April, Simcoe repeated Dorchester's speech to the

Maumee tribes. In March, Henry Dundas, Britain's secretary for home affairs, advised Simcoe to keep the western nations engaged in their campaign against the Americans, hoping that a third Indian victory would give British negotiators added leverage at the peace conference. In July, Simcoe encouraged McKee to continue his efforts to supply arms and provisions to the western nations. "If I know anything of the States they so highly overrate their own importance that Mr. Jay's Embassy will be fruitless," he wrote, "& I conceive War inevitable."[45]

But while Canadian officials seemed to be promising full military assistance to the Indian alliance, they also explicitly understood that Great Britain was unprepared to commit troops to the conflict or take any overt military action that would endanger the peace negotiations or force a declaration of war from the United States. As early as August 1792, Simcoe had advised McKee that it was "neither the Interest nor the Inclination of His Majesty's Government to commence Offensive Hostilities against the United States." The agent clearly understood the limits that British policy placed on his actions. Writing to Maj. Richard Campbell, the commander of Fort Miamis, after the engagement at Fort Recovery, McKee commented that the commitment of British troops on the expedition, "Provided I had been authorized for that purpose," would have materially strengthened the attack. "But we must in that case have taken an active share in the contest and become at least auxiliaries in the War."[46]

The western alliance had fallen victim to a policy that was cynically exploitive and based on tacit promises that could not be kept and commitments that would not be honored. For the second time in eleven years, negotiators in Great Britain had sacrificed native interests in the Ohio Country to further the broader interests of the realm.[47]

Reeling from their encounter with the legion at Fort Recovery, the western nations offered little resistance as Wayne began his final thrust to the Maumee River in July 1794. The army advanced cautiously from Fort Greene Ville, passed Fort Recovery on July 29, and reached the Glaize on August 8. Wayne found that the Indians had abandoned the village in great haste, and he paused only long enough to begin construction of a forward base, Fort Defiance, in the middle of the native stronghold. On August 13, the legion renewed its march down the Maumee River to confront the Indians, who congregated near the foot of the rapids. Wayne reached Roche de Bout on August 18 and spent the

remainder of that day and the next constructing Fort Deposit, a fortified, temporary camp to hold the army's baggage.[48]

McKee had assembled nearly thirteen hundred warriors to oppose
the American army. On August 19, the Indians occupied Fallen Timbers, a dense thicket about four miles west of Fort Miamis, where high
winds had uprooted many of the trees. The Indian force deployed along
a mile-long front that ran in a northerly direction, nearly perpendicular
to the Maumee River, and waited for Wayne's advance.[49]

Wayne began his assault two hours after dawn on August 20. Moving
down the Maumee, the legion engaged the Indians at midmorning. The
alliance's defense, while fierce, was disorganized and quickly collapsed
in the face of the legion's determined onslaught. Within little more than
two hours, Wayne had won a signal victory over the Maumee nations.
Driving the retreating Indians ahead of the legion at bayonet point,
Wayne continued downriver to Fort Miamis, where he destroyed the
crops and burned McKee's post to the ground. McKee watched the
battle from the water's edge, a "respectful distance" from the combat.
As the Indian defense disintegrated, he followed the fleeing warriors to
Fort Miamis. He informed William Campbell, the post's commander,
that the tribes had been "out generaled," then he continued downriver
to Swan Creek, nearly six miles below the British garrison, where he
finally stemmed the Indian retreat.[50]

McKee used every resource at his disposal to bolster the Indians' confidence in the wake of their defeat and to assure them of the Indian
department's continued support. Within a few weeks, thousands of the
Crown's allies had sought refuge at the temporary camp. McKee or an
assistant listed 2,556 Indians from ten different nations at the site on
September 15. One week later, Matthew Elliott ordered provisions for
1,010 men and 1,990 women at the encampment. On September 26,
Capt. William Mayne visited the site and described 3,000 Indian men,
women, and children whose appearance was "grander and more inter-
esting to me than anything I ever beheld since my arrival in Canada." To
keep the Indians at Swan Creek and to demonstrate the Crown's continued commitment to the Northwest nations, Simcoe, upon McKee's
recommendation, fortified the site with a small earthwork and blockhouse. Two artillery pieces, a six-pounder and a four-pounder, manned
by a small detachment from Fort Miamis, guarded the post, while two
bakehouses provided bread for the refugees and their families. Further,

McKee supplied provisions, including 79,560 pounds of flour; 50,330 pounds of pork; and smaller quantities of salt beef, peas, butter, rice, and corn to the assembled nations.[51]

Despite McKee's success in halting the Indians' retreat, his actions had not met with universal approval. Colonel England, in particular, was highly critical of McKee's actions. Complaining to Simcoe a few days after the Battle of Fallen Timbers, the Detroit commander described Indian department efforts at Swan Creek as a waste of valuable supplies and provisions for "Indians who have already in a dastardly, cowardly manner retired to Miamis Bay and left the Fort [Miamis] totally unprotected." Simcoe, though, continued to encourage McKee and to support his activities. By early fall, the lieutenant governor understood that it was only the Indian department's work at Swan Creek that prevented the Indians from leaving the lower reaches of the Maumee and drifting toward the Glaize where Wayne had established his winter cantonment, Fort Defiance. Simcoe urged McKee to continue his efforts to keep the northwest nations attached to the British and away from American negotiators. McKee responded ably, and in September, Joseph Chew truthfully reported that "nothing keeps the Indians from quitting that part of the Country and Separating but his Presence & influence."[52]

Yet no matter how energetic the Crown's efforts, no amount of provisions or supplies could erase the fact that British troops had not taken the field in the battle against Wayne. Throughout the fall, all but the most strident members of the Indian confederacy began to discreetly contact the American commander in anticipation of a formal peace proposal. Wayne seized the initiative early in 1795. On New Year's Day he issued a general invitation to the Northwestern tribes to begin peace negotiations. Claiming he had thanked "the Great Spirit for opening your eyes and changing the Inclination of your Hearts from War to Peace," Wayne told the Indians they could not "come forward too soon" to begin the discussions that would establish a permanent peace. Many of the once-belligerent nations accepted the American proposal, and by January 27, McKee complained that Indians "from all quarters" intended to meet with Wayne and end the British-Indian military alliance.[53]

The alliance also received a severe blow in late January when the Shawnee leader, Blue Jacket, one of the most prominent and visible members of the confederation, took his band to meet with the American general. On February 11, the Shawnees signed a preliminary treaty with the United States and urged others within the confederacy to do likewise. Blue Jacket's example was a powerful inducement, and British observers near the American camp reported that Potowatomis, Chippewas, Ottawas, and Sacs were also eager to enter into negotiations with the Americans. Wayne's spies claimed that in April, McKee's personal emissary to Sandusky was executed as he attempted to restrain the village from treating with the American commander. Furthermore, Wayne learned in early May that McKee and Blue Jacket had nearly come to blows, and as a result the Shawnee leader was using all his efforts to counteract McKee's influence among the western nations. Powerless to act as the alliance broke apart, Crown officials lashed out at their one-time allies. The Indians at Swan Creek were "jealous, stupid wretches," confided George Ironside to McKee in early February. Further, McKee had also learned that Detroit traders were supplying provisions and supplies to Wayne and his army. "We have already more Enemies than Friends in this Country," raged McKee in a letter to Simcoe. "If some steps are not speedily taken there will be an end to all . . . respect for the . . . King's interest."[54]

Joseph Brant seemed to take a particular delight in McKee's difficulties. "It is a pity," he wrote to Joseph Chew, "that Colonel McKee should have lost his influence with the Indians." But Chew, a close friend of McKee, was unwilling to let the insult go unchallenged. Upbraiding the Mohawk leader for allowing his differences with McKee to go too far, too publicly, Chew claimed that Brant's remarks would only "infuse Jealousies" among the Maumee Valley nations and "make them distrust their best Friends." Moreover, Chew continued to praise McKee's "exertions, care, attention and Zeal" in his dealings with the northwest confederacy. But by spring and early summer, no amount of exertion, care, attention, or zeal could preserve the alliance. Simcoe and McKee visited the Shawnee living on Swan Creek in September 1794. The lieutenant governor was awed by the "grand spectacle" of thousands of Indians lining the river bank to greet him. Later that evening, at a dance held in his honor, Simcoe watched in amazement as the Shawnees performed in elaborate costumes decorated with plumage, beadwork, silver, and jewelry that he guessed were worth forty or fifty pounds sterling per man. When Simcoe remarked upon the richness of the Indians' dress, a wistful McKee replied that when he first came to the Ohio Country, the Indians "in their grand Dances frequently changed their dresses eight or ten times a night," and each costume was equal in value to the ones worn this evening. "In this finery," claimed McKee, "consisted their greatest Vanity and Emulation." Although he was not yet ready to admit it to himself, McKee's reply recognized the obvious. The Ohio Country tribes, militarily, politically, and economically, were but a shadow of their former selves. Despite the beauty and pageantry of the evening's festivities, nearly forty years of intermittent warfare had hollowed the Indians' culture to its core. McKee's efforts were fruitless. The Battle of Fallen Timbers had destroyed what little remained of the badly divided western confederation. By spring, the nations responded to Wayne's invitation to negotiate a peace. Meeting at Fort Greene Ville in August 1795, the tribes concluded an agreement, the Treaty of Greenville, that extinguished their title to much of present-day Ohio and established a fifteen-year interval of peace along the Great Lakes frontier.[55]

The Ohio Country tribes had suffered under the provisions of a manipulative Indian policy created, in part, by McKee and administered under his supervision by the British Indian department. The policy sought to preserve British strategic and economic interests along the Detroit frontier by exploiting Great Britain's ties with the western tribes in order to create a coordinated diplomatic and military opposition to American expansion north of the Ohio River. McKee persisted in this policy, hoping that additional military successes along the Maumee River would strengthen the bargaining position of Britain's negotiators who were seeking to reestablish normal relations with the United States.

British officials along the Detroit frontier were fully aware that their Indian policy was based to a considerable degree on half-truths and misrepresentations. Moreover, Simcoe was greatly concerned that if the western nations discovered the full depth of their duplicity, then the Indians might well "destroy the settlement and massacre the unfortunate Inhabitants of Upper Canada." McKee, who had been directly involved in policy development and implementation, was also worried about the possibility of widespread Indian violence, and he was especially concerned for his personal safety. On August 19, 1794, the night before the Battle of Fallen Timbers, the agent wrote his will. The document was short and direct; it left the bulk of his estate to his son, Thomas, and provided support for a second son, James, and a daughter, Catherine.[56]

At first glance, the document seems to indicate that McKee, on the eve of facing his implacable enemy Wayne, attempted to place his affairs in order in case the fortunes of war led to his death. In part, that is exactly what the document represents. On June 2, 1794, William Sullivan, an American deserter, had told McKee that Wayne was offering a reward of one thousand dollars for the scalps of Indian department employees. There is little doubt that Wayne would have summarily executed McKee, whom he considered the "principle stimulator of the war now existing between the United States and the savages," had the agent fallen into American hands. But McKee also knew that neither he nor any other British official was going to participate in the battle. During the engagement, McKee did exactly what he had planned to do; he watched from a distance. There was little real danger of his being captured or killed by the Americans.[57]

McKee realized that, despite his official assertions to the contrary, the Indian department had given the alliance every reason to believe the British would assist their allies with a complete commitment of resources, including troops, to stop Wayne at Fallen Timbers. Immediately following the August 1793 council at the rapids that had ended diplomatic negotiations between the western alliance and the United States, the Indians prepared a war feast at which the Shawnees "sang the War Song encouraging the warriors of all the Nations to be active in defending their Country, saying their Father the English would assist them and Pointed to Col. McKee." Neither British policy nor McKee's actions in the months that followed challenged that assumption. In May 1794, McKee wrote to Joseph Chew that the absence of an "Absolute rupture with the States" was preventing him from supplying British troops to the expedition that was gathering to attack Fort Recovery. But he did tell the tribes that Simcoe had ordered the Twenty-fourth Regiment to garrison Fort Miamis. "This step has given great spirits to the Indians," he observed with satisfaction, "and impressed them with the hope of our ultimately acting with them and affording a security for their families should their Enemy penetrate to their village." McKee also knew that the Indians who opposed the Legion were badly divided and considerably weakened after the Fort Recovery expedition. Defeat was possible. McKee worried that if the Indians suspected they had been intentionally deceived by the British, they would turn on him. McKee had more reason to fear his allies during the engagement than his enemies.[58]

The Battle of Fallen Timbers and the subsequent Treaty of Greenville marked the end of a particularly trying period of Indian-Crown relations along the western frontier. Throughout the post-Revolutionary War era, McKee had demonstrated his unwavering commitment to Great Britain's interests in the region, even if this required him to ignore or sacrifice native interests. The end of the Indian Wars would allow McKee to rebuild the Indian-Crown alliance and to reestablish the Indian department as a credible agency to mediate between the western nations and the British government.

—— ❧ ——

The Peaceful Frontier, 1795–1799

———

The signing of Jay's Treaty in November 1794 marked the beginning of a new era in British-Indian relations along the Great Lakes frontier. The accord ended Great Britain's military occupation in the Great Lakes region of the United States and thus ended the need for an active military alliance with the western tribes. With peace established between the western nations and the United States, McKee worked to reorganize the Indian department at a time when the Crown had little need for a military partnership with the western tribes and little interest in continuing the generous financial support provided to the agency when war between Canada and the United States had seemed likely.

Praising McKee's "loyalty, fidelity, and ability," Lord Dorchester appointed McKee deputy superintendent general and inspector for Indian affairs for Upper and Lower Canada on December 26, 1794. The post was the second highest position for the administration of Indian affairs in British North America. McKee was subordinate only to Sir John Johnson, the superintendent general, who was in Great Britain from 1792 to 1796. McKee found the promotion "extremely gratifying" and promised "all my Exertions in the Various Branches of duty now to be fulfilled."[1]

Unresolved issues revolving around the Jay and Greenville negotiations took up much of McKee's time immediately after his appointment.

In particular, McKee was absorbed in the attempt to provide rations and provisions to the Indians assembled at Swan Creek. His task was made far more difficult by a general lack of supplies in the Detroit region; growing friction between the Indian department and the military, both of whom placed the blame for the disaster at Fallen Timbers on the other; and increasing demands by the British government to bring economy to the administration of Indian affairs. As early as October 1794, Lt. Col. Richard England, the commanding officer at Detroit, was growing alarmed at McKee's extraordinary demands for provisions. There were neither enough contractors nor provisions in the field available for purchase to meet McKee's requests, claimed England. Further, McKee's earlier requisitions had drained the King's stores at Detroit to such an extent that only provisions normally reserved for emergencies were now on hand. England stated, "I feel a considerable share of anxiety lest we should all be reduced to much distress," and he reported that he was unable to send McKee more than a quarter of the supplies he had requisitioned.[2]

McKee attempted to deal with the situation by increasing the number of Indian department vessels deployed to deliver supplies to the Indians and by continuing his pressure on the military to release additional provisions. Nonetheless, McKee was only partially successful in increasing the amount of food and other supplies brought to the site. The crisis continued until the Swan Creek encampment was abandoned and the tribes living there were brought to Canada in late 1796.[3]

McKee also spent much of the summer and early fall of 1795 in Montreal conferring with Dorchester to develop a policy for the Indian department that responded to the new peace along the Detroit frontier. In June 1796, McKee submitted a proposal for the future administration of the Indian department that called for the appointment of a superintendent, storekeeper, and clerk at Forts Malden, George, and St. Joseph (on the Canadian border near the abandoned British posts at Detroit, Niagara, and Michilimackinac, respectively). The superintendents were to oversee distribution of the king's annual presents to the various nations and observe the "temper, disposition, and apparent views or designs of all the Tribes in their districts." Further, they were to promote friendship between the Indians and the military and encourage "that harmony so necessary for the tranquility of . . . the King's posts."[4]

McKee also used the opportunity to recommend his son, Thomas, for the position of superintendent at St. Joseph. McKee had hoped that Thomas would pursue a career in the military. But after "mature reflection . . . with an anxious regard for the King's as well as the Indian's interest," he had determined that his son's frequent dealings with the Indian nations and his familiarity with their languages and customs qualified him above all others for the appointment. Dorchester agreed with both McKee's administrative proposal and his personnel recommendations. By the end of the year, Dorchester enacted the new plan, and Thomas McKee assumed his duties at St. Joseph, along with William Claus (grandson of Sir William Johnson and a long-time Indian department official) at Fort George and Matthew Elliott at Malden.[5]

Sir John Johnson commented on McKee's plan shortly after he returned to Montreal in December 1796. Johnson was disappointed that McKee had not fully recognized the new financial restraints that confronted the government. The Indian department bureaucracy put in place by McKee was too large, he complained, and he refused to approve the hiring of several interpreters McKee had requested. Further, he ordered that in the future, McKee "be particularly attentive to the Necessity of . . . a strict Economy" in all areas of the Indian department under his supervision. McKee responded in late January 1797 by defending his actions. The past few years had been "a long period of difficulties among the Indian tribes," he claimed, and his policy was simply a continuation of a long tradition of the British government to extend support to its allies. Johnson did not return an answer to McKee's observations, but lessening financial resources and increased governmental oversight continued to be the realities of Indian department administration throughout the remainder of the century.[6]

The appointment of the new superintendents freed McKee from most of the routine obligations connected with the Indian department's daily administration. By 1797, he had built a new home on the Thames River where he lived in quiet semiretirement. Given McKee's reluctance to provide day-to-day direction to the agency, Matthew Elliott quickly exploited his lack of direct supervision. Although only a midlevel employee with the Indian department before his promotion in 1796, Elliott had amassed a considerable fortune. His two thousand-acre estate on the Detroit River was staffed by servants and slaves and contained a home that many considered the finest in the Detroit region. Under the rules that now governed the Indian department, the military comander at each Indian department post was responsible for approving the types and amounts of presents given to the Indians. He was also required to be in attendance when presents were distributed, to provide a check that these goods were given in the manner and in the amount claimed by the Indian agent. Elliott, though, had consistently refused to notify military officials when gifts were to be distributed, and he resisted every demand that he account for the goods under his charge that already had been given to the Indians. Elliott and Fort Malden's new commander, Capt. William Mayne, had feuded over this policy ever since Mayne had accepted his post in January 1797. One year earlier, McKee had confided to Joseph Chew that, in his opinion, too many junior officers within the Indian department allowed themselves to be "under too much influence" and "under the Authority" of their post's military commander, "notwithstanding their respective dutys' are perfectly distinct and separate." Nonetheless, in December 1796, McKee urged Elliott to cooperate with Mayne "in such measures as may be deemed expedient to Husband the Provisions now in store for the use of the Indians." But despite McKee's admonition, relations between Elliott and Mayne had begun badly and never recovered.[7]

In late June, Mayne had a conversation with Blackbeard, Captain Johnny, The Borrer, and The Buffalo, four Shawnee headmen who lived near Amherstburg. According to Mayne, the Indians complained that Elliott "gives us but very few presents." Furthermore, the Indians also claimed that "Col. McKee does not now take notice of his children. We know that the greatest part of the fine presents that our great Father sends us he keeps behind for his own use." Mayne defended McKee, saying that he was "a good man" and that "King George puts great confidence in him and leaves him in this country to take care of you," but he also sent a transcript of the meeting to his superiors. Before the rupture between the commanding officer and the Indian department could grow, Mayne was transferred from the post. McKee did not dignify Mayne's insinuations with a denial, but he sent a letter to the new lieutenant governor, Peter Russell, asking him to clarify the policies and procedures the Indian department was to follow. He also enclosed a letter in which he defended Elliott's actions. What Mayne understood to be irregularities were, in reality, the result of informal gifts to visiting tribal delegations. Groups comprising between twenty and one hundred

Indians frequently showed up at McKee's and other Indian department officials' homes, he claimed. When they appeared, they were offered gifts of food, tobacco, pipes, rum, and other amenities, all distributed outside the formal channels required by official regulations. The Indian department officers at Amherstburg had served his majesty with "zeal and fidelity" for over forty years and would continue to do so, said McKee, attempting to reassure the lieutenant governor. Now that Mayne was gone, McKee hoped that the "change in the Garrison might bring the mode of issuing Provisions for this service into its accustomed channel." Russell was satisfied with McKee's response, and there the matter might have ended except that Mayne's replacement, Capt. Hector McLean, proved even more aggressive in his prosecution of Elliott than his predecessor.[8]

Elliott greeted McLean with the same indifference and disdain he had shown Mayne. McLean responded with a blistering attack, sent to his superiors, in which he reported widespread corruption throughout the Indian department at his post. Further, he openly claimed that Elliott's lavish life-style was a result of the theft of government goods and provisions intended for the Indians. "He lives, as I am informed, in the greatest affluence at an expense of above a thousand a year," said McLean.

> He possesses an extensive farm not far from the garrison stock'd with about six or seven hundred head of cattle and I am told employs fifty or sixty persons constantly about his house and farm, chiefly slaves. If the question should be asked, How these people are fed & cloathed & how his wealth has been accumulated, I shall not undertake to give a positive answer, but the general opinion of people better acquainted with these matters is well known.

The blame for the garrison's troubles, said McLean, fell squarely on McKee, who was unwilling to spend time at the garrison and thereby refused to provide the direct supervision necessary to prevent or to change the widespread irregularities. "I have not seen Mr. McKee to converse with him on anything relating to this Department as he lives chiefly at the River Thames at too great a distance for me to think of going from my command," reported McLean, "and he has not been here since my arrival."[9]

Sir John Johnson responded immediately to the charges. On September 15, he wrote to McKee, reminding his assistant that he would allow no deviation from policy when it came to the issue of presents or provisions. Further, in a thinly veiled reprimand, he urged McKee to disperse the "Odium cast on the Department" by "resisting every ill-founded Charge and by a due Attention to the conduct of those intrusted to execute your Orders." McKee responded angrily, calling McLean's accusations "indiscriminate," "highly injurious," and "unjust." "If Capt. McLean has been alarmed at any time during the two months of his Command, it has never been heard of by me," declared McKee, "nor has the most trifling cause for it ever existed as far as relates to the public peace and security, & the quiet demeanor of the Indians." "I can only observe," he concluded, "that during the existence of such an improper Line of conduct as Capt. McLean has, without just grounds adopted and pursued, the King's Service must be materially injured." The situation, though, was beyond salvage. McLean was determined to bring the Indian department to heel at Elliott's expense. By October, he had uncovered discrepancies in Elliott's requisitions for the Indians who lived on the Chenail Ecarte River that he said proved the agent's dishonesty. McKee intervened on Elliott's behalf, claiming that many Indians had recently left the settlement to go on their winter hunt and that any discrepancies could be accounted for by the changing population at the village. Once again, Peter Russell accepted McKee's explanation, but Elliott's and McLean's relationship continued to fester. Eventually McLean's continued complaints forced Governor General Robert Prescott to demand Elliott's resignation. In December 1797, McKee carried out Prescott's wishes and replaced Elliott with his son, Thomas.[10]

While McKee was attempting to contend with McLean and the military, he was also dealing with rumors that whispered of foreign intrigue directed against the British. McKee had first heard accounts of foreign involvement with the Great Lakes nations in the spring of 1796. On June 20, McKee was told that several agents in the pay of the Spanish had arrived at Swan Creek, and "by unjust representations of the Conduct of the British government" they were attempting to lure the Indians there into the Spanish sphere of influence. Although they were never confirmed, the reports persisted throughout that year and into the next. In May 1797, Elliott reported that either the Spaniards or the French were attempting to persuade the Indians to move across the Mississippi and into the southwest. The following month he reported that the Spanish and the French, acting in concert, were making diplomatic overtures to the Great Lakes nations. Their purpose, Elliott warned, was to use the Indians as allies in a joint military venture against the British. Both European nations, he had learned, already had sizable armies and gun boats, mounted with twenty-four-pound cannon, on the Mississippi, poised for the assault.[11]

Unfortunately, these rumors circulated at the time when the Indian department's feud with the military was at its most intense. McLean accused McKee and Elliott of fabricating these reports to artificially enhance the Indian department's importance and to redirect the government's attention away from its internal scandals. But the tales had circulated long before the department's troubles with the military. There is no indication that McKee considered them anything less than genuinely worrisome, though unconfirmed, intelligence. McKee responded appropriately and cautiously, soliciting information from agents in the field, sending observers to live with the western Indian nations, and directing spies to the upper reaches of the Mississippi Valley. In December 1798, he reported that belts and other messages from the Spanish and French had undoubtedly circulated throughout the region during the previous year. But stories telling of armies advancing through the Ohio Country to liberate the Great Lakes nations from either the United States or the British had circulated throughout the region for years, and McKee doubted the region's Indians would believe these latest ones until they saw the soldiers actually marching through their villages. Beyond these few rumors, the situation in the west remained clouded. McKee recommended keeping agents in the field to gather intelligence, bringing Indians known to be friendly to the Crown to Fort Malden, arming the militia, and discreetly asking the United States for permission to cross its boundaries in order to carry out a preemptive raid against the Spanish settlements on the Mississippi. The Crown acted only upon the recommendation to keep its agents alert in the field. Soon, the rumors stopped, and the plot, if it ever existed, evaporated.[12]

Crown officials urged McKee to return to Fort Malden in the wake of Elliott's dismissal and as the Spanish crisis unfolded, but he refused.

Ill health had plagued the agent since 1795, and he showed little enthusiasm for reentering the rough and tumble world of daily Indian department administration. In May 1795, his close friend, Prideaux Selby,
observed that McKee had been extremely ill with a "Rheumatic or Bil-
ious fever, attended with great swellings in his feet, hands, and joints."
After five weeks of illness, McKee was still "incapable of writing" and
"much reduced." In 1797 McKee and Thomas traveled to St. Joseph
Island to purchase it for the Crown's use, but for the most part he remained close to his Thames River estate. In 1798, he injured his leg
just before he was stricken with another attack of the fever that left him
bedridden and lame. On January 10, 1799, McKee wrote to Selby, complaining that a "fever and pain in my breast" had kept him in bed for two
days and that the episode had been followed by the onset of a cold and
fever that afflicted him for another twenty-four hours. The attack was
more serious than McKee realized. He died at his home before dawn on
January 15. His body was interred two days later at Thomas's home, a
few miles north of Fort Malden.[13]

McKee's death marked the end of a remarkable career. Active with
the British Indian Department for nearly fifty years, he had participated
in events that had defined Great Britain's imperial interest in the Great
Lakes frontier from the capture of Fort Duquesne to the surrender of
Detroit. McKee's skills as a cultural mediator, one who brokered the encounters between the British government and the Indian tribes of the
Great Lakes region, had served the Crown well. His activities with the
Indian department had helped build a commercial and political partnership between Great Britain and the Ohio Country tribes that had been
a powerful tool for securing and protecting Britain's interests in the
region during the last half of the eighteenth century. Indeed, the understandings that McKee created and the relationships that he developed during his career continued to form the underlying structure that
shaped Crown policy toward the lower Great Lakes Indian nations until
the end of the War of 1812.[14]

McKee's impact on the Great Lakes nations is more difficult to assess.
There is little doubt his relations with the Ohio Country tribes were
rooted in continuing concern, genuine sympathy, and an abiding respect for people whom he considered "his own" until his death. And yet
there can also be little argument that after 1775 (and particularly after
1790), because he understood that only the Crown could guarantee the

Ohio tribes' well-being, he consistently responded in ways that, when Crown and native interests diverged, supported the government at the expense of the western nations. McKee's decisions during this period were influenced also by more than diplomacy. The slow process through which McKee had created a self-identity as one of Upper Canada's landed aristocracy also molded his behavior in a significant way. Self-interest was always a factor in McKee's life. Clearly, as he worked to protect the Crown's interests in the region, his own fortunes advanced as well. McKee's actions, therefore, can be understood as the result of a complex interaction that required him to balance his obligations to the region's native peoples, the Crown, and himself. Each factor was always present in a dynamic, constantly changing tension with the others. All three shaped the values that guided McKee throughout his career.

England's policy for managing Indian affairs in the Great Lakes region originated at Whitehall and then took a long and perilous journey before it was implemented. After they crossed the Atlantic Ocean, imperial directives were filtered through successive layers of the bureaucracy until, increasingly thin and web-like, they arrived on the trans-Appalachian frontier to be executed by persons like McKee. Therefore, the execution of British Indian policy was derived only partly from the instructions articulated within that policy. Indian affairs were shaped also to a considerable degree by perceptions of self and place held by the agents charged with putting that policy into action. In the fluid, pragmatic environment of the Great Lakes frontier, McKee's actions as a cultural mediator changed over time because his concept of himself changed over time. Who he was defined his implementation of imperial policy as much as what he was.

Cultural mediation along the Ohio Country frontier required agents to seek both cultural change and cultural stability with their Indian clients and to employ both accommodation and opposition in response to European initiatives. Equally Indian and European, McKee was successful as a cultural mediator because he was particularly skilled at exploiting his personal, familial, and economic ties to both the Indian and European worlds, blurring the distinctions between both communities and allowing members of each to see their interests as compatible with the other's. But McKee was also a master of eliciting and manipulating the deep-seated resentment nativist leaders experienced when

American territorial ambitions threatened Indian and British interests. These skills allowed McKee and other British authorities to create a policy that successfully defended native political autonomy for nearly two generations and that, in 1791, came remarkably close to total victory. But it was also a policy that ended in total failure and led ultimately to the subjugation and eventual ruin of the region's native peoples. In a life filled with extraordinary successes, perhaps McKee's greatest failure was in his unrelenting opposition to the United States long after that policy was capable of yielding positive results for the region's native peoples. Yet more than any other, it was this decision that carried long-lasting and serious consequences for the Ohio nations. McKee could employ both adaptation and resistance with equal facility. It is beyond the scope of this study to speculate whether or not a policy of accommodation would have eased the transition between native and United States hegemony within the region. It is tragic, though, that neither McKee nor other British officials seem ever to have considered the idea.

Alexander Fraser attended McKee's funeral and noted that many of the region's political, military, and economic leaders—the British "Grandees," he called them—were on hand to pay their last respects. Solomon McCulloch, a friend of Simon Kenton's, remembered that a few months after the ceremony, several hundred Indians arrived at the grave site. Assisted by Thomas, they began a slow, measured, and dignified dance that celebrated the memory of their departed friend. The ritual began in the morning and continued throughout the night and well into the following day. Simon Girty confided to McCulloch that in all his years among the Ohio tribes, he had seen the ceremony conducted only twice before. The Indians reserved the ritual, he claimed, "Only for men of distinction among them." In death as well as in life, McKee bridged both worlds, defining the British Empire's cultural encounter with the Great Lakes frontier.[15]

—— 𝕏 ——

Notes

———

PREFACE

1. Lorenzo Sabine, *Biographical Sketches of Loyalists of the American Revolution with an Historical Essay*, 2:67.

2. Fontaine's letter to his brother is quoted in James Hugo Johnson, *Race Relations in Virginia and Miscegenation in the South, 1776–1860*, 169–70. See also Colin Calloway, "Neither White Nor Red, White Renegades on the American Frontier" and R. David Edmunds, "Coming of Age: Some Thoughts Upon American Indian History."

3. Isabel Thompson Kelsay, *Joseph Brant, 1743–1807: Man of Two Worlds;* Paul A. Hutton, "William Wells: Frontier Scout and Indian Agent;" Anthony C. Wallace, *King of the Delaware: Teedyuscung, 1700–1763*.

4. Colin G. Calloway, "Simon Girty: Interpreter and Intermediary," 38–58; Nancy L. Hagedorn, "'Faithful, Knowing, and Prudent': Andrew Montour as Interpreter and Cultural Broker, 1740–1772;" 44–60; Everett V. Stonequist, *The Marginal Man: A Study of Personality and Culture Conflict*, especially 2–3.

ONE: CULTURAL MEDIATION, CULTURAL EXCHANGE,
AND THE INVENTION OF THE OHIO FRONTIER

1. This and the following two paragraphs are based on the correspondence found in the John Graves Simcoe Papers, MG23 H11, National Archives of Canada. See also Ernest A. Cruikshank, ed., *The Correspondence of Lieutenant Governor John Graves Simcoe, With Allied Documents Relating to His Administration of Upper Canada* [hereafter cited as Simcoe Correspondence], passim;

Wiley Sword, *President Washington's Indian War: The Struggle for the Old Northwest, 1790–1795;* Reginald Horsman, "The British Indian Department and Resistance to General Anthony Wayne." For general studies, see Robert F. Berkhofer, "Barrier to Settlement: British Indian Policy in the Old Northwest, 1783–1794," 249–76; Reginald Horsman, "American Indian Policy in the Old Northwest, 1783–1812;" Robert S. Allen, *His Majesty's Indian Allies: British Indian Policy in the Defence of Canada, 1774–1815,* 57–87.

2. McKee's life may be traced in the Papers of Alexander and Thomas McKee, MG 19 F16, National Archives of Canada; McKee Papers, Burton Historical Collection, Detroit Public Library; and McKee Family Genealogical File, Fort Malden National Historic Park. For published biographies, see Walter R. Hoberg, "Early History of Colonel Alexander McKee"; Walter R. Hoberg, "A Tory in the Northwest"; John H. Carter, "Alexander McKee, Our Most Noted Tory"; and Raymond McKee, *The Book of McKee.* See also Patricia Talbot Davis, "Alexander McKee, Frontier Tory, 1776–1794" (master's thesis); Frederick Wulff, "Colonel Alexander McKee and British Indian Policy, 1735–1799." (master's thesis).

3. Calloway, "Simon Girty, 38–58; Reginald Horsman, *Matthew Elliott: British Indian Agent;* Hagedorn, " 'Faithful, Knowing and Prudent' "; 25–43; Hutton, "William Wells"; Consul W. Butterfield, *An Historical Account of the Expedition against Sandusky under Col. William Crawford in 1782,* 126–28; Erminie Wheeler-Voegelin, "Ethnohistorical Report on the Wyandot, Ottawa, Chippewa, Munsee, Delaware, Shawnee, and Potawatomi on Royce Areas 53 & 54."

4. Richard White, *The Middle Ground: Indians, Empires, and Republics in the Great Lakes Region, 1650–1815,* ix–x; Jeremy Boissevain, *Friends of Friends: Networks, Manipulators, and Coalitions,* 27; Edward Spicer, "Types of Contact and Process of Change," in *Perspectives in American Indian Cultural Change,* edited by Edward Spicer, 153–67; Christopher L. Miller and George R. Hamell, "A New Perspective on Indian-White Contact: Cultural Symbols and Colonial Trade," 326.

5. Howard Lamar and Leonard Thompson, eds., *The Frontier in History: North American and Southern Africa Compared,* 1–13. For the frontier as a zone of creation, see James Merrell, *The Indians' New World: Catawbas and Their Neighbors from Contact throughout the Era of Removal* and James Merrell, " 'The Customes of Our Countrey': Indians and Colonists in Early America," in *Strangers Within the Realm: Cultural Margins of the First British Empire,* edited by Bernard Bailyn and Philip Morgan, 117–56. For culturally based studies of the Ohio frontier, see White, *Middle Ground;* Michael N. McConnell, *A Country Between: The Upper Ohio Valley and Its Peoples, 1724–1774,* particularly 207–32; Eric Alden Hinderaker, "The Creation of the American Frontier:

Europeans and Indians in the Ohio River Valley, 1673–1800" (Ph.D. diss.). For summaries of recent scholarship, see Gregory Nobles, "Breaking into the Backcountry: New Approaches to the Early American Frontier, 1750–1800" and Stephen Aron, "The Significance of the Kentucky Frontier."

6. Colin G. Calloway, "Beyond the Vortex of Violence: Indian-White Relations in the Ohio Country, 1783–1815." See also Bailyn and Morgan, *Strangers Within the Realm*, 1–31. For the emergence of an ethnically self-conscious, racially mixed community whose people assumed principal roles as economic middlemen and cultural brokers in the upper Great Lakes region during the late eighteenth and early nineteenth centuries, see Jacqueline Peterson, "Prelude to Red River: A Social Portrait of the Great Lakes Metis" and Jacqueline Peterson, "Many Roads to Red River: Metis Genesis in the Great Lakes Region, 1600–1815." For related studies, see Olive P. Dickson, "From 'One Nation' in the Northeast to 'New Nation' in the Northwest: A Look at the Emergence of the Metis" and R. David Edmunds, "'Unacquainted with the Laws of the Civilized World': American Attitudes Toward the Metis Communities in the Old Northwest," 184–94.

7. Boissevain, *Friends of Friends*, 147–69.

8. T. H. Breen, "An Empire of Goods: The Anglicization of Colonial America, 1690–1776" and James H. Merrell, "'Our Bond of Peace,': Patterns of Intercultural Exchange on the Carolina Piedmont, 1650–1750," 198–222. For a general study, see Carolyn Gilman, *Where Two Worlds Meet: The Great Lakes Fur Trade*.

9. "The Crown to Baynton, Wharton, & Morgan For sundry goods delivered at different Times, by order of Capt. Murray and Mr. Alexander McKee assistant agent for Indian Affairs, for the use of the Indians, June 12, 1766," in *The Papers of Sir William Johnson* [hereafter cited as Johnson Papers], edited by James Sullivan, Alexander Flick, Melton W. Hamilton, et al., 5:246–60; "Return of the Amount of Merchandize brought to Fort Pitt in the year 1767," in Sullivan et al., *Johnson Papers*, 397. See also Lawrence S. Thurman, "An Account Book of Baynton, Wharton, and Morgan at Fort Pitt, 1765–1767."

10. Miller and Hamell, "A New Perspective on Indian-White Contact," 318; James Axtell, "The English Colonial Impact on Indian Culture," in *The European and the Indian: Essays in the Ethnohistory of Colonial America*, by James Axtell, 253–54.

11. Lincoln MacVeagh, ed., *The Journal of Nicholas Cresswell: 1774–1777*, 12–21.

12. William C. Reichel, ed., *Memorial of the Moravian Church*, 1:95. See also Hagedorn, "Faithful, Knowing, and Prudent," 57 and Paul A. W. Wallace, *Indians in Pennsylvania*, 178.

13. MacVeagh, *Journal of Nicholas Cresswell*, 83–84, 87.

14. MacVeagh, *Journal of Nicholas Cresswell*, 102–03.

15. John H. Moore, ed., "A Captive of the Shawnees, 1779–1784," 291; Thomas Ridout, "An Account of My Capture by the Shawanese Indians," 10, 17; David Jones, *A Journal of Two Visits Made to some Nations of Indians on the West Side of the River Ohio, In the Years 1772 and 1773*, 53; MacVeagh, *Journal of Nicholas Cresswell*, 111–12.

16. Lt. [John] Boyer, *A Journal of Wayne's Campaign* . . . , 5; "Wayne to the Secretary of War, 14th August, 1794," *American State Papers: Documents Legislative and Executive of the Congress of the United States—Indian Affairs*, 1:490. The extent and wide diversity of native horticulture along the Maumee and Auglaize Rivers astounded Wayne's soldiers, eliciting nearly universal comment within the surviving journals and diaries. For representative observations, see "Isaac Paxton," in *Pioneer History*, by James McBride, 127; Richard C. Knopf, ed., "A Precise Journal of General Wayne's Last Campaign"; Dwight Smith, ed., *With Captain Edward Miller in the Wayne Campaign of 1794*, 3–4; Richard C. Knopf, ed., "Two Journals of the Kentucky Volunteers, 1793 and 1794," 263; Reginald E. McGrane, ed., "William Clark's Journal of Wayne's Campaign," 424. See also Archer B. Hulbert and William N. Schwarze, eds., "David Zeisberger's History of the Northern American Indians," 14–16; O. M. Spencer, *Indian Captivity: A True Narrative of the Capture of Rev. O. M. Spencer by the Indians in the Neighborhood of Cincinnati*, 83; John Heckewelder, *History, Manners, and Customs of The Indian Nations Who Once Inhabited Pennsylvania and the Neighbouring States*, 147, 157. Heckewelder also noted the existence of domesticated house cats. For general discussions of native agricultural practices, see R. Douglas Hurt, *Indian Agriculture in America: Prehistory to the Present*, 27–41 and J. McIver Weatherford, *Indian Givers: How the Indians of the Americas Transformed the World*, 79–115.

17. Jones, *Journal of Two Visits*, 33, 87, 99–101, 104, 108–9.

18. This and the following paragraph are drawn from Jones, *Journal of Two Visits*, 54–55, 87–88; C. F. Volney, *A View of the Soil and Climate of the United States of America* . . . , 378.

19. For Richard Conner, see Charles N. Thompson, *Sons of the Wilderness: John and William Conner*, 11–14.

20. Spencer, *Indian Captivity*, 90–92; Helen Hornbeck Tanner, "The Glaize in 1792: A Composite Indian Community"; Milo M. Quaife, "Fort Wayne in 1790."

21. James Smith, *An Account of the Remarkable Occurrences in the Life and Travels of Col. James Smith*, 18. For descriptions of similar buildings, see John Heckewelder, *Narrative of the Mission of the United Brethren among the Delaware and Mohegan Indians* . . . , 298; Edmund De Schweinitz, *The Life and*

Times of David Zeisberger, 529; Spencer, *Indian Captivity,* 78–81. For a general discussion, see Donald A. Hutslar, *The Architecture of Migration: Log Construction in the Ohio Country, 1750–1850,* particularly 81–94.

22. Hulbert and Schwarze, "David Zeisberger's History," 17–18, 380; William A. Galloway, *Old Chillicothe,* 13.

23. De Schweinitz, *Life and Times of David Zeisberger,* 366; Franklin B. Dexter, *Diary of David McClure, Doctor of Divinity: 1748–1820,* 61.

24. MacVeagh, *Journal of Nicholas Cresswell,* 106; Jones, *Journal of Two Visits,* 56; Hulbert and Schwarze, "David Zeisberger's History," 87.

25. MacVeagh, *Journal of Nicholas Cresswell,* 109–12.

26. Hulbert and Schwarze, "David Zeisberger's History," 115; Charles Johnston, *A Narrative of the Incidents Attending the Capture, Detention, and Ransom of Charles Johnston, of Botetourt County, Virginia,* 16, 40; James Smith, *Account of the Remarkable Occurrences,* 78.

27. Johnston, *A Narrative,* 40; Spencer, *Indian Captivity,* 49–50. "Col. William Christian to Col. William Preston, 15th Oct. 1774," 3QQ121, William Preston Papers, Draper Collection, State Historical Society of Wisconsin.

28. James Smith, *Account of the Remarkable Occurrences,* 42.

29. Heckewelder, *History, Manner, and Customs of the Indian Nations,* 154. David Zeisberger also described this type of marital arrangement but was quick to point out that "there are many cases where husband and wife are faithful to one another throughout life." See Hulbert and Schwarze, "David Zeisberger's History," 79.

30. Jones, *Journal of Two Visits,* 52, 75–76; MacVeagh, *Journal of Nicholas Cresswell,* 98. See also Dexter, *Diary of David McClure,* 91.

31. The British Indian Department was the Crown agency charged with maintaining Great Britain's economic and military alliance with the Ohio Country Indian nations. "Captain Hector McLean to Major James Green, August 27, 1799," in *Michigan Pioneer and Historical Collections* [hereafter cited as *MPHC*], 12:305; MacVeagh, *Journal of Nicholas Cresswell,* 102–8, 113–14, 112; Dexter, *Diary of David McClure,* 54. See also J. B. Brebner, "Subsidized Intermarriage with the Indians: An Incident in British Colonial Policy" and Merrell, "Our Bond of Peace," 198–201. See also Clara Sue Kidwell, "Indian Women as Cultural Mediators."

32. "Extracts From A Journal of John Parrish, 1773"; John Lacey, "Journal of a Mission to the Indians in Ohio by Friends from Pennsylvania, July–September, 1773," in *Notes and Queries: Historical, Biographical, and Genealogical, Relating Chiefly to Interior Pennsylvania,* by William H. Egle, 7:103–7.

33. John W. Jordan, "Journal of James Kenny, 1761–1763," For Thomas McKee's tribal affiliation, see *American Archives: Consisting of a Collection of*

Authentick Records, State Papers, Debates, and Letters and other Notices of Publick Affairs . . . In Six Series, 1:478.

34. James Smith, *Account of the Remarkable Occurrences,* 10–11. See also James Axtell, "The White Indians," in *The Invasion Within: The Contest of Cultures in Colonial North America,* by James Axtell, 302–28; Daniel K. Richter, "War and Culture: The Iroquois Experience," 528–29.

35. T. H. Breen, "Creative Adaptations: Peoples and Cultures," 195–232; Merrell, "'The Customes of Our Countrey,'" 131–37. See also Colin G. Calloway, *Crown and Calumet: British-Indian Relations, 1783–1815,* 98–128.

36. For an overview of this period, see Randolph C. Downes, *Council Fires on the Upper Ohio: A Narrative of Indian Affairs in the Upper Ohio Valley until 1795.* Other studies include White, *Middle Ground;* Gregory E. Dowd, *A Spirited Resistance: The North American Indian Struggle for Unity, 1745–1815;* Francis Jennings, *Empire of Fortune: Crowns, Colonies, and Tribes in the Seven Years War in America;* McConnell, *Country Between;* Colin G. Calloway, *The American Revolution in Indian Country: Crisis and Diversity in Native American Communities,* 158–81; Sword, *President Washington's Indian War;* R. David Edmunds, *The Shawnee Prophet.* While mediators work to reconcile diverse cultural interests, the maintenance of cultural barriers is also necessary for the mediator's continued utility. See Edna Bonacich, "A Theory of Middleman Minorities," 588. The Delaware description of Americans and English is found in Heckewelder, *History, Manner, and Customs of the Indian Nations,* 104.

37. Nancy L. Hagedorn, "'A Friend to Go Between Them': The Interpreter as Cultural Broker During Anglo-Iroquois Councils, 1740–79," 68–80; Yohuside Kawashima, "Forest Diplomats, The Role of Interpreters in Indian-White Relations on the Early Frontier"; Daniel K. Richter, "Cultural Brokers and Intercultural Politics: New York-Iroquois Relations, 1664–1701."

38. "Account of Henry Wilson, a participant, 16 July, 1843," 9J21–35, Lyman C. Draper Collection, State Historical Society of Wisconsin; Ridout, "Account of My Capture," 10.

39. Calloway, "Beyond the Vortex of Violence," 21.

40. Calloway, "Beyond the Vortex of Violence," 21; Calloway, "Simon Girty, Interpreter and Intermediary," 38–58.

TWO: FROM THE SUSQUEHANNA TO THE OHIO, 1735–1763

1. Thomas McKee (c. 1695–1769) awaits a biographer. McKee family genealogical information is found in the MacDonald Papers, Windsor's Community Museum; McKee Family Genealogical File, Fort Malden National Historic Park; and McKee, *The Book of McKee,* particularly chapter 12. For

McKee's career in the Indian trade, see *Colonial Records of Pennsylvania*, 4:630, 642, 5:761; Charles A. Hanna, *The Wilderness Trail*, passim. Scattered references are also found throughout Egle, *Notes and Queries*. Thomas McKee's grandson, Thomas McKee (c. 1769/1700–1814), was the third member of the McKee dynasty to take a prominent role in western Indian affairs. An officer in the Sixtieth Regiment Foot stationed at Detroit in the 1790s, Thomas was appointed superintendent of Indian affairs for the Northwestern District in 1796. At the outbreak of the War of 1812, he took an active part in the engagements fought along the Detroit frontier. He died shortly before the war's end, while on the way to Montreal. See *Dictionary of Canadian Biography*, vol. 5, *1801–1820*, s.v. "Thomas McKee," by John Clark.

2. For McKee's military service, see "Officers of the Associated Regiment of the West End of Lancaster County on the Susquehanna, 1747–48" and "Officers of the Provincial Service (1755–56)," in *Pennsylvania Archives: Selected and Arranged from Original Documents in the Office of the Secretary of the Commonwealth*, 5/1:22–24, 31; Thomas L. Montgomery, *Report of the Commission To Locate the Site of the Frontier Forts of Pennsylvania*, passim; William A. Hunter, *Forts on the Pennsylvania Frontier, 1753–1758*, passim. For McKee's activities in land speculation and Indian diplomacy, see Sullivan et al., *Johnson Papers*, passim; Julian P. Boyd, et al., eds., *The Susquehanna Company Papers*, passim; and Paul A. W. Wallace, *Conrad Weiser, 1696–1760: Friend of Colonist and Mohawk*. Standard biographies of George Croghan include Nicholas B. Wainwright, *George Croghan, Wilderness Diplomat* and Albert T. Volwiler, *George Croghan and the Western Movement, 1741–1782*.

3. Hanna, *Wilderness Trail*, 2:207–212; Egle, *Notes and Queries*, 1/2: 265–67; Paul A. W. Wallace, *Conrad Weiser*, 145–46. For Mary McKee's identification as the Half King's sister, see "The McKee Family, by Francis Cleary," MacDonald Collection, no. 3076. For the McKee family tradition that links Mary McKee to Tecumseh, see McKee, *The Book of McKee*, 435–36.

4. John W. Jordan, ed., "Bishop J. C. F. Cammerhoff's Narrative of a Journey to Shamokin, Pennsylvania, in the Winter of 1748," 169; Hanna, *Wilderness Trail*, 1:113, 207–12.

5. "Proclamation of Attainder Against Certain Named Persons Adjudged Guilty of High Treason, June 15, 1778," and "An Alphabetical List of All Persons Attainted of High Treason in Pursuance of the Treason Laws of the State of Pennsylvania, November 28, 1783," *Pennsylvania Archives*, 4/3:680–89, 937–45; "Inventories and Sales: Estate of James Rankin, May ye 28th, 1779," *Pennsylvania Archives*, 6/12:265; "Decrees Made by the Judges of the Supreme Court in Favor of the Claimants to Real Estate of Persons Attainted of Treason Before the 18th December 1780," *Pennsylvania Archives*, 6/13:502.

6. The western Pennsylvanian Indian traders were described in "Baynton and Wharton to Richard Neave, July 1, 1760," Baynton and Wharton Letter Book, (1758–60), 403, Historical Society of Pennsylvania.

7. For brief biographies of McKee's early contemporaries, see Paul A. W. Wallace, *Indians in Pennsylvania* 171–80. See also Howard Lewin, "A Frontier Diplomat: Andrew Montour" and Hagedorn, "'Faithful, Knowing, and Prudent,'" 44–60.

8. For McKee's military activities during the period, see MacDonald Papers, nos. 3045–3063; "Officers and Soldiers, Province of Pennsylvania, 1744–1765," *Pennsylvania Archives* 5/1:47–267, passim. For his activities as a scout during the Forbes expedition, see "James Burd to Henry Bouquet, 26 August, 1758," in *The Papers of Henry Bouquet* [hereafter cited as *Bouquet Papers*], edited by S. K. Stevens, Donald Kent, Autumn L. Leonard, et al., 2:427–28. Burd's activities may be traced in "James Burd Journal, 1756–57," *Pennsylvania Archives* 2/2:743–820 and Lily Lee Nixon, "Colonel James Burd in the Forbes Campaign." For Fort Augusta, see Thomas L. Montgomery, *Report of the Commission*, 1: passim; and William H. Hunter, *Forts on the Pennsylvania Frontier*, passim, especially 481–543.

9. Bouquet to Forbes, 17th September 1758, S. K. Stevens et al., *Bouquet Papers* 2:513–522. For Forbes' account of Grant's defeat, see Alfred P. James, ed., *Writings of General John Forbes Relating to his Service in North America*, 215–17. Clark's comments concerning the Pennsylvania troops are quoted in Nixon, "Burd in the Forbes Campaign," 121.

10. This and the following paragraph are drawn from Wainwright, *George Croghan*, 47–183 and Volwiler, *George Croghan and the Westward Movement*, 115–208. For Sir William Johnson, see *Dictionary of Canadian Biography*, 4, *1771–1800*, s.v. "Sir William Johnson," by Julian Gwyn.

11. "Thomas Lloyd to Bouquet, January 12, 1759," S. K. Stevens et al., *Bouquet Papers*, 3:39.

12. Nicholas Wainwright, ed., "George Croghan's Journal, 1759–1763, From the Original in the Cadawalader Collection of the Historical Society of Pennsylvania," 314, 316–17.

13. "Conference Held at Fort Pitt, April 6–12, 1760," Sullivan et al., *Johnson Papers*, 3:208–217.

14. This and the following paragraph are based on Robert Rogers, *Journals of Major Robert Rogers: Containing An Account of the several Excursions he made*, 197–236 and Robert Rogers, *A Concise Account of North America*, 240–41.

15. Rogers to Bouquet, December 7, 1760," S. K. Stevens et al., *Bouquet Papers*, 5:162–63.

16. "Proceedings of An Indian Conference Held at Detroit By George Croghan, December 3–5, 1760," Sullivan et al., *Johnson Papers*, 10: 198–206; "Bouquet to Monckton, 11th August, 1760," S. K. Stevens et al., *Bouquet Papers* 5:162–63.

17. This and the following paragraph are based upon Robert Rogers, *Journals*, 229–30; "Robert Rogers to McKee, c. December 7, 1760," Stevens et al., *Bouquet Papers*, 5:165; Wainwright, "George Croghan's Journal," 399; "Croghan to Johnson, January 13, 1761," Sullivan et al., *Johnson Papers*, 3:301–4. Descriptions of the Lower Shawnee Town are found in William M. Darlington, ed., *Christopher Gist's Journals*, 44, and "A List of Indian Nations, 1759," Bouquet Papers, Add. MSS 21655, National Archives of Canada. See also Helen Hornbeck Tanner and Erminie Wheeler-Voegelin, *Indians of Ohio and Indiana Prior to 1795: The Greenville Treaty, 1795, & Ethnohistory of Indian Use and Occupancy in Ohio and Indiana Prior to 1795*, 1:382.

18. Wainwright, "George Croghan's Journal," 404–5; "A Return of People Employed in the Western Indian Department, February 12th, 1761," Sullivan et al., *Johnson Papers*, 3:300–1.

19. "John Langdale to Col. Henry Bouquet, March 5th, 1761," S. K. Stevens et al., *Bouquet Papers*, 5:328–31.

20. Wainwright, "George Croghan's Journal," 409–11.

21. "Johnson to Gage, January 12, 1764," Sullivan et al., *Johnson Papers*, 4:296.

22. Wainwright, "George Croghan's Journal," 409–11, 430–31.

23. "Instructions for Mr Alexander McKee, October 5th, 1762," Sullivan et al., *Johnson Papers*, 10:546–48; "George Croghan to Jeffery Amherst, October 5th, 1762," Sullivan et al., *Johnson Papers*, 543–44; John W. Jordan, ed., "Journal of James Kenny," 172.

24. "Instructions for Mr. Alexander McKee, October 5th, 1762," Sullivan et al., *Johnson Papers*, 10:546–48. See also Michael K. Foster, "Another Look at the Function of Wampum in Iroquois-White Councils," 99–114, and "Glossary of Figures of Speech in Iroquois Political Rhetoric," 115–26; Mary Druke, "Linking Arms: The Structure of Iroquois Intertribal Diplomacy," 29–40.

25. "Mr. McKee's Journal of Transactions with the Shawaneze, &c, from Octr. 12th to Novr. 27th, 1762," Sullivan et al., *Johnson Papers*, 10:576–80; Edward Rondthaler, *Life of John Heckewelder*, 386–91.

26. "Mr. McKee's Journal of Transactions with the Shawaneze, &c, from Octr. 12th to Novr. 27th, 1762," Sullivan et al., *Johnson Papers*, 10:576–80; Wainwright, "George Croghan's Journal," 432; "Croghan to Bouquet, Dec. 10th, 1762," S. K. Stevens et al., *Bouquet Papers*, 6:137–38.

27. "Mr. Alexander McKee's Journal of Transactions with the Shawaneze &c, from Octo. 12th to Novr. 27th, 1762," Sullivan et al., *Johnson Papers*, 10:576–80; "McKee to Bouquet, 22 November 1762," S. K. Stevens et al., *Bouquet Papers*, 6:133; Wainwright, "George Croghan's Journal," 432; Jordan, "Journal of James Kenny," 174.

28. For McKee's return to Pittsburgh, see "Mr. McKee's Journal of Transactions with the Shawaneze, &c, from Octr. 12th to Novr. 27, 1762," Sullivan et al., *Johnson Papers*, 10:576–80. Croghan's views regarding Amherst's policies are found in "George Croghan to Henry Bouquet, Dec. 10th, 1762," Sullivan et al., *Johnson Papers*, 596–98; "George Croghan to Sir William Johnson, Decr. 10th, 1762," Sullivan et al., *Johnson Papers*, 3:964–66; Wainwright, "George Croghan's Journal," 432. For McKee's return to Ohio, see "Croghan to Bouquet, Dec. 10, 1762," S. K. Stevens et al., *Bouquet Papers*, 6:137–38.

29. This and the following paragraph are based on McKee's Journal, found in Wainwright, "George Croghan's Journal," 437–39. See also "Croghan to Bouquet, Feby. 4th, 1763," Bouquet Collection, Add. MSS. 21649, National Archives of Canada.

30. Jordan, *Journal of James* "Kenny," 193–94; "Captain Simeon Ecuyer to Col. Henry Bouquet, April 9, 1763," Bouquet Collection, Add. MSS. 21649, National Archives of Canada.

31. "McKee: Indian Conference Minutes, April 16–18, 1763," S. K. Stevens et al., *Bouquet Papers*, 6:182–86.

32. Wainwright, "George Croghan's Journal," 444.

THREE: FROM COMMISSARY TO AGENT

1. Dowd, *A Spirited Resistance*, 1–36; Howard H. Peckham, *Pontiac and the Indian Uprising*, 98–101; Anthony F. C. Wallace, *The Death and Rebirth of the Seneca*, 115–21. See also Charles E. Hunter, "The Delaware Nativist Revival of the Mid-Eighteenth Century."

2. Jordan, "Journal of James Kenny," 197–98; "S. Ecuyer to Henry Bouquet, May 29, 1763," S. K. Stevens et al., *Bouquet Papers*, 6:193.

3. "Ecuyer to Bouquet, May 29, 1763," S. K. Stevens et al., *Bouquet Papers*, 6:193; A. T. Volwiler, ed., "William Trent's Journal at Fort Pitt, 1763," 393–94; "Intelligence brought to Fort Pitt by Mr. Calhoun June 1st, 1763," Sullivan et al., *Johnson Papers*, 10:685–88.

4. "S. Ecuyer to Col. Bouquet, June 16, 1763," S. K. Stevens et al., *Bouquet Papers* 6:228–33; "Ecuyer to Bouquet," June 18, 1763," ibid., 236; "Lieut. Alexander McKee: Memorandum, c. June, 1763," Bouquet Papers, Add. MSS 21655, National Archives of Canada; Volwiler, "Trent's Journal," 399.

5. "S. Ecuyer to Col. Bouquet, June 26, 1763," Stevens, *Bouquet Papers* 6:258–60; Volwiler, "William Trent's Journal," 400.

6. "S. Ecuyer to Col. Bouquet, June 26, 1763," S. K. Stevens et al., *Bouquet Papers*, 6:258–60; "Discourse Between Delawares and Ecuyer, June 24th, 1763," S. K. Stevens et al., *Bouquet Papers*, 261–62; Volwiler, "William Trent's Journal," 400. See also, Bernhard Knollenberg, "General Amherst and Germ Warfare."

7. Volwiler, "William Trent's Journal," 403–7. "S. Ecuyer to Col. Bouquet, Aug. 2, 1763," S. K. Stevens et al., *Bouquet Papers*, 6:332; "Indian Speeches at Fort Pitt, July 26th, 1763," S. K. Stevens et al., *Bouquet Papers*, 333–35; "Ecuyer: Reply to Indians, July 27th, 1763," S. K. Stevens, *Bouquet Papers*, 336–37; "Alexander McKee to George Croghan, August 2nd, 1763," Sullivan et al., *Johnson Papers*, 4:180.

8. Bouquet's account of the Battle of Bushy Run are found in "Bouquet to Amherst, 5 August 1763," and "Bouquet to Amherst, 6 August 1763," S. K. Stevens et al., *Bouquet Papers*, 6:338–40, 342–44. For the relief of Fort Pitt, see "Bouquet to Amherst, 11 August 1763," S. K. Stevens et al., *Bouquet Papers*, 361–62.

9. "Sir William Johnson to Alexander McKee, 1st December, 1763," Sullivan et al., *Johnson Papers*, 4:256–57.

10. Thomas McKee to Johnson, Feb. 15, 1764," Sullivan et al., *Johnson Papers*, 11:55–57.

11. "Bouquet to Bradstreet, 12th Sept., 1764," *MPHC*, 19:274; Sullivan et al., *Johnson Papers*, 4:550–51.

12. For Bouquet's departure from Fort Pitt, see "Bouquet to Gage, 2nd October 1764,: S. K. Stevens et al., *Bouquet Papers*, 6:657–58. Bouquet's preparations are discussed in William Smith, *An Historical Account of the Expedition against the Ohio Indians, in the Year 1764, Under the Command of Henry Bouquet, Esq.*, 1–6.

13. "Bouquet: Speech to the Delawares, 20th Sept., 1764," S. K. Stevens et al., *Bouquet Papers*, 6:649–50; and "Onondaga and Oneida Indians: Speech to Bouquet, 2 October 1764," S. K. Stevens et al., *Bouquet Papers*, 653–54.

14. Bouquet's negotiations with the Ohio tribes can be followed in "Indian Proceedings, October 13–November 16, 1764," Sullivan et al., *Johnson Papers*, 11:435–68.

15. William Smith, *An Historical Account of the Expedition Against the Ohio Indians*, 26–27; "Copy of the Conferences and Messages which passed between Colonel Bouquet, and the Delawares, Shawanese &c from his Arrival at the Camp of Tuscarawas on the 13th of October 1764 to the Conclusion of the Peace with those Nations.—Transmitted to Sir Wm. Johnson by Alexander McKee assist. Agt. for Indian Affairs, October 13–November 16, 1764,"

Sullivan et al., *Johnson Papers*, 11:435–68; "McKee to Johnson, October 21st, 1764," Sullivan et al., *Johnson Papers*, 385–86; "Bouquet to Johnson, November 15, 1764," Sullivan et al., *Johnson Papers*, 4:585–86; "Alexander McKee to Sir William Johnson, November 17, 1764," Sullivan et al., *Johnson Papers*, 11:474–75; "Johnson to Bouquet, December 17, 1764," Sullivan et al., *Johnson Papers*, 4:619–20.

16. Wainwright, *George Croghan*, 208–9.

17. "George Croghan to Alexander McKee, December 6th, 1764," Bouquet Collection, Add. MSS. 21653, National Archives of Canada.

18. "Col. Henry Bouquet to General Thomas Gage, 22nd December, 1764," S. K. Stevens et al., *Col. Bouquet Papers*, 21653:341–43.

19. "Journal of the Transactions of Geo. Croghan, Esq., Deputy Agent for Indian Affairs, with different tribes of Indians at Fort Pitt, from Feb. 28, 1765 to May 12, 1765," in Israel D. Rupp, *Early History of Western Pennsylvania, and of the West*, appendix, 166–79.

20. *Colonial Records of Pennsylvania*, 9:250–64; Edmund B. O'Callaghan and Berthold Fernow, eds., *Documents Relative to the Colonial History of the State of New York*, 7:750.

21. Croghan's journey to the Ohio Country nations can be traced in "Croghan's Journal; May 15–September 26, 1765," in *Early Western Travels, 1748–1846*, edited by Reuben G. Thwaites, 1:126–66. See also "Croghan to McKee, July 13, 1765" Gage Papers, American Series, William L. Clements Library.

22. "George Croghan to Alexander McKee, July 13, 1765," Sullivan et al., *Johnson Papers*, 11:845–87; "Alexander McKee to Sir William Johnson, August 2nd, 1765," Sullivan et al., *Johnson Papers*, 877; "Alexander McKee to Sir William Johnson, August 12, 1765," Sullivan et al., *Johnson Papers*, 884. "Croghan to McKee, August 3rd, 1765," Gage Papers, American Series, William L. Clements Library; "Croghan to McKee, January 5, 1766," Gage Papers, American Series, William L. Clements Library.

23. "Sir William Johnson to George Croghan, March 15, 1766," Sullivan et al., *Johnson Papers*, 5:75–76; "Warrant and Instructions to Alexander McKee, March 24, 1766," Sullivan et al., *Johnson Papers*, 12:49–52. For the full extent of the Indian department's reorganization, see "List of the Officers of the Northern Department of William Johnson Bart., with the respective Salarys, for the better management of Indian Affairs &c. [December, 1766]," Sullivan et al., *Johnson Papers*, 442–44; "Thomas Gage to Right Honourable Lord Viscount Barrington, 28 October, 1766," in *The Correspondence of General Thomas Gage with the Secretaries of State and with the War Office and the Treasury, 1763–1775*, edited by Clarence E. Carter, 2:384–87. "Warrant and Instructions to Alexan-

der McKee, March 24, 1766," Sullivan et al., *Johnson Papers*, 12:49–52. McKee's new administrative duties can be traced in "Account of Alexander McKee, March 24, 1766," "Dennis McElhenney's Receipt to Alexander McKee," "Robert Love's Receipt to Alexander McKee," and "John Meanner's Receipt to Alexander McKee," Sullivan et al., *Johnson Papers*, 5:100–101.

24. R. A. Humphreys, "Lord Shelburne and the Proclamation of 1763"; Jack Sosin, *Whitehall and the Wilderness: The Middle West in British Colonial Policy, 1760–1775*, 27–47.

25. "Joseph Spear, et al. to Sir William Johnson, October 4, 1766," Sullivan et al., *Johnson Papers*, 5:384–85. For Croghan and McKee's involvement with the firm, see "Baynton, Wharton and Morgan to Sir William Johnson, August 28, 1766," Sullivan et al., *Johnson Papers*, 12:164–66; "Sir William Johnson to Baynton, Wharton, and Morgan, April 1, 1767," Sullivan et al., *Johnson Papers*, 291–92.

26. "Alexander McKee to George Croghan, February 24, 1767," Sullivan et al., *Johnson Papers*, 5:504; "Alexander McKee to George Croghan, March 6, 1767," Sullivan et al., *Johnson Papers*, "Alexander McKee to Sir William Johnson, September 20, 1767," Sullivan et al., *Johnson Papers*, 686–87.

27. "George Croghan to Sir William Johnson, September 25, 1767," Sullivan et al., *Johnson Papers*, 5:700–02; "George Croghan to Sir William Johnson, October 18, 1767," Sullivan et al., *Johnson Papers*, 738; "George Croghan to Sir William Johnson, October 18, 1767," Sullivan et al., *Johnson Papers*, 12:372–75; "Journal of a Conference with Indians, Fort Pitt, December 17(?), 1767," Sullivan et al., *Johnson Papers*, 6:10–11.

28. "Alexander McKee to Sir William Johnson, February 13, 1768," Sullivan et al., *Johnson Papers*, 6:101–02; "George Croghan to Sir William Johnson, February 17, 1768," Sullivan et al., 108–10; "Croghan to Thomas Gage, February, 1768," Sullivan et al., 110–11; "Croghan to Sir William Johnson, March 11, 1768," Sullivan et al., 127–30. "Croghan to Gage, March 1, 1768," Gage Papers, American Series, William L. Clements Library; McKee to Croghan, February 13, 1768," Gage Papers; "Minutes of conferences held at Fort Pitt, in April and May, under the direction of George Croghan, Esq., Deputy Agent for Indian Affairs, with the Chiefs and warriors of the Ohio, and other western Indians," Rupp, *Early History of Western Pennsylvania*, appendix, 181–202.

29. For an overview of British policy during this period, see Downes, *Council Fires on the Upper Ohio*, 123–50; Peter Marshall, "Sir William Johnson and the Treaty of Fort Stanwix, 1768."

30. "Alexander McKee to Sir William Johnson, September 18, 1769," Sullivan et al., *Johnson Papers*, 7:183; "Journal of Alexander McKee [September,

1769]," Sullivan et al., *Johnson Papers*, 184–85; "George Croghan to Sir William Johnson, September 18, 1769," Sullivan et al., *Johnson Papers*, 182.

31. "McKee to Croghan, February 20th, 1770," Sullivan et al., *Johnson Papers*, 7:404–6; "Speech of Red Hawk," Sullivan et al., *Johnson Papers*, 406–8; "Croghan to Johnson, April 28, 1770," Sullivan et al., *Johnson Papers*, 609–10; "Croghan to Johnson, May 10th, 1770," Sullivan et al., *Johnson Papers*, 650–54.

32. "McKee to Croghan, May 19th, 1770," Sullivan et al., *Johnson Papers*, 7:685; "Croghan to Johnson, May 19th, 1770," Sullivan et al., *Johnson Papers*, 688–89; "Croghan to Johnson, August 24th, 1770," Sullivan et al., *Johnson Papers*, 855–57.

33. "Information Concerning an Indian Conspiracy, March 7th, 1771," and "Intelligence of An Indian Conspiracy, March 7th, 1771," Sullivan et al., *Johnson Papers*, 8:6–9.

34. "McKee's Journal, April 20–August 24, 1771," Gage Papers, American Series, William L. Clements Library. See also "Speech of the Shawnees, July 1771," and "Extract of Mr McKee's Letter Containing his Thoughts, and Observations made during his Journey. &c," Sullivan et al., *Johnson Papers*, 12:914–17; "Johnson to Gage, September 19, 1771," Sullivan et al., *Johnson Papers*, 8:258–62.

35. "McKee's Journal," April 20–August 24, 1771," Gage Papers.

36. Walter Hoberg, "Early History of Colonel Alexander McKee," 26–27; Raymond McKee, *The Book of McKee*, 456.

37. Wainwright, *George Croghan*, 257, 261, 270; "Sir William Johnson to Goldsbrow Banyar, March 17, 1770," Sullivan et al., *Johnson Papers*, 12:794; "Claim of Alexr. McKee, Esq., late of Pensilva., Aug. 31 [1787]," *Second Report of the Bureau of Archives for the Province of Ontario*, edited by Alexander Fraser; 987–88; "Deed, June 15th, 1777," McKee Family Genealogical File, Fort Malden National Historic Park; "Alexander Ross to William Preston, July 8th, 1775," 4QQ 24, William Preston Papers, Draper Collection.

38. John C. Fitzpatrick, ed., *The Diaries of George Washington, 1748–1799*, 1:412; see also Hugh Cleland, *George Washington in the Ohio Valley*, 233–72.

39. William H. Smith, ed., *The St. Clair Papers: The Life and Public Services of Arthur St. Clair*, 1:283; McKee Family Genealogical File, Fort Malden National Historical Park; "Sir William Johnson to Thomas Gage, May 20, 1772," Sullivan et al., *Johnson Papers*, 8:491–92; Howard Glenn Clark, "John Fraser, Western Pennsylvania Frontiersman," 150–75. Scattered references to McKee's actions as a Justice of the Peace are found in Boyd Crumrine, ed., "The Records of Deeds for the District of West Augusta, Virginia, for the Court held at Fort Dunmore (Pittsburgh, Pennsylvania), 1775–1776," *Annals*

of the Carnegie Museum, especially 255, 266, 285, 287, 288, 290. "John Johnson to Lyman Draper, July 10, 1848," Tecumseh Papers, 11YY 33, Draper Historical Collection, State Historical Society Wisconsin.

40. "George Croghan to Sir William Johnson, September 18, 1969," Sullivan et al., *Papers of Sir William Johnson*, 7:182.

41. "Sir William Johnson to Thomas Gage, May 20, 1772," Sullivan et al., *Johnson Papers*, 8:491–92; Wainwright, *George Croghan*, 281–82.

FOUR: DUNMORE'S WAR, 1772–1774

1. For this and the following paragraph, see Sosin, *Whitehall and the Wilderness*, 79–238; Downes, *Council Fires on the Upper Ohio*, 123–51; Louise P. Kellogg, *The British Regime in Wisconsin and the Northwest*, 93–114; John W. Huston, "The British Evacuation of Fort Pitt, 1772," 319–29.

2. Thomas Gage to Lord Hillsborough, June 16, 1768, Gage Papers, American Series, William L. Clements Library.

3. "Gage to Capt. Charles Edmonstone, August 31, 1772," Gage Papers, American Series, William L. Clements Library; "McKee to Gage, September 2, 1772," Gage Papers, American Series, William L. Clements Library.

4. "Johnson to Gage, May 20, 1772," Sullivan et al., *Johnson Papers*, 8:491–92.

5. "Johnson to Croghan, June 11, 1772," Sullivan et al., *Johnson Papers*, 12:966–67.

6. "Accounts Against the Crown, August 16, 1772," Sullivan et al., *Johnson Papers*, 12:1001; "Johnson to Gage, September 2, 1772," Sullivan et al., *Johnson Papers*, 8:586–88; Jones, *Journal of Two Visits*, 57.

7. "Johnson to Gage, September 2, 1772," Sullivan et al., *Johnson Papers*, 8:586–88; Downes, *Council Fires on the Ohio*, 144–49.

8. "Henry Lyons to Sir William Johnson, October 21, 1772," Sullivan et al., *Johnson Papers*, 8:618–19; "McKee to Johnson, November 26, 1772," Sullivan et al., *Johnson Papers*, 8:644–47.

9. "McKee to Johnson, November 26, 1772," Sullivan et al., *Johnson Papers*, 8:644–47; "McKee to Gage, November 26, 1772," K. G. Davies, ed., *Documents of the American Revolution, 1770–1783*, 4:248.

10. This and the following six paragraphs are drawn from "McKee to Johnson, December 31, 1772," Sullivan et al., *Johnson Papers*, 8:678–80. See also Paul L. Stevens, "His Majesty's 'Savage' Allies" (Ph.D. dissertation), 96–101; George Brown, et al., eds., *Dictionary of Canadian Biography*, vol. 4, 1775–1800, s.v. "Kayashota," by Thomas S. Abler.

11. "Return of Provisions turned over to Alex. McKee 18 December, 1772," Sullivan et al., *Johnson Papers*, 8:662; "Alexander Ross to Alexander McKee, 23 December, 1772," Sullivan et al., *Johnson Papers*, 666–67.

12. Sosin, *Whitehall and the Wilderness*, 181–210; Thomas P. Abernathy, *Western Lands and The American Revolution*, 40–58; Peter Marshall, "Lord Hillsborough, Samuel Wharton, and the Ohio Grant, 1769–1775."

13. "McKee to Johnson, December 31, 1772," Sullivan et al., *Johnson Papers*, 8:678–80; Croghan to Thomas Wharton, December 23rd, 1772," in "Letters of Colonel George Croghan."

14. "McKee's Journal—Plains of Scioto, April 3–6, 1773," Sullivan et al., *Johnson Papers*, 8:755–61; Samuel Wharton, *Plain Facts: Being an Examination into the Rights of the Indian Nations of America*, appendix 1:154.

15. Downes, "Dunmore's War," 311–30; Sosin, "The British Indian Department and Dunmore's War," 34–45; Irene Brand, "Dunmore's War"; John W. Huston, "The British Evacuation of Fort Pitt, 1772."

16. This and the following two paragraphs are based on "Speech of Six Shawanese Indians, June 28, 1773," Sullivan et al., *Johnson Papers*, 8:834–35; "Talk from Shawnese to Keashuta and Alexander McKee, 28 June 1773," in *Documents of the American Revolution, 1770–1783*, edited by K. G. Davies, 4:375; "Talk brought by Shawnese to Alexander McKee, 28 June 1773," Davies, *Documents*, 4:382; "Shawnese Deputies to Keashuta and Alexander McKee, June 28, 1773," Davies, *Documents*, 6:166–67. See also Paul L. Stevens, "His Majesty's 'Savage' Allies" (Ph.D. dissertation), 156–57.

17. "Journal of Alexander McKee, October 7, 1773," Sullivan et al., *Johnson Papers*, 12:1032–34.

18. "An Indian Conference, Pittsburgh October 9, 1773," Sullivan et al., *Johnson Papers*, 12:1034–36.

19. "McKee to Johnson, October 16, 1773," Sullivan et al., *Johnson Papers*, 12:1038–39.

20. "Conference with Kayaghshota, January 5–15, 1774," Sullivan et al., *Johnson Papers*, 12:1044–79.

21. Sullivan et al., *Johnson Papers*, 12:1044–79.

22. John Connolly, "A Narrative of the Transactions, Imprisonment, and Sufferings of John Connolly, An American Loyalist and Lieutenant-Colonel in His Majesty's Service," 310–24; Percy B. Caley, "The Life Adventures of Lieutenant-Colonel John Connolly: The Story of a Tory," 26–49.

23. Downes, *Council Fires on the Upper Ohio*, 159; Paul L. Stevens, "His Majesty's 'Savage' Allies," 159–60; for Connolly's actions during the crisis, see Clarence M. Burton, "John Connolly: A Tory of the Revolution"; Percy B. Caley, "Lord Dunmore and the Pennsylvania-Virginia Boundary Dispute"; Caley, "Life Adventures of Lieutenant-Colonel John Connolly," 26–49; Con-

nolly, "Narrative of the Transactions, Imprisonment and Sufferings of John Connolly," 310–24.

24. *American Archives*, 4th series, vol. 1:484.

25. "Johnson to McKee, January 20, 1774," Sullivan et al., *Johnson Papers*, 8:1011–13; "Alexander Ross to McKee, February 14, 1774," Sullivan et al., *Johnson Papers*, 1034; "McKee to Johnson, February 15, 1774," Sullivan et al., *Johnson Papers*, 1035–36; Nicholas B. Wainwright, ed., "Turmoil at Pittsburgh: Diary of Augustine Prevost, 1774," 129, 132.

26. "Journal of Alexander McKee, February 26–March 1, 1774," Sullivan et al., *Johnson Papers*, 12:10799–81; "McKee to Johnson, March 2, 1774," Sullivan et al., *Johnson Papers*, 8:1057; "McKee to Johnson, March 3, 1774," Sullivan et al., *Johnson Papers*, 1057–59; "McKee to Johnson, March 3, 1774," Sullivan et al., *Johnson Papers*, 12:1081–83; "Journal of Alexander McKee, March 8–13, 1774," Sullivan et al., *Johnson Papers*, 1083–86. See also Paul L. Stevens, "His Majesty's 'Savage' Allies," 162–63.

27. [Alexander McKee], Extract from a Journal of Indian Transactions, February 27th–March 8th, 1774, Chalmers Collection, Indians 1750–75, New York Public Library.

28. "Journal of Alexander McKee, April 16–May 5, 1774," Sullivan et al., *Johnson Papers*, 12:1087–1100.

29. "Journal of Alexander McKee, April 16–May 5, 1774," Sullivan et al., *Johnson Papers*, 12:1087–1100. John Minor's recollection is found in John J. Jacob, *A Biographical Sketch of the Life of the Late Captain Michael Creasap*, 140–42.

30. "Logan—The Mingo Chief, 1710–1780."

31. "Journal of Alexander McKee, April 16–May 5, 1774," Sullivan et al., *Johnson Papers*, 12:1087–1100. Other accounts of the Yellow Creek incident as related by some of the participants are found in Reuben G. Thwaites and Louise P. Kellogg, eds., *Documentary History of Dunmore's War, 1774*, 9–19.

32. "Recollections of Capt. Michael Myers, Newburgh, Ohio, given to Dr. Draper February 25 and 26, 1850," Thwaites and Kellogg, *Dunmore's War*, 17–19. Much later Baker's wife testified that Greathouse and the others came to the trading post at her request because a few nights earlier an Indian women living at Logan's camp had secretly crossed the river to tell her that Logan's band was planning to attack the Virginia trader. This explanation, especially viewed within the light of the Indians' subsequent actions, seems transparently disingenuous.

33. Accounts of the Yellow Creek murders are found in Thwaites and Kellogg, *Dunmore's War*, 9–17; Thomas Jefferson, *Notes on Virginia*, in *The Writings of Thomas Jefferson*, edited by Albert E. Bergh, 89–93, 304–29.

34. Jefferson, *Notes on Virginia*, 89–93, 304–29.

35. "Journal of Alexander McKee, April 16–May 5, 1774," Sullivan et al., *Johnson Papers*, 12:1087–1100; [Alexander McKee], Extract taken from a Journal of Indian Transactions, 1–26 May 1774, Chalmers Collection, Indians 1750–1775, New York Public Library; [Alexander McKee], Extract from my Journal from the 1st of May 1774 containing Indian Transactions & ca., Chalmers Collection, Indians 1750–1775, New York Public Library. See also "Extract Taken From a Journal of Indian Transactions," *American Archives*, fourth series, 2:475–82; "Extract from the Journal of Alexander McKee, Sir William Johnson's Resident on the Ohio & etc., March the 8th, 1774," Edmund B. O'Callaghan and B. Fernow, eds., *Documents Relative to the Colonial History of the State of New York*, 8:461–66; "Extract of the Diary of Alexander McKee," Neville B. Craig, ed., *The Olden Time: A Monthly Publication, Devoted to the Preservation of Documents and other Authentick Information in Relation to Early Explorations and the Settlement and Improvement of the Country Around the Head of the Ohio,* 2:13–26; "Extract Taken From Alexander M'Kee, Esqr's., Journal of Transactions with the Indians at Pittsburgh, &c., from the 1st of May, to the 10th of June, 1774" Israel D. Rupp, *Early History of Western Pennsylvania, and of the West,* appendix, 203–13. Extract from Alexander McKee Esq. Journal of Transactions with Indians at Pittsburgh &c from the 4th of May to the 10th of June, 1774, Peter Force Papers, Library of Congress, Series 8D: Ac. #17,147, item 93.

36. [John Connolly], Journal of my Proceedings & etc. Commencing from the late Disturbances with the Cherokees upon the Ohio, Chalmers Collection, Indians 1750–75, New York Public Library.

37. "Extract Taken from a Journal of Indian Transactions," *American Archives*, 479; Paul L. Stevens, "His Majesty's 'Savage' Allies," 171–73; Downes, *Council Fires on the Ohio*, 163–65; "Arthur St. Clair to Governor Penn, May 29, 1774," William H. Smith, *The St. Clair Papers*, 1:296–302.

38. Connolly, "Narrative of the Transactions, Imprisonment, and Sufferings of John Connolly," 312–13.

39. "Extract of a Letter From Alexander M'Kee, esq., Agent for Indian Affairs at Fort Pitt, dated June 10, 1774," *American Archives*, fourth series, 1:466. Johnson's reply is found in "Johnson to McKee, June 20, 1774," Sullivan et al., *Johnson Papers*, 8:1172–73.

40. Alexander McKee, Extract from my Journal from the 1st May 1774 containing Indian Transactions &ca, Chalmers Collection, Indians 1750–1775, New York Public Library.

41. Alexander McKee, Extract from my Journal from the 1st May 1774 containing Indian Transactions &ca, Chalmers Collection, Indians 1750–1775,

New York Public Library. 179–86. See also "White Eye's Speech, Pittsburgh, July 23, 1774," William H. Smith, *St. Clair Papers*, 1:331–333.

42. "Arthur St. Clair to Governor Penn, August 8, 1774," William H. Smith, *St. Clair Papers*, 1:338–40; McKee to Connolly, July 28th, 1774, Chalmers Collection, Indians 1750–75; New York City Library; Sosin, "The British Indian Department and Dunmore's War," 48–49.

43. [Alexander McKee], Extract from my Journal from the 1st May 1774 Containing Indian Transactions & etc., entries for August 29 and 30, 1774, Chalmers Collection, Indians 1750–1775, New York Public Library.

44. "Synopsis of a letter of Lord Dunmore to Capt. John Connolly, June 20, 1774," Thwaites and Kellogg, *Dunmore's War*, 37–38; "Governor's Instructions to Colonel Lewis, July 12th, 1774," Thwaites and Kellogg, *Dunmore's War*, 86–87. The descriptions of Pittsburgh are found in MacVeagh, ed. *Journal of Nicholas Cresswell: 1774–177*, 65–66; Jones, *Journal of Two Visits*, 20; Dexter, *Diary of David McClure*, 45, 109.

45. Accounts of the battle by its participants are found in Thwaites and Kellogg, *Dunmore's War*, 257–97.

46. For the terms of the Camp Charlotte treaty, see "Affairs in Virginia; The Indian Expedition: Dunmore's Account," Thwaites and Kellogg, *Dunmore's War*, 368–95. See also McConnell, *A Country Between*, 280–82. The impact of the Camp Charlotte agreement is also discussed in Franklin B. Wickwire, "'Go On and Be Brave:' The Battle of Point Pleasant."

47. "Journal of James Newell Across the Ohio," Thwaites and Kellogg, *Dunmore's War*, 364. Point Pleasant's daily return of troops for October 19 shows that the camp housed 114 wounded and 170 "Fit for Duty." The document makes no mention of unattached civilians or government officials being present at the encampment. "A Morning Return of the Troops Campt on Point Pleasant Under the Command of Colo. William Fleming Octr. 19th 1774," Thwaites and Kellogg, *Dunmore's War*, 418–19.

48. "Arthur St. Clair to Governor Penn, August 8, 1774," William H. Smith, *St. Clair Papers*, 1:338–40; "McKee to Sir John Johnson, August 13, 1774," Sullivan et al., *Johnson Papers*, 8:1196.

49. "Governor John Penn to the Shawnee, August 6, 1774," *American Archives*, fourth series, 1:675.

50. "Alexander Ross to William Preston, July 8th, 1775," 4QQ 24, William Preston Papers, Draper Collection, State Historical Society of Wisconsin. Boyd Crumrine, ed., "Minute Book of the Virginia Court Held at Fort Dunmore (Pittsburgh) For the District of West Augusta, 1775–1776," 533, 565.

51. For Dunmore's possible recall, see John E. Selby, *The Revolution in Virginia, 1775–1783*, 16–17.

FIVE: THE REVOLUTIONARY WAR, 1775–1778

1. "Inhabitants of Transmontane Augusta to Dunmore, May 1775," Colonial Office: Canada, Original Correspondence, M.G.11, C.O. 42, National Archives of Canada; For general overviews, see Edward G. Williams, "Fort Pitt and the Revolution on the Western Frontier," 131–36; Edgar W. Hassler, *Old Westmoreland: A History of Western Pennsylvania During the Revolution*, 14–16; Anne M. Ousterhout, *A State Divided: Opposition in Pennsylvania to the American Revolution*, 253–55.

2. *American Archives*, fourth series, 2:612–15.

3. *American Archives*, fourth series, 2:615. Few studies focus on Loyalist activities in the Upper Ohio Valley. See Wilbur H. Seibert, "The Tories of the Upper Ohio"; Wilbur H. Seibert, "The Loyalists of Pennsylvania"; Wilbur H. Seibert, "Kentucky's Struggle with Its Loyalist Proprietors"; Wilbur H. Seibert, "The Tory Proprietors of Kentucky Lands."

4. Connolly, "Narrative of John Connolly, 315–17. Percy B. Caley, "The Life and Adventures of Lieutenant-Colonel John Connolly: The Story of a Tory," 95–109.

5. Minutes of the treaty negotiations are scattered in Robert L. Scribner and Brent Tarter, eds., *Revolutionary Virginia, The Road to Independence: A Documentary Record*, vols. 3, 4, 7, passim.

6. Scribner and Tarter, *Revolutionary Virginia*, 4:143; Walter H. Mohr, *Federal Indian Relations: 1774–1788*, 33–34. See also Reuben G. Thwaites and Louise P. Kellogg, eds., *The Revolution on the Upper Ohio, 1775–1777*, 25–136.

7. Connolly, "Narrative of John Connolly," 316–17.

8. Thwaites and Kellogg, *Revolution on the Upper Ohio*, 136–42; Scribner and Tarter, *Revolutionary Virginia*, 4:82–83; Neville B. Craig, *Olden Time*, 2:522–23; "Thomas Gage to the Right Honorable Earl of Dartmouth, September 20th, 1775," Clarence E. Carter, ed., *The Correspondence of General Thomas Gage with the Secretaries of State and with the War Office and the Treasury 1763–1775*, 414–17; "Governor Earl of Dunmore to Earl of Dartmouth, 11 January 1776," Davies, *Documents of the American Revolution*, 10:218; Gage to McKee, 12th September, 1775, Gage Papers, American Series, William L. Clements Library.

9. *American Archives*, fourth series, 4:615–17; Connolly, "Narrative of John Connolly," 411–20; J. F. D. Smyth, *A Tour in the United States of America: Containing An Account of the Present Situation of that Country*, 2:243–69.

10. John Connolly to Susanna Connolly, December 16, 1775 and John Connolly to Alexander McKee, December 16, 1775, Papers of the Continental Congress, Letters, C-78, 5:5–6. National Archives of the United States of

America. See also "John Connolly to Alexander McKee," December 16, 1775," Craig, *Olden Time*, 2:107; *American Archives*, 4th series, 4:617–18.

11. "Colonel John Butler to Alexander McKee, February 29, 1776," Scribner and Tarter, *Revolutionary Virginia*, 6:153–54; *American Archives*, fourth series, 5:818–19; Craig, *Olden Time*, 2:102.

12. "Richard Butler to Colonel James Wilson, April 8, 1776," *American Archives*, fourth series, 5:816; "Committee of West Augusta to Pennsylvania Delegates, April 9, 1776," *American Archives*, fourth series, 5:820; "Minutes of the Continental Congress, April 29, 1776," *American Archives*, fourth series, 5:1692; see also Scribner and Tarter, *Revolutionary Virginia*, 6:362–63, 490–91; Craig, *Olden Time*, 2:97–101, 104; Worthington C. Ford, ed., *Journals of the Continental Congress, 1774–1789*, 4:308, 317.

13. George Morgan to Lewis Morris, May 16, 1776; George Morgan to Lewis Morris, July 27th, 1776, George Morgan Letter Book—1776 [typescript], Pennsylvania Historical and Museum Commission; Scribner and Tarter, *Revolutionary Virginia*, 7:218, 479–81; Isaac S. Harrell, *Loyalism in Virginia: Chapters in the Economic History of the Revolution*, 43; "Minutes of the Continental Congress, Monday, April 29, 1776," *American Archives*, fourth series, 5:1692.

14. John Neville to the President of the Committee of Safety, June 13, 1776, in "Virginia Legislative Papers," *Virginia Magazine of History and Biography*.

15. Paul Long to Morgan, July 23, 1776, George Morgan Letter Book, 1776 [typescript], Pennsylvania Historical and Museum Collection.

16. George Morgan's Itinerary of Journey to Indians Towns, June 4–July 19, 1776, George Morgan Letterbook, 1776 [typescript], Pennsylvania Historical and Museum Collection. For Morgan's career, see Max Savelle, *George Morgan, Colony Builder*, especially chapter 6, "Fort Pitt: Indian Affairs, 1776–1779," 130–66; and Walter Fee,"Colonel George Morgan at Fort Pitt."

17. For Dunmore's comments to Lord Dartmouth, see Harrell, *Loyalism in Virginia*, 52.

18. Paul L. Stevens, "Placing Proper Persons at Their Head: Henry Hamilton and the Establishment of the British Revolutionary-Era Indian Department at Detroit, 1777" ; Jack M. Sosin, "The Use of Indians in the War of the American Revolution" ; Nelson Vance Russell, "The Indian Policy of Henry Hamilton: A Re-valuation." For British Indian policy prior to 1777 see Paul L. Stevens, "The Indian Diplomacy of Capt. Richard B. Lernoult, British Military Commandant of Detroit, 1774–1775." For studies that examine native response to the British proposal, see Francis Jennings, "The Indian Revolution," in *The American Revolution: Explorations in the History of American*

Radicalism, edited by Alfred F. Young, 319–48; Peter Marshall, "First Americans and Last Loyalists: An Indian Dilemma in War and Peace," and Francis Jennings, "Tribal Loyalty and Tribal Independence," both in *Red, White, and True Blue: The Loyalists in the Revolution*, edited by Esmond Wright, 33–53, 19–31; Russell L. Barsh, "Native American Loyalists and Patriots: Reflections on the American Revolution in Native-American History."

19. General Edward Hand to Richard Henry Lee, Richard Law and Daniel Roberdeau, December 21, 1777, in "Letters From the Ferdinand J. Dreer Collection of Manuscripts," *Pennsylvania Magazine of History and Biography*"; 467–69; see also Reuben G. Thwaites, Louise P. Kellogg, eds., *Frontier Defense on the Upper Ohio, 1777–1778*, 184–86 and Mary C. Darlington, *Fort Pitt and Letters from the Frontier*, 224.

20. "General Edward Hand to Committee of Congress, 21st Decr. 1777," Thwaites and Kellogg, *Frontier Defense*, 184–86; "Gen. Edward Hand to Jasper Yeates, 9th Octr. 1777," Thwaites and Kellogg, *Frontier Defense*, 128; "Extracts from a Letter of Gen. Hand to Richard Peters, Secretary to Board of War, November 9th, 1777," Thwaites and Kellogg, *Frontier Defense*, 155–56.

21. "Col. John Gibson to Gen. Edward Hand, Oct. 22nd, 1777," Thwaites and Kellogg, *Frontier Defense*, 142.

22. "Extracts from a Letter of Gen. Hand to Richard Peters, Secretary to Board of War, November 9th, 1777," Thwaites and Kellogg, *Frontier Defense*, 155–56. McKee's parole is found in Boyd Crumrine, ed., "Minute Book of the Virginia Court Held for Yohogania County, First at Augusta (Now Washington, Pennsylvania), and Afterwards on the Andrew Heath Farm Near West Elizabeth: 1776–1780," 106; "Deposition of John Campbell, 4 May, 1778," 2U 14, Frontier Wars, Draper Collection, State Historical Society of Wisconsin.

23. "Committee of Congress to Unknown, 24th Octr. 1777," Paul H. Smith ed., *Letters of Delegates to Congress, 1774–1789*, 8:174–75; see also Edmund C. Burnett, ed., *Letters of Members of the Continental Congress*, 2:533.

24. Ford, *Journals of the Continental Congress*, 9:942–45; "Disposition of Joseph Nicholson, January 20, 1778," Dreer Collection, Historical Society of Pennsylvania.

25. "General Hand to Jasper Yeates, 17th January, 1778," Thwaites and Kellogg, *Frontier Defense*, 200–01; "General Hand to General Horatio Gates, 30th March, 1778," Thwaites and Kellogg, *Frontier Defense*, 234–35; Ewing to Yeates, March 30, 1778," Thwaites and Kellogg, *Frontier Defense*, 253. For McKee's land transfer with James, see "Deed, June 25th, 1777," McKee Family Genealogical File, Fort Malden National Historic Park.

26. "General Hand to General Horatio Gates, 30th March, 1778," Thwaites and Kellogg, *Frontier Defense*, 249.

27. The expedition became derisively known as the "Squaw Campaign." For accounts by various participants, see Thwaites and Kellogg, *Frontier Defense*, 215–23.

28. This and the following paragraph are based upon "General Hand to General Horatio Gates, 30th March, 1778," Thwaites and Kellogg, *Frontier Defense*, 249–56; "George Morgan to The Hon'ble Henry Laurens, Esq'r, March 31, 1778," Thwaites and Kellogg, *Frontier Defense*. For Elliott, see Horsman, *Matthew Elliott*, 14–17.

29. "General Hand to General Horatio Gates, 30th March, 1778," Thwaites and Kellogg, *Frontier Defense*, 249–56; "George Morgan to the Hon'ble Henry Laurens, Esq'r, March 31, 1778," Thwaites and Kellogg, *Frontier Defense*.

SIX: THE REVOLUTIONARY WAR, 1778–1783

1. "General Hand to Gen. Horatio Gates, 24th April, 1778," Thwaites and Kellogg, *Frontier Defense on the Upper Ohio*, 278–79; "Commissioners at Pittsburgh to H. Laurens, March 31, 1778," M247, Papers of the Continental Congress, item 78, Letters Addressed to Congress, 2:437–44, National Archives of the United States. See also "John Proctor to President Thomas Wharton, April 26, 1778," Papers of the Continental Congress, item 69, Pennsylvania State Papers, 1775–1791, vol. 1:503. Paul A. W. Wallace, ed., *Thirty Thousand Miles with John Heckewelder*, 146; "Deposition of John Campbell, 4 May 1778," 2U14, Frontier Wars, Lyman C. Draper Collection, State Historical Society of Wisconsin.

2. "Lieut. Gov. Hamilton to Gen. Carleton, April 25, 1778," *MPHC*, 9:433–37; Paul A. W. Wallace, *Thirty Thousand Miles*, 148–49. McKee's route can be traced on Map 16, "Frontier in Transition 1772–1781: The Ohio Country and Canada," in *Atlas of Great Lakes Indian History*, edited by Helen H. Tanner, 80.

3. This and the following paragraph are based on Butterfield, *History of the Girtys*, 1–8, 60–61. See also Colin G. Calloway, "Simon Girty: Interpreter and Intermediary," 38–58 and the dated Thomas Boyd, *Simon Girty, The White Savage*. An historiographical review of Girty biographies is found in John B. Ingham, "Simon Girty: Degeneration Through Violence" (master's thesis), 1–15.

4. "Lieut. Gov. Hamilton to Captain McKee, Apl. 23d 1778," *MPHC* 10: 285; "Mr. Hay to Captain McKee, April 23d 1778," *MPHC*, "Lieut.-Governor Henry Hamilton to Lord George Germain, 7 June, 1778," Davies, *Documents of the American Revolution*, 15:134–35.

5. "Council held at Detroit June 14th 1778 with the Ottawas, Chippoweys, Hurons, Poutconattamies, Delawares, Shawanese, Miamis, Mingoes, Mohawks, & the Tribes of Ouashtanon, Saguinan &c. Delawares, Senecas," *MPHC*, 9:442–58; "Hamilton to Germain, 7 June, 1778," Davies, *Documents of the American Revolution*, 15:134–35.

6. "Hamilton to Germain, 7 June, 1778," Davies, *Documents of the American Revolution*, 15:134–35; Ibid.; "List of Officers, Interpreters, & etc. in the Indian Department, District of Detroit, Sept'r 5th, 1778," *MPHC*, 9:470; "Return of Officers & etc. for the Enterprise Against the Rebels, Detroit, Sept'r 30th, 1778," *MPHC*, 485; "Henry Hamilton to Gen. Haldimand, Sept. 22nd to 3rd Oct., 1778," *MPHC*, 9:477–82; "Report of a Council held at Detroit June 29–July 3, 1778," Add. MSS. 21782, ff. 52–54, National Archives of Canada. See also John D. Barnhart, ed., *Henry Hamilton and George Rogers Clark in the American Revolution with the Unpublished Journal of Lieut. Gov. Henry Hamilton*, 104–05. Clark's exploits can be traced in *George Rogers Clark Papers, 1771–1781*, vol. 8 of *Collections of the Illinois State Historical Library*, edited by James A. James, 20–63.

7. Barnhart, *Henry Hamilton*, 113–14, 120; William A. Evans, ed., *Detroit to Fort Sackville, 1778–1779: The Journal of Normand MacLeod*, 14, 60, 80, 96; "McKee to Lernoult, October 25, 1778," *MPHC*, 19:360; Thomas I. Pieper and James B. Gidney, *Fort Laurens, 1778–1779: The Revolutionary War in Ohio*, 1–42.

8. Barnhart, *Henry Hamilton*, 174.

9. "McKee to General Haldimand, July 16, 1779," *MPHC*, 10:341–42; "Captain Alexander McKee to Capt. R. B. Lernoult," *MPHC*, 19:423–34. For McKee's activities during the remainder of 1779 and the early months of 1780 see "MacLeod to Capt. McKee, 6 April, 1778," *MPHC*, 10:283–84; "D. Brehm to Haldimand, July 5, 1779," *MPHC*, 9:416–18; "Major DePeyster to Capt. McKee, 2 November, 1779," *MPHC*, 10:370–71; "DePeyster to McKee, 2 January, 1780," *MPHC*, 10:373; McKee to DePeyster, November 16, 1779," Add. Mss. 21670, 256–57, National Archives of Canada. For McKee's promotion in June, 1779, see "Alexander McCormick to Col. Daniel Brodhead, June 29th, 1779," Kellogg and Thwaites, *Frontier Advance*, 382–83. For accounts of Bowman's raid see "Bowman's Expedition against Chillicothe, May–June 1779"; "Bowman's Campaign of 1779."

10. "John Butler to Haldimand, June 1780," Haldimand MSS B105, 293 and "Sir Guy Johnson to Haldimand, June 1, 1780," Add. MSS. 21767, 73–74, National Archives of Canada.

11. "Major DePeyster to General Haldimand, March 8, 1780," *MPHC*, 10:378–79. See also Nancy O'Malley, *"Stockading Up": A Study of Pioneer Sta-*

tions in the Inner Bluegrass Region of Kentucky and Charles G. Talbert, "A Roof for Kentucky."

12. "DePeyster to McKee, May 8, 1780," *MPHC*, 10:394–95; "Summary of letter of John Heckewelder, Coshocton, June 30, 1779," Kellogg, *Frontier Advance*, 383.

13. "Major DePeyster to Captain McKee, 2nd, Nov. 1779," *MPHC*, 10:370–71, "DePeyster to McKee, 8 Sept. 1780," *MPHC*, 10:426; "McKee to Walls, May 29, 1783," *MPHC*, 20:125–26; "McKee to Maclean, June 5, 1783," *MPHC*, 20:126.

14. Pay Roll of Volunteers with Captn. Bird, from the 25th May to the 4th August, 1780, Macomb, Edgar & Macomb Papers, Burton Historical Collection, Detroit Public Library; "McKee to DePeyster, June 4, 1780," *MPHC*, 19:530–31.

15. "Bird to DePeyster, June 3rd, 1780," *MPHC*, 19:527–29; "Bird to DePeyster, June 11, 1780" *MPHC*, 19:533–34; "McKee to DePeyster, July 8, 1780," *MPHC*, 19:541–43.

16. "Bird to DePeyster, July 1st, 1780," *MPHC*, 19:538–39. "Interview of Jere Morrow," 29J23, Draper Historical Collection, State Historical Society of Wisconsin.

17. "Capt. Bird to DePeyster, June 11th, 1780," *MPHC*, 19:533–34; "McKee to DePeyster, July 8th, 1780," *MPHC*, 19:541–43; "DePeyster to McKee, June 22nd, 1780," *MPHC*, 10:404; DePeyster to McKee, 8 May 1780," *MPHC*, 10:394–95.

18. "Brodhead to Indian Penn, December 2, 1780," Louise Kellogg, ed., *Frontier Retreat on the Upper Ohio*, 299; "Big Cat to Col. Daniel Brodhead, September 12, 1780," Kellogg, *Frontier Retreat*, 273.

19. "McKee to DePeyster, 22 August, 1780," Haldimand Collection, B 122, 529, National Archives of Canada; "DePeyster to Haldimand, 31st August, 1780," *MPHC*, 10:423–24. See also James A. James, *Clark Papers*, 451–84 and J. Martin West, ed., *Clark's Shawnee Campaign of 1780: Contemporary Accounts*.

20. James A. James, *Clark Papers*, 485–608.

21. "McKee to DePeyster, March 1, 1781," *MPHC*, 19:597–98; "At A Council Held at Detroit April 5, 1781 with a Deputation of Principal Chiefs of the Shawanese, Delawares, and Cherokees," *MPHC*, 10:462–65; "At a Council held at Detroit the 26th April 1781, by Major de Peyster Commanding Detroit and its Dependencies, with the several Nations," *MPHC*, 10:472–76; "Intelligence from the Shawnese, July 14th, 1781," *MPHC*, 19: 646–67; "McKee to DePeyster, July 15th, 1781," *MPHC*, 19:647–48; "Brant to McKee, August 21, 1781," *MPHC*, 19:655–54. McKee to DePeyster, February 27, 1781, Haldimand Papers, 21761, folio 16, 16–17 and Intelligence from

Indian Country, April 17, 1781, Haldimand Papers, folio 53, 56–57, National Archives of Canada.

22. A. Thompson & Alex. McKee to Major DePeyster, August 29, 1781, 6Q 163–64, Historical Miscellanies, Draper Collection, State Historical Society of Wisconsin; Downes, *Council Fires on the Upper Ohio*, 270. Brant's role in the victory is detailed in Kelsay, *Joseph Brant*, 306–19.

23. "McKee to DePeyster, Sept'r 26th, 1781," *MPHC*, 10:516–18.

24. "McKee to DePeyster, Sept'r 26th, 1781," *MPHC*, 10:516–18.

25. "DePeyster to McKee, 7th Sept. 1781," *MPHC*, 10:509–10; "DePeyster to Capts. Thompson and McKee, 13th Sep. 1781," *MPHC*, 10:512; "McKee to DePeyster, Sept'r 26th 1781," *MPHC*, 10:516–18; DePeyster to McKee, Oct'r 4th, 1781," *MPHC*, 10:522–23; "Speech of Chiefs to the Shawanese, Mingoes and Delawares to Col. A. McKee, 20th Septr 1781," *MPHC*, 10:24:5.

26. "Guy Johnson to McKee, 7 April, 1781," Kellogg, *Frontier Retreat*, 299; Kelsay, *Joseph Brant*, 306–08.

27. "Joseph Munger to Lyman Draper, March 8, 1848," 10E, 144–51, Brady and Wetzel Papers, Draper Collection, Historical Society of Wisconsin; Butterfield, *History of the Girtys*, 130–31.

28. Earl P. Olmstead, *Blackcoats among the Delaware: David Zeisberger on the Ohio Frontier*, 34–50; Horsman, *Matthew Elliott*, 30–36.

29. "McKee to DePeyster, Sept'r 26th, 1781," *MPHC*, 10:516–18, 13:41; John Heckewelder, *Narrative of the Mission of the United Brethren*, 229–62; Paul A. W. Wallace, ed., *The Travels of John Heckewelder in Frontier America*, 170–81. For a general discussion, see Olmstead, *Blackcoats among the Delaware*, 34–39.

30. "McKee to DePeyster, September 26, 1781," *MPHC*, 10:516–18; "DePeyster to McKee, October 4th, 1781,' *MPHC*, 10:522–23; "McKee to DePeyster, October 10, 1781," *MPHC*, 13:42; Heckewelder, *Narrative of the Mission of the United Brethren*, 285–95; Eugene F. Bliss, ed., *Diary of David Zeisberger: A Moravian Missionary Among the Indians of Ohio*, 1:23–29.

31. "McKee to DePeyster, Sept'r 26, 1781," *MPHC*, 10:516–18.

32. This and the following paragraph are based on Heckewelder, *Narrative of the Mission of the United Brethren*, 299–324.

33. Girty to DePeyster, April 8, 1782, Haldimand Papers, Add. MSS. 21762, folios 13–14, National Archives of Canada; McKee to DePeyster, April 10th, 1782, Haldimand Papers, Add. MSS. 21783, folios 139–40, National Archives of Canada.

34. Butterfield, *An Historical Account*, 1–80.

35. "Indian Council, 15th May, 1782," *MPHC*, 10:576–78; "To Major DePeyster, 31st May '82," *MPHC*, 13:46–47; "A Person at Sandusky to

DePeyster, April, 1782" and Girty to DePeyster, 12th April, 1782, Haldimand Papers, Add. MSS. 21762, folios 13–14, National Archives of Canada.

36. "Capt. Wm. Caldwell to DePeyster, June 11th, 1782," *MPHC*, 20:25–26. The standard account for Crawford's defeat is Butterfield, *An Historical Account*, 202–32. For recent treatments, see Parker B. Brown, "The Battle of Sandusky: June 4–6, 1782" and Parker B. Brown, "The Historical Accuracy of the Captivity Narrative of Doctor John Knight," 53–67.

37. Dr. Knight, *A Narrative of a Late Expedition Against the Indians, with an Account of the Barbarous Execution of Col. Crawford and the Wonderful Escape of Dr. Knight and John Slover, from Captivity in 1782*, 24; "McKee to DePeyster, August 28, 1782," *MPHC*, 20:51.

38. "DePeyster to McKee, 19th August 1782," *MPHC*, 10:377–78; "McKee to DePeyster, August 28, 1782," *MPHC*, 20:51.

39. "McKee to DePeyster, July 22nd, 1782," *MPHC*, 20:32–33.

40. "McKee to DePeyster, August 28, 1782," *MPHC*, 20:49–50; "DePeyster to McKee, August 6th, 1782," *MPHC*, 20:37–38.

41. This and the following paragraph are based upon "McKee to DePeyster, August 28, 1782," *MPHC*, 20:49–50.

42. John Dabney Shane interview with Jacob Stevens, 12CC134–35, Lyman C. Draper Collection, State Historical Society of Wisconsin.

43. McKee to DePeyster, August 28, 1782, Colonial Office 42, vol. 43, folio 389–93, National Archives of Canada. For McKee's treatment of American captives following the Battle of Blue Licks, see 3Q 160, Historical Miscellanies, Draper Collection, State Historical Society of Wisconsin.

44. "McKee to Caldwell, September 21, 1782," *MPHC*, 10:46; "McKee to DePeyster, September 22, 1782," *MPHC*, 20:60; "DePeyster to McKee, September 27, 1782," *MPHC*, 10:648–49; "DePeyster to McKee, October 1, 1782," *MPHC*, 10:651; "DePeyster to McKee, October 23, 1782," *MPHC*, 10:664–65; "McKee to DePeyster, October 25, 1782," *MPHC*, 20:68–69.

45. McKee to DePeyster, November 15, 1782, Add. MSS. 21783, 270, National Archives of Canada.

46. "McKee to Haldimand, July 16, 1779," *MPHC*, 10:341; "DePeyster to Haldimand, 10 March 1780," *MPHC*, 10:379–80; "DePeyster to Haldimand, August 18, 1780, *MPHC*, 10:419–20; "Samuel Robertson to Frederick Haldimand, 21 August 1780," *MPHC*, 9:621–26; "McKee to Haldimand, May 25, 1782," *MPHC*, 10:581–82; "Haldimand to DePeyster, 11 July 1782," *MPHC*, 10:598; "Edgar to McKee, 19 August 1782," *MPHC*, 10:630.

47. "DePeyster to McKee, 3rd April 1782," *MPHC*, 10:565–66; "McKee to DePeyster, 10th April, 1782," Haldimand Papers, Add. MSS. 21783, folios 139–40, National Archives of Canada.

48. "DePeyster to McKee, April 20, 1783," *MPHC*, 11:359–60; "DePeyster to McKee, May 6, 1873," *MPHC*, 11:363–64.

49. "McKee to DePeyster, 24 May 1783," *MPHC*, 20:122–23. For the negotiations that led to the Treaty of Paris, see Samuel F. Bemis, *The Diplomacy of the American Revolution*, 189–256. For the treaty's impact on the Great Lakes region, see Abernathy, *Western Lands*, 274–87; Colin G. Calloway, "Suspicion and Self-Interest: The British Indian Alliance and the Peace of Paris."

50. "Transactions with the Indians at Sandusky, 26 August to 8 September, 1783," *MPHC*, 20:174–83; "McKee to DePeyster, September 8, 1783," *MPHC*, 11:385–86; "McKee to Sir John Johnson, September 9th, 1783," *MPHC*, 20:183–84.

SEVEN: LAND ACQUISITION, PUBLIC AFFAIRS,
AND POLITICS, 1783–1799

1. "Col. McKee to James McKee, July 10th, 1783," *MPHC*, 11:375; Peter D. James, "Report on the British Indian Department in the Detroit-Amherstburg Region in the Period 1785–1812," ii.

2. "DePeyster to Maclean, 1 August 1783," *MPHC*, 20:157–58; "DePeyster to Maclean, August 18, 1783," *MPHC*, 20:171; "Hay to Haldimand, August 5, 1784," *MPHC*, 11:444; "Lord Dorchester to Dundas, March 28th, 1794," *MPHC*, 24:655; "Simcoe to Dundas, June 21st, 1794," *MPHC*, 24:666; "Dorchester to Grenville, 15th March, 1790," Cruikshank, *Simcoe Correspondence*, 1:10; "Dorchester to Simcoe, 16th April, 1794," Cruikshank, *Simcoe Correspondence*, 2:207.

3. "Smith to Simcoe, 30 April, 1792," Cruikshank, *Simcoe Correspondence*, 1:149. Documents relating to McKee's administration of the militia are scattered throughout Milo M. Quaife, ed., *The John Askin Papers*, passim. See also Paul Couture, "War and Society on the Detroit Frontier, 1791–1815," 55–56.

4. *Askin Papers*, 1:301; Clarence M. Burton, Scrapbook, 4:49, Burton Historical Collection, Detroit Public Library.

5. "Memorandum of Captain William Mayne, October, 1794," Cruikshank, *Simcoe Correspondence*, 3:77.

6. Ernest J. Lajeunesse, ed., *The Windsor Border Region, Canada's Southernmost Frontier: A Collection of Documents*, cii–cix; Dean Jacobs, "Indian Land Surrenders," 62–64. The early land distribution along the southern Detroit River area is documented in "The Farney Collection," Fort Malden Nation Historic Park. For a general discussion, see also David Farrell, "Settlement Along the Detroit Frontier, 1760–1796" and Hamish A. Leach, *The Founding*

of *Fort Amherstburg (Malden) Along the Detroit Frontier-1796*, particularly chapters 1 and 2.

7. "McKee to Johnson, 11 October, 1783," *MPHC*, 20:190–91; "Captain Bird to Captain Mathews, 15 October, 1783," *MPHC*, 20:191–92; "Indian Deed to Jacob Schieffelin, October 13, 1783," *MPHC*, 20:193–94. See also Lajeunesse, *Windsor Border Region*, 155–57 and David Farrell, "Settlement Along the Detroit Frontier, 1760–1796, 96–99.

8. "Captain Alex. McKee to Sir John Johnson, November, 1783," *MPHC*, 20:203; In Council—Detroit, 10 October–22 October, 1783, RG10, series 2, 261–86, National Archives of Canada.

9. "Haldimand to Johnson, 15th Nov. 1783," "Haldimand to Hay, 26th April, 1784," Lajeunesse, *Windsor Border Region*, 157–58.

10. "Haldimand to Hay, 14 August 1784," Lajeunesse, *Windsor Border Region*, 159–60.

11. "Haldimand to Hay, 14th August, 1784," Lajeunesse, *Windsor Border Region*, 157–58; "Documents Relative to Land on Detroit River Granted to Lt. Col. H. Bird, August 31, 1784," *MPHC*, 24:14–15. The grant was not legally completed until 1788. Schlieffelin's comments are found in J. Schlieffelin to Sir John Johnson, Minutes and records of the land board for the District of Hesse, Detroit, 18 October 1798, RG1, L4, 2, 125, National Archives of Canada.

12. Lajeunesse, *Windsor Border Region*, ciii–civ.

13. "The Chiefs of the Ottawa and Chippewa Nations of Detroit Ceding Land at River Canard and Bois Blanc, May 15, 1786," Lajeunesse, *Windsor Border Region*, 165–66. For McKee's later acquisitions, see appendix, book B., Cruikshank, *Simcoe Correspondence*, 5:201–20, passim. McKee's Loyalist claims may be traced in "Memorial of Alexander McKee," American Loyalist Claims, AO12, Exchequer and Audit Department, series 1 (1776–1831), 40:388–90, National Archives of Canada; for settlement of his claim, see 66:79 and 109:232. Elliott's affidavit is found in "Claim of Alexr. McKee, Esqu., late of Pensilva., Aug. 31, 1787," in Alexander Fraser, ed., *Second Report of the Bureau of Archives for the Province of Ontario*, 987–88.

14. Henry Hamilton to Lord Sydney, 29 August 1785, MG11, CO 42, 48:132 and Hamilton to Nepean, September 1, 1785, 48:285–88, National Archives of Canada.

15. "Appointment of Justices and Officers for the District of Hesse, 24th July 1788," Lajeunesse, *Windsor Border Region*, 105–6.

16. Lajeunesse, *Windsor Border Region*, cix; "Lands for Settlement in Canada, 2nd September 1789," *MPHC*, 8:489–90. For McKee's actions during his tenure on the board, see Alexander Fraser, ed., "Board of Land Office for the District of Hesse, 1789–1794: Minutes of Meetings, etc.," in Alexander

Fraser, ed., *Third Report of the Bureau of Archives for the Province of Ontario,* passim.

17. "Indian Deed of Present Southwestern Ontario to King George III, May 19, 1790," Lajeunesse, *Windsor Border Region,* 171–73. McKee's acquisitions are detailed on the map "Indian Land Surrenders & Treaties," found in Dean Jacobs, "Indian Land Surrenders," 63.

18. Lajeunesse, *Windsor Border Region,* cv; McKee's correspondence with the land board regarding the Canard River reserve is found in *MPHC,* 12:24–28, passim. The area is shown on the map "The Above is a plan of a Tract of land called the Huron Reserve, Feb. 20, 1790," Ontario Ministry of Natural Resources—Survey Records Branch.

19. Dean Jacobs, "Indian Land Surrenders," 64.

20. "J. G. Simcoe to Alured Clark, 31 May 1793," Cruikshank, *Simcoe Correspondence,* 1:338; "Minutes of a Council with the Chippewas and Ottawas At a Council held at Chenail Ecarte this 30th August, 1796," Ernest A. Cruikshank and A. F. Hunter, *The Correspondence of the Honourable Peter Russell with Allied Documents Relating to His Administration of the Government of Upper Canada during the Official Term of Lieut-Governor J. G. Simcoe while on Leave of Absence* [hereafter cited as *Russell Correspondence*], 1:34–35. See also Dean Jacobs, "Indian Land Surrenders," 64–66; the purchase is shown on the map "We The Chiefs of the Chippewa Nations do hereby agree with Alexander McKee, Esquire, Deputy Sup. General & Deputy Inspector General of Indian Affairs . . . 9 Sept. 1795" (sic. 1796), Cartographic Archives and Architectural Drawings Division, National Archives of Canada.

21. Biographical information concerning Ainse is found in George Brown, et al., eds., *Dictionary of Canadian Biography* vol. 6, *1821–1835,* s.v. "Sarah Ainse," by John Clark; C. Hamil, *Sally Ainse, Fur Trader.*

22. For Ainse's original purchases, see "Detroit Notarial Registers, vol. 6, 1776–1784," 143 and "Upper Canada Land Petitions A, vol. 4, no. 45," National Archives of Canada, and also for the testimony given by the eight Chippewa chiefs March 7, 1794. See also "Brant to Smith, April 3rd, 1795," Cruikshank and Hunter, *Russell Correspondence,* 1:2–3. McKee's response in September, 1795 is found in "Upper Canada Land Petitions A, vol. 4, no. 45." See also Fraser, "Board of Land Office," 213, 238–39.

23. "Sarah Ainse," in Brown et al., *Dictionary of Canadian Biography.*

24. John Clarke, "Geographical Aspects of Land Speculation in Essex County to 1825: The Strategy of Particular Individuals," in K. G. Pryke and L. L. Kulisek, eds., *The Western District: Papers from the Western District Conference,* 82.

25. Entries for February 15, 1785; February 23, 1785; September 29, 1785; and October 26, 1785, in Bliss, *Diary of David Zeisberger*, 1:218–19, 245, 247. See also Olmstead, *Blackcoats Among the Delaware*, 64–106.

26. Entries for February 1 and March 30, 1790, Bliss, *Diary of David Zeisberger*, 83–84, 96.

27. Entry for March 25, 1791, Bliss, *Diary of David Zeisberger*, 2:165; "Zeisberger to McKee, March 10, 1791," CO 42, 73:419–22, National Archives of Canada.

28. Entry for February 25, 1792, Bliss, *Diary of David Zeisberger*, 2:249. The new settlement is located on the map "A Sketch of the River Thames, from the Delaware Village to the Upper Forks, General's Office Upper Canada, 22nd March, 1793," Cartographic Archives and Architectural Drawings Division, National Archives of Canada.

29. Lajeunesse, *Windsor Border Region*, lxxxvii–lxxxix; "Legislative Candidacy of David W. Smith, 26 July 1792," and "Entertainment For Detroit Electors, 14 August, 1792," in Quaife, *Askin Papers*, 1:416–19, 427–28.

30. Lajeunesse, *Windsor Border Region*, lxxxviii; "J. G. Simcoe to Henry Dundas, November 4th, 1792," *Simcoe Correspondence*, 1:249–50; "D. W. Smith to John Askin, 7th November, 1792," *Simcoe Correspondence*, 1:254–55.

31. "Names of Persons recommended for Seats in the Executive Council for the intended Province of Upper Canada, 15 March 1790," *Simcoe Correspondence*, 1:11; "Simcoe to Dundas, 20th June, 1794," *Simcoe Correspondence*, 2:279–87.

32. "Phyn, Ellice & Co. to Col. McKee, 8th June 1793," *MPHC*, 20:317; "Phyn, Ellice & Inglis to McKee, 9 August 1792 (93)," *MPHC*, 20:319–20.

33. John Clarke, "The Role of Political Position and Family and Economic Linkage in Land Speculation in the Western District of Upper Canada, 1788–1815." "Miami Company Ledger Books" and "Ledger Book D," John Askin Papers, Burton Collection, Detroit Public Library.

EIGHT: INDIAN AFFAIRS, 1783–1794

1. For an overview of the post-Revolutionary period, see Downes, *Council Fires on the Upper Ohio*, 277–338 and Allen, *His Majesty's Indian Allies*, 40–87. Simcoe had commanded a Loyalist corps, the Queen's Rangers, during the Revolution and accepted the post of lieutenant governor to vindicate British imperialism in the wake of the 1783 Treaty of Paris. See Brown, *Dictionary of Canadian Biography*, vol. 5. *1801–1820*, s.v. "John Graves Simcoe," by S. R. Mealing.

2. "McKee to DePeyster, September 8th, 1783," *MPHC*, 11:385–86.

3. "McKee to DePeyster, September 8th, 1783," *MPHC*, 11:385–86; "McKee to Sir John Johnson, Sept. 9th, 1783," *MPHC*, 20:183–84.

4. Quoted in Erminie Wheeler Voegelin, "Ethnohistorical Report on the Wyandot, Ottawa, Chippewa, Munsee, Delaware, Shawnee, and Potawatomi of Royce Areas 53 and 54," 181.

5. "McKee to Johnson, June 2, 1784," *MPHC*, 20:229–30; "Robertson to Haldimand, June 26th, 1784," Reuben G. Thwaites, et al., eds, *Collections of the State Historical Society of Wisconsin*, 12:69–70.

6. Reginald Horsman, "United States Indian Policies, 1776–1815," 4:29–30.

7. For the text and negotiations that led to the Treaty of Fort McIntosh, see *American State Papers*, 1:11. For McKee's actions during the spring and summer of 1785, see A Letter from the Shawnee & etc. to Col. McKee complaining against the Indians that treated at Beaver's Creek, March 20th, 1785, 23U 16–21, Frontier Wars and Extracts of letters from Col. McKee to the Superintendent General representing the uneasiness of many Indians on Account of the Americans attempting to settle on their land, 24th April, 1785, May 29th, 1785, and August 6th, 1785, 23U 22–24, Frontier Wars, Draper Collection, State Historical Society of Wisconsin.

8. *American State Papers*, 1:11.

9. Logan's objective was a cluster of seven Shawnee villages, including Piqua, Wapakoneta, Wapatomica, Mequashake, McKee's Town, and Blue Jacket's Town, located in southern Logan and northern Champaign Counties. See the map "Frontier in Transition 1782–1786: The Ohio Country and Canada," in Tanner, *Atlas of Great Lakes Indian History*, 85.

10. Simon Girty to Capt. A. McKee, 11th Octr. 1786," *MPHC*, 24:34–35; Parts of a Letter from Col. McKee to the Superintendent General, undated, 23U 38, Frontier Wars, Draper Collection, State Historical Society of Wisconsin. The description of McKee's home is found in Conversation with Simon Kenton 13th February, 1833 from the Original Notes by John H. James, 5BB 107–08, Simon Kenton Papers, Draper Collection, State Historical Society of Wisconsin. Another member of Logan's party remembered that McKee's home was "a large blockhouse that the English had built there of a huge size." See "Personal Narrative of William Lytle," 18.

11. "Intelligence From Sandusky, May 15th, 1786," *MPHC*, 24:27; [Samuel Montgomery], "A Journey Through the Indian Country Beyond the Ohio, 1785," 266, 272; Pacanne to the Messengers sent by the Indian Commissioners, September 25th, 1785, 301–2 and Deposition of William Doleman, Spring 1786, 291–93, both in M247, Papers of the Continental Congress, item 56, Papers Relating to Indian Affairs 1765–1789, National Archives.

12. "Indian Council, Detroit 24th December 1786," *MPHC*, 11:470–72.

13. Col. McKee's Speech to the Miamis & etc., etc., at Detroit the 7th September, 1787, 23U 60, Frontier Wars, Draper Collection, State Historical Society of Wisconsin; Copy of a letter from William Wilson to Co. Wm. Butler, dated Mouth of the Detroit River, June 30th, 1788, M247, Papers of the Continental Congress, item 150, Letters from Maj. Gen. Henry Knox, Secretary at War 1785–1788, 3:445–46. See also "Hamtramck to Harmar, January 1, 1788," Gayle Thornbrough, ed., *Outpost on the Wabash; 1787–1791: Letters of Brigadier General Josiah Harmar and Major Francis Hamtramck and Other Letters and Documents Selected from the Harmar Papers in the William C. Clements Library*, 58–63.

14. "Hamtramck to Harmar, August 31, 1788," Thornburg, *Outpost on the Wabash*, 114–20.

15. Downes, *Council Fires on the Upper Ohio*, 305; Horsman, "United States Indian Policies, 1776–1815," 31. The Treaty of Fort Harmar is found in *American State Papers*, 1:5–7.

16. "Lord Dorchester to Lord Sidney, 25 June 1789," *MPHC*, 12:9–10.

17. "St. Clair to Henry Knox, November 26, 1790," William H. Smith, *St. Clair Papers*, 2:192–97.

18. For the location of McKee's post and Grant's Blockhouse at the foot of the Maumee River rapids, see the map "A Sketch of the Bass Islands, Miamis Bay and a part of the Miamis River, 1794, by Robert Pilkington," *Simcoe Correspondence*, 2:284–85. McKee's post at the Glaize is described in Spencer, *Indian Captivity of O. M. Spencer*, 96. See also "Information of Thomas Rhea, undated [July, 1791]," *MPHC*, 24:277–78. Freeman's comments are found in "John Cleves Symmes to Jonathan Dayton, July 17, 1789," Beverley W. Bond, ed., *The Correspondence of John Cleves Symmes, Founder of the Miami Purchase*, 100–106. The Glaize is described in Helen Hornbeck Tanner, "The Glaize in 1792: A Composite Indian Community," especially 25–35.

19. "George Sharp to McKee, October 17, 1790," *MPHC*, 24:105–06; "McKee to Johnson, October 18, 1790," *MPHC*, 106–7; "Elliott to McKee, 23 October 1790," *MPHC*, 108–9; "Information of Capt. Matthew Elliott, November 29, 1790," *MPHC*, 133–34.

20. "McKee to Johnson, April 1, 1791," *MPHC*, 24:200–201; "McKee to Johnson, April 29, 1791," *MPHC*, 213; "McKee to Johnson, 20th June, 1791," *MPHC*, 262–64.

21. "Copy of a letter from A. McKee to Major Smith dated Foot of the Rapids Miamis, 5th July 1791," *MPHC*, 24:285–86; "Colo. McKee's Speech to the Following Nations of Indians, at the Foot of the Miamis Rapids, 1st July, 1791," Cruikshank, *Simcoe Correspondence*, 1:36.

22. "Simon Girty to McKee, October 28, 1791," *MPHC*, 24:329–30; "McKee to Johnson, 5 December 1791," *MPHC*, 335–37.

23. "McKee to Johnson, 5th December 1791," *MPHC*, 24:335–36.

24. "Brant to McKee, May 23, 1792," *MPHC*, 24:417.

25. "Brant to McKee, May 23, 1792," *MPHC*, 24:417. For Brant's discussions with Knox and other American officials, see Kelsay, *Joseph Brant 1743–1807*, 458–75.

26. "J. G. Simcoe to Henry Dundas, June 21st, 1792," Cruikshank, *Simcoe Correspondence*, 1:171–73; "Memorandum by J. G. Simcoe and Alexander McKee, undated [June, 1792]," Cruikshank, *Simcoe Correspondence*, 173–74. For discussions of the Indian buffer state, see Samuel F. Bemis, *Jay's Treaty: A Study in Commerce and Diplomacy*, 109–33; Dwight L. Smith, "A North American Neutral Indian Zone: Persistence of a British Idea," 46–63; Malcolm MacLeod, "Fortress Ontario or Forlorn Hope: Simcoe and the Defence of Upper Canada."

27. "Simcoe to McKee, Augt. 30, 1792," Cruikshank, *Simcoe Correspondence*, 1:207–9.

28. "Indian Council at the Glaize, 1792," Cruikshank, *Simcoe Correspondence*, 1:218–29; "Simcoe to McKee, Novr. 1st, 1792," Cruikshank, *Simcoe Correspondence*, 5:24–25; "Simcoe to McKee, Novr. 10th, 1792," Cruikshank, *Simcoe Correspondence*, 5:25.

29. "Simcoe to McKee, January 23, 1793," Cruikshank, *Simcoe Correspondence*, 1:278–79; "Simcoe to Alured Clarke, January 27, 1793," Cruikshank, *Simcoe Correspondence*, 1:280–82.

30. "Simcoe to McKee, Novr. 10th, 1792," Cruikshank, *Simcoe Correspondence*, 5:25. For a discussion of the western tribes' demands, see "From the Western Indians to the Five Nations, February 27, 1793," Cruikshank, *Simcoe Correspondence*, 34–35.

31. "Brant to McKee, March 23rd, 1793," Cruikshank, *Simcoe Correspondence*, 5:37.

32. "McKee to Simcoe, June 2nd, 1793," Cruikshank, *Simcoe Correspondence*, 5:47. Simcoe and McKee were correct. Jefferson later wrote to Charles Pinckney, claiming that the United States had agreed to the negotiations only "to prove to all our citizens that peace was unattainable on terms which any one of them would admit," quoted in Reginald Horsman, "The British Indian Department and the Abortive Treaty of Lower Sandusky, 1793," 195. For the creation and movements of the Legion, see Richard C. Knopf, ed., *Campaign into the Wilderness: The Wayne-Knox-Pickering-McHenry Correspondence*, vols. 1–3, passim.

33. "McKee to Simcoe, June 29, 1793," Cruikshank, *Simcoe Correspondence*, 1:371–72; "Instructions to Mr. Sheehan and Mr. Johnson, Indian

Interpreters at the Approaching Treaty at Sandusky," Cruikshank, *Simcoe Correspondence*, 368. McKee's dealings with the southern nations is detailed in Philip M. Hamer, "The British in Canada and the Southern Indians, 1790–1794." For an overview of the proceedings, see Horsman, "British Indian Department," 189–213.

34. "Captain Brant's Journal of the Proceedings at the General Council Held at the Foot of the Rapids of the Miamis," Cruikshank, *Simcoe Correspondence*, 2:5–7; see also Kelsay, *Joseph Brant*, 475–82.

35. "Brant's Journal," Cruikshank, *Simcoe Correspondence*, 2:7; "McKee to Simcoe, June 29, 1793," Cruikshank, *Simcoe Correspondence*, 1:371–72; "McKee to Simcoe, July 1st, 1793," Cruikshank, *Simcoe Correspondence*, 1:374. The American delegation's actions can be traced in "The Journal of the Commissioners of the United States, Appointed to Hold a Treaty at Sandusky for the Purpose of Making Peace with the Western Indians," *American State Papers*, 1:342–60.

36. "Simcoe to Clarke, July 10th, 1793," Cruikshank, *Simcoe Correspondence*, 1:383.

37. "Journal of the Commissioners," *American State Papers*, 1:352–54.

38. "Brant to McKee, August 4, 1793," Cruikshank, *Simcoe Correspondence*, 5:66–67; "Simcoe to Hammond, September 8th, 1793," Cruikshank, *Simcoe Correspondence*, 2:49–50; "McKee to Simcoe, 22d August, 1793," Cruikshank, *Simcoe Correspondence*, 2:34–35; "Simcoe to McKee, September 8, 1793," Cruikshank, *Simcoe Correspondence*, 5:72–73.

39. For the Legion's movements in 1793 and 1794, see Knopf, *Campaign Into the Wilderness*, vols. 3 and 4, passim. See also Anthony Wayne Papers, Ohio Historical Society. McKee's efforts to supply the Maumee tribes may be traced in War of 1812 Papers of the Department of State, 1789–1815, General Records of the Department of State [RG 59], National Archives of the United States of America. For Fort Miamis, see F. Clever Bald, "Fort Miamis, Outpost of Empire." The actions of the British Indian Department during the 1793–1795 period are summarized in Horsman, "The British Indian Department,"

40. "Diary of an Officer in the Indian Country," Cruikshank, *Simcoe Correspondence*, 5:90–94. For the Indian response to the Indian department's actions near the rapids, see "Extract of a Letter From Colo. Alexr. McKee to Joseph Chew, Secretary of Indian Affairs, Dated Miamis Rapids, May the 8th, 1794," Cruikshank, *Simcoe Correspondence*, 2:234–35.

41. "Diary of an Officer," Cruikshank, *Simcoe Correspondence*, 5:90–94.

42. "Diary of an Officer," Cruikshank, *Simcoe Correspondence*, 5:90–94; "McKee to Chew, July 7, 1794," Cruikshank, *Simcoe Correspondence*, 1:310; "McKee to Simcoe, July 5, 1794," Cruikshank, *Simcoe Correspondence*, 5:95–96.

43. Larry L. Nelson, "'Never Have They Done So Little:' The Battle of Fort Recovery and the Collapse of the Miami Confederacy," 51; see also Sword, *President Washington's Indian War*, 277–78.

44. The standard treatment for the diplomatic negotiations that revolved around the northern posts is Bemis, *Jay's Treaty*. See also Robert Berkhofer, "Barrier to Settlement," 246–76.

45. "Dorchester to the Seven Nations of Canada, 10 February 1794," Cruikshank, *Simcoe Correspondence*, 2:149–50; "Dundas to Simcoe, 16 March 1794," Cruikshank, *Simcoe Correspondence*, 187." Simcoe to McKee, July 10, 1794," Cruikshank, *Simcoe Correspondence*, 5:97.

46. "Simcoe to McKee, August 30, 1792," Cruikshank, *Simcoe Correspondence*, 1:207–09; "McKee to England, July 10, 1794," Cruikshank, *Simcoe Correspondence*, 2:315.

47. Canada's reluctance to give unqualified support to the Indian resistance was not lost on Little Turtle. The Miami chief withdrew from the Indian alliance's leadership in July 1794 after he became convinced that British authorities would not furnish troops to fight against Wayne's advance. See Harvey L. Carter, *The Life and Times of Little Turtle: First Sagamore of the Wabash*, 132. The administration of British Indian policy along the Maumee River during 1790–1794 is discussed in Allen, *His Majesty's Indian Allies*, 57–86. Allen concludes that Indian policy during the period was "based fundamentally on denial and deception, Machiavellian in style—manipulative, cruel, and successful."

48. Wayne's movements can be traced in Copy of a Letter from Major General Wayne to the Secretary of War, 28th August, 1794, *American State Papers—Indian Affairs*, 1:491. See also Paul D. Nelson, *Anthony Wayne: Soldier of the Early Republic*, 249–68; Downes, *Council Fires on the Upper Ohio*, 335–36.

49. "McKee to Chew, August 27, 1794," Cruikshank, *Simcoe Correspondence*, 3:7–8.

50. Wayne's account of the battle is found in "Copy of a Letter from Major General Wayne to the Secretary of War, 28th August, 1794," *American State Papers—Indian Affairs*, 1:491. See also "Campbell to England, August 20, 1794," Cruikshank, *Simcoe Correspondence*, 2:395–96; "McKee to Chew, 27 August 1794," Cruikshank, *Simcoe Correspondence*, 3:7–8; "McKee to England, August 30, 1794," Cruikshank, *Simcoe Correspondence*, 3:23. For McKee's location during the battle, see "Examination of Antoine Laselle," Cruikshank, *Simcoe Correspondence*, 3:13.

51. For estimates of the number of Indians found at Swan Creek, see "Return of Indians at Swan Creek, 15 September, 1794," Cruikshank, *Simcoe Correspondence*, 5:110; "Certificate of Matthew Elliott, 22 September, 1794," Cruik-

shank, *Simcoe Correspondence*, 5:110–11; "Memoranda by Lieut. Wm. Mayne on the Expedition to Detroit, Turtle Island, Fort Miamis, & Etc.," Cruikshank, *Simcoe Correspondence*, 3:73–79. For the site's fortification, see "Simcoe to England, October 10, 1794;" "Instruction By Lieut. Gov. Simcoe, October 13, 1794," and "Smith to McKee, October 16, 1794," Cruikshank, *Simcoe Correspondence*, 3: 119–20, 125, 129. For provisions sent to Swan Creek, see "England to Francis LeMaistre, October 28, 1794," and "Account of Provisions, October 10 through November 11, 1794," Cruikshank, *Simcoe Correspondence*, 3:156, 181.

52. "England to Simcoe, August 24, 1794," Cruikshank, *Simcoe Correspondence* 2:419. For Simcoe's instructions to McKee, see "Simcoe to McKee, October 22, 1794," "Simcoe to McKee, October 25, 1794," and "Simcoe to McKee, October 31, 1794," Cruikshank, *Simcoe Correspondence*, 5:115–16, 118, 121. Chew's comments are found in "Chew to Coffin, September 22, 1794," Cruikshank, *Simcoe Correspondence*, 3:105.

53. "Anthony Wayne to the Indians of Sandusky, January 1, 1795," Cruikshank, *Simcoe Correspondence*, 3:252–53; "England to Simcoe, January 27, 1795," Cruikshank, *Simcoe Correspondence*, 274–75.

54. "McKee to England, January 27, 1795," Cruikshank, *Simcoe Correspondence*, 3:276; "Antoine Laselle to Jacques Laselle, January 31, 1795," Cruikshank, *Simcoe Correspondence*, 3:281; "George Ironside to McKee, February 6, 1795," Cruikshank, *Simcoe Correspondence*, 3:288–89; "Preliminary Articles of a Treaty of Peace, February 11, 1795," Cruikshank, *Simcoe Correspondence*, 3:290–92; "Simcoe to Dorchester, February 15, 1795," Cruikshank, *Simcoe Correspondence*, 3:297–98; "Simcoe to the Duke of Portland, March 17, 1795," Cruikshank, *Simcoe Correspondence*, 3:328–29. "Wayne to Pickering, April 7, 1795," and "Hunt to Wayne, May 1, 1795," Anthony Wayne Papers, Ohio Historical Society.

55. For the negotiations that led to the Treaty of Greenville, see *American State Papers—Indian Affairs*, 1:562–84. For Brant's comments, see "Brant to Joseph Chew, February 24, 1795," Cruikshank, *Simcoe Correspondence*, 3:310 and "Joseph Chew to Thomas Aston, March 26, 1795," Cruikshank, *Simcoe Correspondence*, 3:333–34. For Simcoe's journey to Swan Creek, see "J. G. Simcoe's Diary of Journey to the Miamis River September [1794]," Cruikshank, *Simcoe Correspondence*, 3:97–100 and "Simcoe to the Committee of the Privy Council for Trade and Plantations, December 20th, 1794," Cruikshank, *Simcoe Correspondence*, 3:226–29.

56. "Simcoe to Hammond, August 24, 1793," Cruikshank, *Simcoe Correspondence*, 2:44. McKee's will is found in the Alexander McKee Reading Room File, Burton Historical Collection, Detroit Public Library.

57. "Information from William Sullivan," Cruikshank, *Simcoe Correspondence*, 2:257–58; "Wayne to the Secretary of War, August 28th, 1794," *American State Papers—Indian Affairs*, 1:491.

58. "Brant's Journal," Cruikshank, *Simcoe Correspondence*, 2:17; "Extract of a Letter from Colo. Alexr. McKee to Joseph Chew, Secretary of Indian Affairs, Dated Miamis Rapids, May the 8th, 1794," Cruikshank, *Simcoe Correspondence*, 2:234–34. See also Donald H. Kent and Merle Deardorff, eds., "John Adlum on the Allegheny: Memoirs for the Year 1794."

NINE: THE PEACEFUL FRONTIER, 1795–1799

1. "Dorchester to McKee, December 26, 1794," *MPHC*, 25:73; "McKee to Chew, 27th March, 1795," Cruikshank, *Simcoe Correspondence*, 3:335.

2. "Lieut. Col. England to Mr. Lemaistre, October 28th, 1794," *MPHC*, 12:148–49.

3. "England to James Green, Sept. 20th, 1795," *MPHC*, 23:347; "England to Green, December 15, 1795," *MPHC*, 347–48; "McKee to Chew, April 21, 1796," *MPHC*, 12:201–2.

4. "Proposed Plan for the Future Government of the Indian Department, Humbly Submitted to His Excellency Lord Dorchester—Commander in Chief, &c., &c., &c.," Cruikshank, *Simcoe Correspondence*, 4:294–95.

5. "McKee to Dorchester, 7th June, 1796," Cruikshank, *Simcoe Correspondence*, 4:293–94.

6. "Sir John Johnson to Alexander McKee, 30th Decr. 1796," and "McKee to Sir John Johnson, 20th January, 1797," Cruikshank and A. F. Hunter, *Russell Correspondence*, 1:103–04, 130–31.

7. "Extract of a Letter From Col. McKee D.S.G. of Indian Affairs to Joseph Chew, Jan'y 29th, 1796," *MPHC*, 12:195–96; "McKee to Prideaux Selby, December 2nd, 1796," Cruikshank and A. F. Hunter, *Russell Correspondence*, 1:102–03. For a contemporary description of Elliott's estate, see Isaac Weld, *Travels in the States of North America and the Provinces of Upper and Lower Canada during the Years 1795, 1796, and 1797*, 2:210–15. Elliott's brief tenure as superintendent at Fort Malden is detailed in Horsman, *Matthew Elliott*, 119–42.

8. "Talk Between Capt. William Mayne and Indian Chiefs, June 30, 1797," *MPHC*, 20:519–21; "Peter Russell to Robert Prescott, 21st August, 1797," Cruikshank and A. F. Hunter, *Russell Correspondence*, 1:258–61; "Peter Russell to Robert Prescott, 6th Septr. 1797—Enclosure No. II, dated 24th August 1797," Cruikshank and A. F. Hunter, 1:272–73.

9. "Capt. Hector McLean to Capt. James Green," Sept. 14th, 1797," *MPHC*, 20:535–39.

10. "John Johnson to McKee, 15th Sept. 1797," Cruikshank and A. F. Hunter, *Russell Correspondence*, 1:283; "Russell to Robert Prescott, 4th Novr. 1797—Inclosure dated 26th Octr. 1797," Cruikshank and A. F. Hunter, *Russell Correspondence*, 2:5–6; "McLean to McKee, Oct. 28, 1797," *MPHC*, 20:565–66; "McKee to McLean, Nov. 5, 1797," *MPHC*, 20:567–68; "McLean to Green, Nov. 11, 1797," *MPHC*, 20:580–81; "McKee to Prescott, Nov. 11, 1797," *MPHC*, 20:581; "Prescott to Russell, December 15, 1797," *MPHC*, 20:584–85.

11. "Col. Alexander McKee to Joseph Chew, June 20, 1796," *MPHC*, 20:456; "George Ironside to Prideaux Selby, 9th May 1797," Cruikshank and A. F. Hunter, *Russell Correspondence*, 1:172; "Matthew Elliott to Sir John Johnson, 23rd June 1797," Cruikshank and A. F. Hunter, *Russell Correspondence*, 1:194–95.

12. "McKee to Russell, 12th October 1797," Cruikshank and A. F. Hunter, *Russell Correspondence*, 1:302–3; "McKee to Russell, 23rd December, 1798," Cruikshank and A. F. Hunter, *Russell Correspondence*, 3:41–43; "Prideaux Selby to Peter Russell, 23rd January, 1799," Cruikshank and A. F. Hunter, *Russell Correspondence*, 3:60–62.

13. "Prescott to Russell, 15th December 1797," *MPHC*, 20:584–85; "Selby to Chew, 3rd May 1795," *MPHC*, 12:168; "England to Simcoe, May 2nd, 1797," Cruikshank, *Simcoe Correspondence*, 4:1; "McKee to Selby, December 2nd, 1798," Cruikshank and A. F. Hunter, *Russell Correspondence*, 3:16; "McKee to Selby, 10th January, 1799," Cruikshank and A. F. Hunter, *Russell Correspondence*, 3:49; "John Drake to Thomas McKee, Jany. 16, 1799," Cruikshank and A. F. Hunter, *Russell Correspondence*, 3:53; "Peter Audrain to Judge James May, January 14–19, 1799," Alexander David Fraser Papers, Burton Historical Collection, Detroit Public Library. For the negotiations at St. Joseph Island, see "Capt. Peter Drummond to Capt. James Green, June 29, 1797," *MPHC*, 20:518–19. Many years later, Simon Kenton told a colleague of Lyman Draper that McKee died when a pet deer gored him in the leg. This story has gained wide circulation, in part because the author, Allan Eckert, included it in his popular novel *The Frontiersmen*. I have found no other reference to an injury of this nature or of a pet deer. However, on December 2, 1798, McKee wrote to Prideaux Selby claiming, "The Fever has left me and my Wound almost Heal'd but my Leg so weak [it] does not allow me to lay any weight on it. I fear it will be some time before I am able even to walk & I do not expect ever to have the Use I had of it, The Sinews are so materially Injur'd." Later, he indicates that the injury had been inflicted some six weeks previously. If this is the

same injury mentioned by Kenton, then the timing of the event, mid- to late October, would place the incident at a time when male deer are particularly aggressive.

14. Although British policy remained stable, Elliott's dismissal and McKee's unexpected passing threw the Indian department into administrative turmoil. The military, seeking to increase its influence over Indian affairs, appointed John Connolly to replace McKee. Old-line Indian department officials led by Sir John Johnson objected to the selection, and several interim administrators occupied the position until the post was permanently filled in July 1800 by William Claus. Matthew Elliott rejoined the Indian department as tensions between the United States and Great Britain rose during the early nineteenth century. Clause called Elliott the "only man capable of calling forth the loyalties of the Indians," and he reinstated Elliott as superintendent of Indian affairs at Fort Malden in 1808. See Robert S. Allen, "The British Indian Department and the Frontier in North America, 1755–1830," 64–67.

15. Peter Audrain to Judge James May, Jan. 14–19, 1799, Alexander David Fraser Papers, Burton Historical Collection, Detroit Public Library; "John H. James Notes on Conversations with General Simon Kenton, February 13, 1832," 5BB 97–125, Simon Kenton Papers, Draper Collection, State Historical Society of Wisconsin.

Bibliography

MANUSCRIPT REPOSITORIES

Darlington Memorial Library, University of Pittsburgh
  Edward Hand Papers
  Pittsburgh Papers, 1759–65
  Yohogania County, Virginia Court Records, 1776–79
Detroit Public Library
  Burton Historical Collection
    McKee Papers
    John Askin Papers
    Alexander David Fraser Papers
    Alexander McKee Reading Room File
    Macomb, Edgar, and Macomb Papers
Fort Malden National Historic Park, Amherstburg, Ontario
  McKee Family Genealogical File
  Farney Collection
Historical Society of Pennsylvania, Harrisburg
  Baynton and Wharton Letterbook, 1758–60
Library of Congress, Washington, D.C.
  Peter Force Papers
National Archives of the United States of America, Washington, D.C.
  Records of the Continental Congress and the Constitutional Convention
      (RG 30)
    Papers of the Continental Congress, 1774–89
  General Records of the Department of State (RG 59)
    War of 1812 Papers of the Department of State, 1789–1815

National Archives of Canada, Ottawa, Ontario
  Papers of Alexander and Thomas McKee (MG19, F16)
  Records Received in the Office of the Lieutenant Governor of Upper
    Canada (RG10)
  Bouquet Collection (MG21 Add. MSS. 21631-21660)
  Haldimand Papers (MG21 Add. MSS. 21661-21892)
  Colonial Office: Canada Original Correspondence (MG11, C.O. 42)
  Governors General Office: Dispatches from the Colonial Office (RG7, G1)
  Audit Office, Loyalist Claims (MG14, A.O.12, vol. 40)
  Executive Council Land Records (RG1, L3)
  Brant Family Records (MG19, A3)
  John Graves Simcoe Papers (MG23 HI1)
  Peter Russell Papers (MG23 HI2)
  E. A. Cruikshank Papers (MG30, E66, vol. 19, Files 48–50)
New York Public Library, New York, New York
  Chalmers Collection, Indians 1750–75
Ohio Historical Society, Columbus, Ohio
  Anthony Wayne Papers, Historical Society of Pennsylvania, Transcribed
    and Typewritten for the Ohio Historical Society by the Anthony
    Wayne Parkway Board, 1952–56
Pennsylvania Historical and Museum Commission, Harrisburg
  George Morgan Letter Book, 1776
State Historical Society of Wisconsin, Madison, Wisconsin
  Lyman C. Draper Collection
    Frontier Wars [series U]
    Historical Miscellanies [series Q]
    Brady and Wetzel Papers [series E]
    William Preston Papers [series QQ]
    Tecumseh Papers [series YY]
    Simon Kenton Papers [series BB]
    Pittsburgh & Northwest Virginia Papers [series NN]
    Draper's Notes [series S]
William L. Clements Library, University of Michigan
  Clinton Papers
  Gage Papers, American Series
  Simcoe Papers
  John Graves Simcoe Letterbook, July 4, 1792–July 25, 1793
Windsor's Community Museum, Windsor, Ontario
  McKee Papers
  MacDonald Papers

PUBLISHED WORKS

Abernathy, Thomas Perkins. *Western Lands and the American Revolution.* Russel and Russell, Inc., 1959.

Ackerknecht, Erwin H. "White Indians: Psychological and Physiological Peculiarities of White Children Abducted and Reared By North American Indians." *Bulletin of the History of Medicine* 15 (1944): 14–36.

Adams, John Arthur. "The Indian Trader of the Upper Ohio Valley." *Western Pennsylvania Historical Magazine* 17 (1934): 163–74.

Adams, Paul K. "Colonel Henry Bouquet's Ohio Expedition in 1764." *Pennsylvania History* 40 (1973): 139–48.

Allen, Robert S. "The British Indian Department and the Frontier in North America, 1755–1830." In *Occasional Papers in Archaeology and History.* Ottawa: Parks Canada, 1975. 5–125.

———. *His Majesty's Indian Allies: British Indian Policy in the Defence of Canada, 1774–1815.* Toronto: Dundurn Press, 1992.

Alvord, Clarence, and Clarence Carter, eds. *British Trade and Politics in the Northwest.* Collections of the Illinois State Historical Library, vol. 16. Springfield: Illinois State Historical Library, 1903.

American Archives: Consisting of a Collection of Authentick Records, State Papers, Debates, and Letters and other Notices of Publick Affairs . . . In Six Series. Washington: M. St. Clair Clarke and Peter Force, 1833.

American State Papers. Documents Legislative and Executive, of the Congress of the United States—Indian Affairs. 2 vols. Washington: Gales and Seaton, 1832.

Anderson, Gary C. "Joseph Renville and the Ethos of Biculturalism." In *Being and Becoming Indian: Biographical Studies of North American Frontiers,* edited by James A. Clifton. Chicago: Dorsey Press, 1989. 59–81.

Aron, Stephen. "The Significance of the Kentucky Frontier." *Register of the Kentucky Historical Society* 91 (1993): 298–323.

Aquila, Richard. *The Iroquois Restoration: Iroquois Diplomacy on the Colonial Frontier, 1701–1754.* Detroit: Wayne State University Press, 1983.

Axtell, James. "The Ethnohistory of Early America: A Review Essay." *William and Mary Quarterly* 35 (1978): 110–40.

———. *The European and the Indian: Essays in the Ethnohistory of Colonial North America.* New York: Oxford University Press, 1981.

———. *The Invasion Within: The Contest of Cultures in Colonial North America.* Oxford: Oxford University Press, 1985.

Bailyn, Bernard, and Philip D. Morgan, eds. *Strangers Within the Realm: Cultural Margins of the First British Empire.* Chapel Hill: University of North Carolina Press, 1991.

Bald, F. Clever. "Fort Miamis, Outpost of Empire." *Northwest Ohio Quarterly* 16 (1944): 75–111.

Barnhart, John D., ed. *Henry Hamilton and George Rogers Clark in the American Revolution, with the Unpublished Journal of Lieut. Gov. Henry Hamilton.* Crawfordsville, Ind.: R. E. Banta, 1951.

Barsh, Russell L. "Native American Loyalists and Patriots: Reflections on the American Revolution in Native-American History." *Indiana History* 10 (1977): 9–19.

Beers, Paul B. "A Wild Beast in Human Form." *American History Illustrated* 3 (1968): 20–24.

Bemis, Samuel F. *The Diplomacy of the American Revolution.* Bloomington: Indiana University Press, 1957.

———. *Jay's Treaty: A Study in Commerce and Diplomacy.* New York: Yale University Press, 1962.

Berkhofer, Robert F. "Barrier to Settlement: British Indian Policy in the Old Northwest, 1783–1794." In *The Frontier in American Development: Essays in Honor of Paul Wallace Gates,* edited by David M. Ellis. Ithaca: Cornell University Press, 1969. 249–76.

Bliss, Eugene L., ed. *Diary of David Zeisberger: A Moravian Missionary Among the Indians of Ohio.* Cincinnati: Robert Clarke and Co., 1885.

Boissevain, Jeremy. *Friends of Friends: Networks, Manipulators, and Coalitions.* New York: St. Martin's Press, 1974.

Bonacich, Edna. "A Theory of Middleman Minorities." *American Sociological Review* 38 (1973): 583–94.

Bond, Beverley W., ed. *The Correspondence of John Cleves Symmes, Founder of the Miami Purchase.* New York: Macmillan, 1926.

"Bowman's Campaign of 1779." *Ohio Archaeological and Historical Publications* 22 (1913): 502–19.

"Bowman's Expedition against Chillicothe, May–June 1779." *Ohio Archaeological and Historical Publications* 19 (1910): 446–59.

Boyd, Julian P., et al., eds. *The Susquehannah Company Papers.* 11 vols. Ithaca: Cornell University Press, 1962–71.

Boyd, Thomas. *Simon Girty, the White Savage.* New York: Minton, Balch and Co., 1928.

Boyer, Lt. John. *A Journal of Wayne's Campaign . . . .* Cincinnati: William Dodge, 1886.

Brand, Irene. "Dunmore's War." *West Virginia History* 40 (1978): 28–46.

Brebner, J. B. "Subsidized Intermarriage with the Indians: An Incident in British Colonial Policy." *Canadian Historical Review* 6 (1925): 33–36.

Breen, T. H. "Creative Adaptations: Peoples and Cultures." In *Colonial British North America: Essays in the New History of the Early Modern Era,* edited by Jack P. Greene and J. R. Pole. Baltimore: Johns Hopkins University Press, 1984. 195–232.

———. "An Empire of Goods: The Anglicization of Colonial America, 1690–1776." *Journal of British Studies* 25 (1986): 467–99.

Brown, George, et al., gen. eds. *Dictionary of Canadian Biography.* 12 vols. Toronto: University of Toronto Press, 1966–90.

Brown, Parker B. "The Battle of Sandusky: June 4–6, 1782." *Western Pennsylvania Historical Magazine* 65 (1982): 116–51.

———. "The Historical Accuracy of the Captivity Narrative of Dr. John Knight." *Western Pennsylvania Historical Magazine* 70 (1985): 53–56.

Bryant, Thomas Julian. "Bryant's Station and Its Founder William Bryant." *Register of the Kentucky Historical Society* 24 (1926): 47–58.

Burnett, Edmund C., ed. *Letters of Members of the Continental Congress.* 8 vols. Washington, D.C.: Carnegie Institution, 1926.

Burt, A. L., Jr. *The United States, Great Britain, and British North America: From the Revolution to the Establishment of Peace After the War of 1812.* New Haven: Yale University Press, 1940.

Burton, Clarence Monroe. "John Connolly: A Tory of the Revolution." *Proceedings of the American Antiquarian Society* 20 (1909): 70–78.

Butterfield, Consul Wilshire. *History of the Girtys: Being a Concise Account of the Girty Brothers . . . .* Cincinnati: Robert Clarke and Co., 1890.

———, ed. *The Washington-Crawford Letters, Being the Correspondence between George Washington and William Crawford, from 1767 to 1781, Concerning Western Lands.* Cincinnati: Robert Clarke and Co., 1877.

Caley, Percy B. "The Life and Adventures of Lieutenant-Colonel John Connolly: The Story of a Tory." *Western Pennsylvania Historical Magazine* 11 (1928): 26–49, 76–111, 144–79, 225–59.

———. "Lord Dunmore and the Pennsylvania-Virginia Boundary Dispute." *Western Pennsylvania Historical Magazine* 22 (1939): 87–100.

Calloway, Colin G. *The American Revolution in Indian Country: Crisis and Diversity in Native American Communities.* Cambridge: Cambridge University Press, 1995.

———. "Beyond the Vortex of Violence: Indian-White Relations in the Ohio Country, 1783–1815." *Northwest Ohio Quarterly* 64 (1992): 16–26.

———. *Crown and Calumet: British-Indian Relations, 1783–1815.* Norman: University of Oklahoma Press, 1987.

———. "Neither White Nor Red, White Renegades on the American Frontier." *William and Mary Quarterly* 17 (1986): 43–66.

———. "Simon Girty: Interpreter and Intermediary." In *Being and Becoming Indian: Biographical Studies of North American Frontiers,* edited by James A. Clifton, Chicago: Dorsey Press, 1989. 38–58.

―――. "Suspicion and Self-Interest: The British Indian Alliance and the Peace of Paris." *The Historian* 48 (1985): 41–60.

―――. "'We Have Always Been the Frontier': The American Revolution in the Shawnee Country." *American Indian Quarterly* 16 (1992): 39–52.

Carter, Clarence Edwin, ed. *The Correspondence of General Thomas Gage with the Secretaries of State and with the War Office and the Treasury, 1763–1775.* 2 vols. New Haven: Yale University Press, 1931–33.

Carter, Harvey Lewis. "A Frontier Tragedy: Little Turtle and William Wells." *The Old Northwest* 6 (1980): 3–18.

―――. *The Life and Times of Little Turtle: First Sagamore of the Wabash.* Urbana: University of Illinois Press, 1987.

Carter, John H. "Alexander McKee, Our Most Noted Tory." *Northumberland County Historical Society Proceedings* 22 (1958): 60–75.

Chaput, Donald. "The Family of Drouet de Richerville: Merchants, Soldiers, and Chiefs of Indians." *Indiana Magazine of History* 74 (1978): 103–16.

Clark, Howard Glenn. "John Fraser, Western Pennsylvania Frontiersman." *Western Pennsylvania Historical Magazine* 39 (1956): 150–75.

Clarke, John. "Geographical Aspects of Land Speculation in Essex County to 1825: The Strategy of Particular Individuals." In *The Western District: Papers from the Western District Conference,* edited by K. G. Pryke and L. L. Kulisek. Windsor: Essex County Historical Society and The Western District Council, 1983. 68–111.

―――. "The Role of Political Position and Family and Economic Linkage in Land Speculation in the Western District of Upper Canada, 1788–1895." *Canadian Geographer* 19 (1975): 18–34.

Cleland, Hugh. *George Washington in the Ohio Valley.* Pittsburgh: University of Pittsburgh Press, 1955.

Clifton, James A. "Alternate Identities and Cultural Frontiers." In *Being and Becoming Indian: Biographical Studies of North American Frontiers,* edited by James A. Clifton. Chicago: The Dorsey Press, 1989. 1–37.

―――. *Being and Becoming Indian: Biographical Studies of North American Frontiers.* Chicago: The Dorsey Press, 1989.

―――. "Personal and Ethnic Identity on the Great Lakes Frontier: The Case of Billy Caldwell, Anglo-Canadian." *Ethnohistory* 25 (1978): 68–94.

Coleman, Winston J., Jr. *The British Invasion of Kentucky.* Lexington: Winburn Press, 1951.

Collins, Lewis, and Richard H. Collins. *History of Kentucky: By the Late Lewis Collins, Revised, Enlarged Four-fold, and Brought Down to the Year 1874 by his Son, Richard H. Collins . . . .* 2 vols. Covington: Collins and Co., 1882.

Collins, Richard H., and Willard R. Jillson. "The Siege of Bryant's Station." *Register of the Kentucky Historical Society* 36 (1938): 15–25.

Colonial Records of Pennsylvania. 16 vols. Harrisburg: The State of Pennsylvania, 1838–53.

Connolly, John. "Narrative of the Transactions, Imprisonment and Sufferings of John Connolly, an American Loyalist and Lieutenant-Colonel in His Majesty's Service." *Pennsylvania Magazine of History and Biography* 12 (1888): 310–24, 407–20; 13 (1889): 61–70, 153–67, 281–91.

Craig, Gerald M. *Upper Canada: The Formative Years: 1784–1841.* London: Oxford University Press, 1963.

Craig, Neville B., ed. *The Olden Time: A Monthly Publication, Devoted to the Preservation of Documents and other Authentick Information in Relation to Early Explorations and the Settlement and Improvement of the Country Around the Head of the Ohio.* 2 vols. Pittsburgh, 1846–47.

Crary, Catherine S. *The Price of Loyalty: Tory Writings from the Revolutionary Era.* New York: McGraw-Hill Book Co., 1973.

Cruikshank, Ernest A., ed. *The Correspondence of Lieutenant Governor John Graves Simcoe, with Allied Documents Relating to His Administration of Upper Canada.* 5 vols. Toronto: Ontario Historical Society, 1923–31.

Cruikshank, Ernest A., and A. F. Hunter, eds. *The Correspondence of the Honourable Peter Russell with Allied Documents Relating to His Administration of the Government of Upper Canada during the Official Term of Lieut-Governor J. G. Simcoe while on Leave of Absence.* 3 vols. Toronto: Ontario Historical Society, 1932–36.

Crumrine, Boyd, ed. "Minute Book of the Virginia Court Held at Fort Dunmore (Pittsburgh) for the District of West Augusta, 1775–1776." *Annals of the Carnegie Museum* 1 (1901): 525–68.

———, ed. "Minute Book of the Virginia Court Held for Yohogania County, First at Augusta (Now Washington, Pennsylvania), and Afterwards on the Andrew Heath Farm Near West Elizabeth; 1776–1780." *Annals of the Carnegie Museum* 2 (1902): 71–140.

———, ed. "The Records of Deeds for the District of West Augusta, Virginia, for the Court held at Fort Dunmore (Pittsburgh, Pennsylvania), 1775–1776." *Annals of the Carnegie Museum* 3 (1902): 237–327.

Davies, K. G., ed. *Documents of the American Revolution, 1770–1783.* 21 vols. Shannon, Ireland: Irish University Press, 1972–81.

Darlington, Mary C. *Fort Pitt and Letters from the Frontier.* Pittsburgh: J. R. Weldin and Co., 1892.

Darlington, William M., ed. *Christopher Gist's Journals.* Cleveland: The Arthur Clark Company, 1893.

DePeyster, J. Watts, ed. *Appendix, Explanatory Notes, &c., &c., &c., &c., to 'Miscellanies by an Officer.'* New York: C. H. Ludwig, 1888.

―――――. *Miscellanies by an Officer of Arent Schuyler de Peyster*. Dumfries, Scotland: C. Monro, at the Dumfries and Galloway Courier Office, 1813.

De Schweinitz, Edmund. *The Life and Times of David Zeisberger: The Western Pioneer and Apostle of the Indians*. Philadelphia: J. B. Lippincott and Co., 1870.

"Destruction of Ruddle's and Martin's Forts." *Register of the Kentucky Historical Society* 54 (1956): 311–38.

Dexter, Franklin B. *Diary of David McClure, Doctor of Divinity: 1748–1820*. New York: Knickerbocker Press, 1899.

Dickson, Olive Patricia. "From 'One Nation' in the Northeast to 'New Nation' in the Northwest: A Look at the Emergence of the Metis." In *The New Peoples: Being and Becoming Metis in North America*, edited by Jacqueline Peterson and Jennifer S. H. Brown. Winnipeg: University of Manitoba Press, 1985. 19–36.

Dowd, Gregory Evans. "The French King Wakes Up in Detroit: 'Pontiac's War' in Rumor and History." *Ethnohistory* 37 (1990): 254–78.

―――――. *A Spirited Resistance: The North American Indian Struggle for Unity, 1745–1815*. Baltimore: Johns Hopkins University Press, 1991.

Downes, Randolph C. *Council Fires on the Upper Ohio: A Narrative of Indian Affairs in the Upper Ohio Valley until 1795*. Pittsburgh: University of Pittsburgh Press, 1940.

―――――. "Dunmore's War, An Interpretation." *Mississippi Valley Historical Review* 16 (1929/30): 311–30.

―――――. "Indian War on the Upper Ohio, 1779–1782." *Western Pennsylvania Historical Magazine* 17 (1934): 93–115.

Druke, Mary. "Linking Arms: The Structure of Iroquoi Intertribal Diplomacy." In *Beyond the Covenant Chain: The Iroquois and Their Neighbors in Indian North America, 1600–1800*, edited by Daniel Richter and James Merrell, Syracuse: Syracuse University Press, 1984. 29–40.

Edmunds, R. David. "Coming of Age: Some Thoughts Upon American Indian History." *Indiana Magazine of History* 85 (1989): 312–21.

―――――. *The Shawnee Prophet*. Lincoln: University of Nebraska Press, 1983.

―――――. "'Unacquainted with the Laws of the Civilized World': American Attitudes Toward the Metis Communities in the Old Northwest." In *The New Peoples: Being and Becoming Metis in North America*, edited by Jacqueline Peterson and Jennifer S. H. Brown. Winnipeg: University of Manitoba Press, 1985. 184–94.

Egle, William Henry. *Notes and Queries: Historical, Biographical, and Genealogical, Relating Chiefly to Interior Pennsylvania*. 12 vols. Harrisburg: Harrisburg Publishing Co., 1893–1900.

Ellis, David M., ed. *The Frontier in American Development: Essays in Honor of Paul Wallace Gates*. Ithaca: Cornell University Press, 1969.

Elliott, John B., ed. *Contest for Empire, 1500–1775*. Indianapolis: Indiana Historical Society, 1979.

Evans, William A., ed. *Detroit to Fort Sackville, 1778–1779: The Journal of Normand MacLeod*. Detroit: Wayne State University Press, 1978.

"Extracts From Journal of John Parrish, 1773." *Pennsylvania Magazine of History and Biography* 16 (1892): 443–48.

Farrell, David. "Settlement Along the Detroit Frontier, 1760–1796." *Michigan History* 52 (1968): 89–107.

Fee, Walter. "Colonel George Morgan at Fort Pitt." *Western Pennsylvania Historical Magazine* 11 (1928): 217–24.

Fitzpatrick, John C., ed. *The Diaries of George Washington, 1748–1799*. 4 vols. Boston: Houghton Mifflin Co., 1925.

Fliegel, Carl John, comp. *Index to the Records of the Moravian Mission Among the Indians of North America*. New Haven: Research Publications, Inc., 1970.

Ford, Worthington Chauncy, ed. *Journals of the Continental Congress, 1774–1789*. 39 vols. Washington, D.C.: Government Printing Office, 1904–37.

Foster, Michael K. "Another Look at the Function of Wampum in Iroquois-White Councils." In *The History and Culture of Iroquois Diplomacy*, edited by Francis Jennings, William N. Fenton, et al. Syracuse: Syracuse University Press, 1985. 99–114.

———. "On Who Spoke First at Iroquois-White Councils: An Exercise in the Method of Upstreaming." In *Extending the Rafters: Interdisciplinary Approaches to Iroquois Studies*, edited by Michael K. Foster, et al. Albany: State University of New York Press, 1984. 183–208.

Foster, Michael K., et al., eds. *Extending the Rafters: Interdisciplinary Approaches to Iroquois Studies*. Albany: State University of New York, 1984.

Franklin, W. Neil. "Pennsylvania-Virginia Rivalry for the Indian Trade of the Ohio Valley." *Mississippi Valley Historical Review* 20 (1934): 463–80.

Fraser, Alexander, ed. *Second Report of the Bureau of Archives for the Province of Ontario*. Toronto: The Legislative Assembly of Toronto, 1904.

———. *Third Report of the Bureau of Archives for the Province of Ontario*. Toronto: The Legislative Assembly of Toronto, 1905.

Galloway, Albert. *Old Chillicothe*. Xenia, Ohio: Buckeye Press, 1934.

Gates, Lillian F. *The Land Policies of Upper Canada*. Toronto: University of Toronto Press, 1968.

Gilman, Carolyn. *Where Two Worlds Meet: The Great Lakes Fur Trade*. St. Paul: Minnesota Historical Society, 1982.

Gipson, Lawrence Henry. *The Triumphant Empire: New Responsibilities Within the Enlarged Empire: 1763–1766*. New York: Alfred A. Knopf, 1956.

"Glossary of Figures of Speech in Iroquois Political Rhetoric." In *The History and Culture of Iroquois Diplomacy*, edited by Francis Jennings, William N. Fenton, et al. Syracuse: Syracuse University Press, 1985. 115–26.

Gray, Elma E. *Wilderness Christians: The Moravian Mission to the Delaware Indians.* Ithaca: Cornell University Press, 1956.

Graymont, Barbara. *The Iroquois in the American Revolution.* Syracuse: Syracuse University Press, 1972.

Hagan, William T. *Longhouse Diplomacy and Frontier Warfare: The Iroquois Confederacy in the American Revolution.* Albany: New York State Revolution Bicentennial Commission, 1976.

Hagedorn, Nancy L. "'Faithful, Knowing, and Prudent': Andrew Montour as Interpreter and Cultural Broker, 1740–1772." In *Between Indian and White Worlds: The Cultural Broker,* edited by Margaret Connell Szasz. Norman: University of Oklahoma Press, 1994.

———. "'A Friend To Go Between Them': The Interpreter as Cultural Broker During Anglo-Iroquois Councils, 1740–70." *Ethnohistory* 35 (1988): 60–80.

Hamer, Philip M. "The British in Canada and the Southern Indians, 1790–1794." *East Tennessee Historical Society's Publications* 2 (1930): 107–34.

Hamil, F. C. *Sally Ainse, Fur Trader.* Detroit: The Algonquin Club, 1939.

Hanna, Charles. *The Wilderness Trail.* 2 vols. New York: G. P. Putnam's Sons, 1911.

Harpster, John W., ed. *Pen Pictures of Early Western Pennsylvania.* Pittsburgh: University of Pittsburgh Press, 1938.

Harrell, Isaac Samuel. *Loyalism in Virginia: Chapters in the Economic History of the Revolution.* New York: AMS Press, 1965.

Hassler, Edgar W. *Old Westmoreland: A History of Western Pennsylvania During the Revolution.* Pittsburgh: J. R. Weldin and Co., 1900.

Heard, Norman. *White into Indian: A Study of the Assimilation of White Persons Captured by Indians.* Metuchen, N.J.: The Scarecrow Press, 1973.

Heckewelder, John. *History, Manners, and Customs of the Indian Nations Who Once Inhabited Pennsylvania and the Neighbouring States . . . .* Philadelphia: Historical Society of Pennsylvania, 1876.

———. *Narrative of the Mission of the United Brethren among the Delaware and Mohegan Indians . . . .* Philadelphia: McCarty and Davis, 1820.

Henning, William Waller. *The Statutes at Large: Being a Collection of all the Laws of Virginia . . . .* Vols. 10–11. Richmond: George Cochran, 1822–23.

Herskovits, Melville J. *Acculturation: The Study of Cultural Contact.* New York: J.J. Augustin, 1938.

Hicks, George L., and Philip E. Leis, eds. *Ethnic Encounters: Identities and Contexts.* North Scituate, Mass.: Duxbury Press, 1977.

Hinderaker, Eric. *Elusive Empires: Constructing Colonialism in the Ohio Valley, 1673–1800.* Cambridge: Cambridge University Press, 1997.

Hoberg, Walter R. "Early History of Colonel Alexander McKee." *Pennsylvania Magazine of History and Biography* 58 (1934): 26–36.

————. "A Tory in the Northwest." *Pennsylvania Magazine of History and Biography* 59 (1934): 32–41.

Holton, Woody. "The Ohio Indians and the Coming of the American Revolution in Virginia." *The Journal of Southern History* 60 (1994): 453–78.

Horsman, Reginald. "American Indian Policy in the Old Northwest, 1783–1812." *William and Mary Quarterly* 18 (1961): 35–53.

————. "The British Indian Department and the Abortive Treaty of Lower Sandusky, 1793." *Ohio Historical Quarterly* 70 (1961): 189–213.

————. "The British Indian Department and Resistance to General Anthony Wayne." *Mississippi Valley Historical Review* 49 (1962): 269–90.

————. *Expansionism and American Indian Policy, 1783–1812*. East Lansing: Michigan State University Press, 1967.

————. *Matthew Elliott: British Indian Agent*. Detroit: Wayne State University Press, 1964.

————. "United States Indian Policies, 1776–1815." In *Handbook of North American Indians*, edited by William C. Sturtevant and Wilcomb E. Washburn. 20 vols. Washington, D.C.: Smithsonian Institute, 1978–.

Hulbert, Archer Butler, and William Nathaniel Schwarze, eds. "David Zeisberger's History of the Northern American Indians." *Ohio State Archaeological and Historical Society Quarterly* 19 (1910): 1–184.

Humphreys, R. A. "Lord Shelburne and the Proclamation of 1763." *English Historical Review* 49 (1934): 241–50.

Hunter, Charles E. "The Delaware Nativist Revival of the Mid–Eighteenth Century." *Ethnohistory* 18 (1971): 39–49.

Hunter, William A. *Forts on the Pennsylvania Frontier, 1753–1758*. Harrisburg: Pennsylvania Historical and Museum Commission, 1960.

Hurt, R. Douglas. *Indian Agriculture in America: Prehistory to the Present*. Lawrence: University Press of Kansas, 1987.

————. *The Ohio Frontier: Crucible of the Old Northwest, 1720–1830*. Bloomington: Indiana University Press, 1996.

Huston, John W. "The British Evacuation of Fort Pitt, 1772." *Western Pennsylvania Historical Magazine* 48 (1965): 317–29.

Hutslar, Donald A. *The Architecture of Migration: Log Construction in the Ohio Country, 1750–1850*. Athens: Ohio University Press, 1986.

Hutton, Paul A. "William Wells: Frontier Scout and Indian Agent." *Indiana Magazine of History* 74 (1978): 183–222.

Jacob, John J. *A Biographical Sketch of the Life of the Late Captain Michael Creasap*. Cincinnati: Jno. F. Uhlhorn, Printer, 1866.

Jacobs, Dean. "Indian Land Surrenders." In *The Western District: Papers from the Western District Conference*, edited by K. G. Pryke and L. L. Kulisek. Windsor: Essex County Historical Society and the Western District Council, 1983. 61–67.

Jacobs, Wilbur R. "British Indian Policies to 1783." In *Handbook of North American Indians*, edited by William C. Sturtevant and Wilcomb E. Washburn. 20 vols. Washington, D.C.: Smithsonian Institution, 1978–.

_____. *Wilderness Politics and Indian Gifts: The Northern Colonial Frontier, 1748–1763*. Lincoln: University of Nebraska Press, 1966.

James, Alfred Procter. "Decision at the Forks." *Western Pennsylvania Historical Magazine* 41 (1958): 1–56.

———, ed. *Writings of General John Forbes Relating to His Service in North America*. Menasha, Wisc.: Collegiate Press, 1937.

James, James A., ed. *Collections of the Illinois State Historical Library*. Vol. 8: *George Rogers Clark Papers, 1771–1781*. Springfield: Illinois State Historical Library, 1912.

James, Peter. "The British Indian Department in the Ohio Country, 1784–1795." *Northwest Ohio Quarterly* 64 (1992): 78–95.

Jefferson, Thomas. *Notes on Virginia*. In *The Writings of Thomas Jefferson*, edited by Albert E. Bergh. Vol. 2. Washington, D.C.: The Thomas Jefferson Memorial Association, 1907.

Jennings, Francis. *The Ambiguous Iroquois Empire: The Covenant Chain Confederation of Indian Tribes with English Colonies*. New York: W. W. Norton and Co., 1984.

———. *Empire of Fortune: Crowns, Colonies, and Tribes in the Seven Years War in America*. New York: W. W. Norton and Co., 1988.

———. "The Indian Revolution." In *The American Revolution: Explorations in the History of American Radicalism*, edited by Alfred F. Young. Dekalb: Northern Illinois University, 1976. 319–48.

———. "Tribal Loyalty and Tribal Independence." In *Red, White, and True Blue: The Loyalists in the Revolution*, edited by Esmond Wright. New York: AMS Press, 1976. 19–31.

Jennings, Francis, et al., eds. *The History and Culture of Iroquois Diplomacy; An Interdisciplinary Guide to the Treaties of the Six Nations and Their League*. Syracuse: Syracuse University Press, 1985.

Johnson, Allen, ed. *Dictionary of American Biography*. 10 vols. New York: Charles Scribner's Sons, 1964.

Johnston, Charles. *A Narrative of the Incidents Attending the Capture, Detention, and Ransom of Charles Johnston, of Botetourt County, Virginia . . . .* New York: J. & J. Harper, 1827.

Johnson, James Hugo. *Race Relations in Virginia and Miscegenation in the South, 1776–1860*. Amherst: University of Massachusetts Press, 1970.

Johnson, L. A. "The Settlement of the Western District, 1749–1850." In *Aspects of Nineteenth-Century Ontario*, edited by F. H. Armstrong, et al. Toronto: University of Toronto Press, 1974.

Johnson, Steven L., ed. *Guide to American Indian Documents in the Congressional Serial Set, 1817–1899.* New York: Clearwater Publishing Company, Inc., 1977.

Jones, David. *A Journal of Two Visits Made to Some Nations on the West Side of the River Ohio in the Years 1772 and 1773.* Burlington, N.J., 1774.

Jordan, John W., ed. "Bishop J. C. F. Cammerhoff's Narrative of a Journey to Shamokin, Pennsylvania, in the Winter of 1748." *Pennsylvania Magazine of History and Biography* 29 (1905): 160–79.

———. "Journal of James Kenny, 1761–1763." *Pennsylvania Magazine of History and Biography* 7 (1913): 1–47, 152–201.

Kawashima, Yohuside. "Forest Diplomats, The Role of Interpreters in Indian-White Relations on the Early Frontier." *American Indian Quarterly* 13 (1989): 1–14.

Kellogg, Louise Phelps. *The British Regime in Wisconsin and the Northwest.* Madison: State Historical Society of Wisconsin, 1935.

———. *Frontier Retreat on the Upper Ohio, 1779–1781.* Madison: State Historical Society of Wisconsin, 1917.

———, ed. *Frontier Advance on the Upper Ohio, 1778–1779.* Madison: State Historical Society of Wisconsin, 1916.

Kelsay, Isabel Thompson. *Joseph Brant, 1783–1807: Man of Two Worlds.* Syracuse: Syracuse University Press, 1984.

Kent, Donald H., and Merle Deardorff, eds. "John Adlum on the Allegheny: Memoirs for the Year 1794." *Pennsylvania Magazine of History and Biography* 84 (1960): 265–324, 435–80.

Kidwell, Clara Sue. "Indian Women as Cultural Mediators." *Ethnohistory* 39 (1992): 97–107.

Knight, Dr. [John]. *A Narrative of a Late Expedition Against the Indians, with an Account of the Barbarous Execution of Col. Crawford and the Wonderful Escape of Dr. Knight and John Slover, from Captivity in 1782.* Philadelphia: Francis Bailey, 1783.

Knollenberg, Bernhard. "General Amherst and Germ Warfare." *Mississippi Valley Historical Review* 41 (1954): 489–94.

Knopf, Richard C., ed. *Campaign into the Wilderness: The Wayne-Knox-Pickering-McHenry Correspondence.* 5 vols. Columbus: Anthony Wayne Parkway Board, Ohio State Museum, 1955.

———. "A Precise Journal of General Wayne's Last Campaign." *Proceedings of the American Antiquarian Society* 64 (1955): 273–302.

———. "Two Journals of the Kentucky Volunteers, 1793 and 1794." *Filson Club Quarterly* 27 (1953): 247–81.

Lafferty, Maude Ward. *Destruction of Ruddle's and Martin's Forts in the Revolutionary War.* Frankfort: Kentucky Historical Society, 1957.

Lajeunesse, E. J., ed. *The Windsor Border Region, Canada's Southernmost Frontier: A Collection of Documents.* Toronto: The Champlain Society, 1960.

Lamar, Howard, and Leonard Thompson, eds. *The Frontier in History: North America and Southern Africa Compared.* New Haven: Yale University Press, 1981.

Landon, Fred. *Western Ontario and the American Frontier.* Toronto: McClelland and Stewart, 1967.

Leach, Hamish A. *The Founding of Fort Amherstburg (Malden) Along the Detroit Frontier—1796.* Houston: Veldt Protea Institute, 1984.

"Letters From the Ferdinand J. Dreer Collection of Manuscripts." *Pennsylvania Magazine of History and Biography* 40 (1916): 467–69.

"Letters of Colonel George Croghan." *Pennsylvania Magazine of History and Biography* 15 (1891): 432–34.

Lewin, Howard. "A Frontier Diplomat: Andrew Montour." *Pennsylvania History* 33 (1966): 153–86.

"Logan—The Mingo Chief, 1710–1780." *Ohio Archaeological and Historical Society Publications* 20 (1911): 137–75.

"Logan's Campaign, 1786." *Ohio Archaeological and Historical Publications* 22 (1913): 520–21.

MacLeod, Malcolm. "Fortress Ontario or Forlorn Hope: Simcoe and the Defence of Upper Canada." *Canadian Historical Review* 53 (1972): 149–78.

MacVeagh, Lincoln, ed. *The Journal of Nicholas Cresswell: 1774–1777.* New York: Dial Press, 1924.

Mariott, Louisa J., ed. *Elizabeth Hicks: A True Romance of the American War of Independence, 1775 to 1783, Abridged from Her Own Manuscript by Her Daughter Fanny Bird.* London: William Hardwick, 1902.

McBride, James. *Pioneer History . . . .* Cincinnati: Robert Clarke and Co., 1871.

McConnell, Michael N. *A Country Between: The Upper Ohio Valley and its Peoples, 1724–1774.* Lincoln: University of Nebraska Press, 1992.

———. "People 'In Between': The Iroquois and the Ohio Indians." In *Beyond the Covenant Chain: The Iroquois and Their Neighbors in Indian North America, 1600–1800,* edited by Daniel K. Richter and James Merrell. Syracuse: Syracuse University Press, 1984. 93–112.

McGrane, Reginald, ed. "William Clark's Journal of Wayne's Campaign." *Mississippi Valley Historical Review* 1: (1914–15): 419–44.

McKee, Raymond. *The Book of McKee.* Dublin: Hodges, Figgis and Co., 1959.

McKnight, Charles. *Our Western Border, Its Life, Forays, Scouts, Combats, Massacres, Red Chiefs, Adventures, Captivities, Pioneer Women, One Hundred Years Ago . . . .* Philadelphia: J. C. McCurdy and Co., 1876.

Madill, Dennis F. K. "Reil, Red River, and Beyond: New Developments in Metis History." In *New Directions in American Indian History,* edited by Colin Calloway. Norman: University of Oklahoma Press, 1988. 49–78.

Marshall, Peter. "Colonial Protest and Imperial Retrenchment: Indian Policy, 1764–1768." *Journal of American Studies* 5 (1971): 1–17.

————. "First Americans and Last Loyalists: An Indian Dilemma in War and Peace." In *Red, White, and True Blue,* edited by Esmond Wright. New York: AMS Press, 1978.

————. "Imperial Policy and the Government of Detroit: Projects and Problems, 1760–1774." *Journal of Imperial and Commonwealth History* 2 (1974): 153–89.

————. "Lord Hillsborough, Samuel Wharton, and the Ohio Grant, 1769–1775." *English Historical Review* 80 (1965): 717–39.

————. "Sir William Johnson and the Treaty of Fort Stanwix, 1768." *American Studies* 10 (1967): 149–79.

Merrell, James. "'The Customes of Our Countrey': Indians and Colonists in Early America." In *Strangers Within the Realm: Cultural Margins of the First British Empire,* edited by Bernard Bailyn and Philip D. Morgan. Chapel Hill: University of North Carolina Press, 1991. 117–56.

————. *The Indian's New World: Catawbas and Their Neighbors from Contact throughout the Era of Removal.* Chapel Hill: University of Carolina Press, 1989.

————. "'Our Bond of Peace': Patterns of Intercultural Exchange on the Carolina Piedmont, 1650–1750." In *Powhatan's Mantel: Indians in the Colonial Southeast,* edited by Peter Wood, Gregory Waselkov, and Thomas Hatley. Lincoln: University of Nebraska Press, 1989.

Michigan Pioneer and Historical Collections. 40 vols. Lansing: State Printer, 1877–1929.

Miller, Christopher L., and George R. Hamell. "A New Perspective on Indian-White Contact: Cultural Symbols and Colonial Trade." *Journal of American History* 73 (1986): 311–28.

Mohr, Walter M. *Federal Indian Relations, 1774–1788.* Philadelphia: University of Pennsylvania, 1933.

Montgomery, Samuel. "A Journey Through the Indian Country Beyond the Ohio, 1785." *Mississippi Valley Historical Review* 2 (1915): 261–73.

Montgomery, Thomas Lynch, ed. *Report of the Commission to Locate the Site of the Frontier Forts of Pennsylvania.* 2d ed. 2 vols. Harrisburg: Wm. Stanley Ray, State Printer, 1916.

Moore, John H., ed. "A Captive of the Shawnees, 1779–1784." *West Virginia History* 23 (1962): 287–96.

Nelson, Larry L. "'Never Have They Done So Little': The Battle of Fort Recovery and the Collapse of the Miami Confederacy." *Northwest Ohio Quarterly* 64 (1992): 43–55.

Nelson, Paul David. *Anthony Wayne: Soldier of the Early Republic.* Bloomington: Indiana University Press, 1985.

Newell, William H. "The Augusta Regiment, Second Battalion of Pennsylvania, 1754–1763." *Historical Society of Schuylkill County Publications* 2 (1907): 35–45.

Nixon, Lily Lee. "Colonel James Burd in the Forbes Campaign." *Pennsylvania Magazine of History and Biography* 59 (1935): 106–33.

———. *James Burd: Frontier Defender, 1726–1793.* Philadelphia: University of Pennsylvania Press, 1941.

Nobles, Gregory. "Breaking into the Backcountry: New Approaches to the Early American Frontier, 1750–1800." *William and Mary Quarterly* 46 (1989): 641–70.

O'Callaghan, Edmund B., and B. Fernow, eds. *Documents Relative to the Colonial History of the State of New York.* 15 vols. Albany: Weed, Parson, and Co., 1853–87.

Olmstead, Earl P. *Blackcoats Among the Delaware: David Zeisberger on the Ohio Frontier.* Kent, Ohio: Kent State University Press, 1991.

———. *David Zeisberger: A Life Among the Indians.* Kent, Ohio: Kent State University Press, 1997.

O'Malley, Nancy, *"Stockading Up": A Study of Pioneer Stations in the Inner Bluegrass Region of Kentucky.* Frankfort: Kentucky Heritage Council, 1987.

Ousterhout, Anne M. *A State Divided: Opposition in Pennsylvania to the American Revolution.* New York: Greenwood Press, 1987.

Paltsits, Victor H. "Journal of Robert Rogers the Ranger on His Expedition for Receiving the Capitulation of Western French Posts." *Bulletin of the New York Public Library* 37 (1933): 261–76.

Peckham, Howard H. *Pontiac and the Indian Uprising.* Princeton: Princeton University Press, 1947.

Pennsylvania Archives: Selected and Arranged from Original Documents in the Office of the Secretary of the Commonwealth . . . . 138 vols. Philadelphia, 1852–1935.

Perkins, Elizabeth A. *Border Life: Experience and Memory in the Revolutionary Ohio Valley.* Chapel Hill: University of North Carolina Press, 1998.

"Personal Narrative of William Lytle." *Quarterly Publication of the Historical and Philosophical Society of Ohio* 1 (1906): 3–29.

Peterson, Jacqueline, and Jennifer S. H. Brown, eds. *The New Peoples: Being and Becoming Metis in North America.* Winnipeg: University of Manitoba Press, 1985.

———. "Many Roads to Red River: Metis Genesis in the Great Lakes Region, 1600–1815." In *The New Peoples: Being and Becoming Metis in North America,* edited by Jacqueline Peterson and Jennifer H. S. Brown. Winnipeg: University of Manitoba Press, 1985. 37–72.

———. "Prelude to Red River, A Social Portrait of the Great Lakes Metis." *Ethnohistory* 25 (1978): 41–67.

Phillips, Paul C. "The Fur Trade in the Maumee-Wabash Country." In *Studies in American History Inscribed to James Albert Woodburn, Professor Emeritus of American History in Indiana University by His Former Students.* Bloomington: Indiana University Press, 1926. 91–118.

———. *The West in the Diplomacy of the American Revolution: University of Illinois Studies in the Social Sciences.* Vol. 11. Urbana: University of Illinois Press, 1913.

Pieper, Thomas I., and James B. Gidney. *Fort Laurens, 1778–1779: The Revolutionary War in Ohio.* Kent, Ohio: Kent State University Press, 1976.

Pratt, G. Michael. "The Battle of Fallen Timbers: An Eyewitness Perspective." *Northwest Ohio Quarterly* 67 (1995): 4–34.

Pryke, K. G., and L. L. Kulisek, eds. *The Western District: Papers from the Western District Conference.* Windsor: Essex County Historical Society and the Western District Council, 1983.

Quaife, Milo M. *Calendar of The Preston and Virginia Papers of the Draper Collection of Manuscripts.* Madison: State Historical Society of Wisconsin, 1915.

———. "Fort Wayne in 1790." *Indiana Historical Society Publications* 7 (1921): 294–361.

———. "The Ohio Campaigns of 1782." *Mississippi Valley Historical Review* 17 (1930–31): 515–29.

———, ed. *The John Askin Papers.* 2 vols. Detroit: Detroit Library Commission, 1928.

Reichel, William C., ed. *Memorial of the Moravian Church.* Philadelphia: Lippincott, 1870.

Richter, Daniel K. "Cultural Brokers and Intercultural Politics: New York-Iroquois Relations, 1664–1701." *Journal of American History* 75 (1988): 4–67.

———. "War and Culture: The Iroquois Experience." *William and Mary Quarterly* 40 (1983): 515–45.

Richter, Daniel K., and James Merrell, eds. *Beyond the Covenant Chain: The Iroquois and Their Neighbors in Indian North America, 1600–1800.* Syracuse: Syracuse University Press, 1984.

Riddell, William R. "Practices of the Court of Common Pleas of the District of Hess." *Transactions of the Royal Society of Canada* 7 (1913): 43–57.

Rideout, Thomas. "An Account of My Capture by the Shawanese Indians." *Western Pennsylvania Historical Magazine* 12 (1929): 3–31.

Ritcheson, Charles. *Aftermath of Revolution: British Policy Toward the United States, 1783–1795.* Dallas: Southern Methodist University Press, 1969.

Rogers, Maj. Robert. *A Concise Account of North America . . . .* London, 1765.

———. *Journals of Major Robert Rogers: Containing an Account of the Several Excursions He Made . . . .* London, 1765.

Rogers, T. L. "Simon Girty and Some of His Contemporaries." *Western Pennsylvania Historical Magazine* 8 (1925): 148–58.

Rondthaler, Edward. *Life of John Heckewelder*. Philadelphia: T. Ward, 1847.

Rupp, Israel D. *Early History of Western Pennsylvania, and of the West, and of Western Expeditions and Campaigns* . . . . Pittsburgh: Kaufman and Hickok, 1847.

Russell, Nelson Vance. "The Indian Policy of Henry Hamilton: A Revaluation." *Canadian Historical Review* 11 (1930): 20–37.

Sabine, Lorenzo. *Biographical Sketches of Loyalists of the American Revolution with an Historical Essay*. 2 vols. Boston: Little, Brown and Co., 1864.

Savelle, Max. *George Morgan, Colony Builder*. New York: Columbia University Press, 1932.

Scribner, Robert L., and Brent Tarter, eds. *Revolutionary Virginia, the Road to Independence: A Documentary Record*. 7 vols. Charlotte: University Press of Virginia, 1973–83.

Seibert, Wilbur H. "Kentucky's Struggle with Its Loyalist Proprietors." *Mississippi Valley Historical Review* 7 (1920–21): 113–26.

———. "The Loyalists of Pennsylvania." *The Ohio State University Bulletin: Contributions in History and Political Science* 24 (1905): 9–19.

———. "The Tories of the Upper Ohio." In *West Virginia Biennial Report for 1911–1914, Archives and History*. Charleston, 1914. 1–13.

———. "The Tory Proprietors of Kentucky Lands." *Ohio Archaeological and Historical Quarterly* 28 (1919): 48–71.

Selby, John E. *The Revolution in Virginia, 1775–1783*. Williamsburg: The Colonial Williamsburg Foundation, 1988.

Skaggs, David C. "Between the Lakes and the Bluegrass: An Overview of the Revolution in the Old Northwest." *Northwest Ohio Quarterly* 48 (1976): 89–101.

———. *The Old Northwest in the American Revolution: An Anthology*. Madison: State Historical Society of Wisconsin, 1977.

Smith, Dwight L. "A North American Neutral Indian Zone: Persistence of a British Idea." *Northwest Ohio Quarterly* 61 (1989): 46–63.

———. "The Old Northwest and the Peace Negotiations." In *The French, The Indians, and George Rogers Clark in the Illinois Country*, edited by Thomas Krasean. Indianapolis: Indiana Historical Society, 1977. 92–105.

———, ed. *With Captain Edward Miller in the Wayne Campaign of 1794*. Ann Arbor: The William C. Clements Library, 1965.

Smith, James. *An Account of the Remarkable Occurrences in the Life and Travels of Col. James Smith* . . . . Lexington: John Bradford, 1799.

Smith, Paul H., ed. *Letters of Delegates to Congress, 1774–1789*. 16 vols. Washington, D.C.: Library of Congress, 1976–89.

Smith, Thomas, ed. *Ohio in the American Revolution*. Columbus: Ohio Historical Society, 1976.

Smith, William. *An Historical Account of the Expedition Against the Ohio Indians, in the Year 1764, Under the Command of Henry Bouquet, Esq.* . . . Philadelphia: William Bradford, 1764.

Smith, William Henry, ed. *The St. Clair Papers: The Life and Public Services of Arthur St. Clair* . . . . 2 vols. Cincinnati: Robert Clarke and Co., 1882.

Smyth, J. F. D. *A Tour in the United States of America: Containing an Account of the Present Situation of that Country* . . . . 2 vols. London: Robinson, Robson, and Cornhill, 1784.

Sosin, Jack M. "The British Indian Department and Dunmore's War." *Virginia Magazine of History and Biography* 74 (1976): 34–50.

———. *The Revolutionary Frontier, 1763–1783*. New York: Holt, Rinehart, and Winston, 1967.

———. "The Use of Indians in the War of the American Revolution." *Canadian Historical Review* 46 (1965): 101–21.

———. *Whitehall and the Wilderness: The Middle West in British Colonial Policy, 1760–1775*. Lincoln: University of Nebraska Press, 1962.

Spencer. O. M. *Indian Captivity: A True Narrative of the Capture of Rev. O. M. Spencer by the Indians in the Neighborhood of Cincinnati* . . . . New York: Waugh and T. Mason, 1835.

Spicer, Edward, ed. *Perspectives in American Indian Cultural Change*. Chicago: University of Chicago Press, 1961.

Spiller, Roger J., ed. *Dictionary of American Military Biography*. 3 vols. Westport, Conn.: Greenwood Press, 1984.

Stevens, Paul L. "The Indian Diplomacy of Capt. Richard B. Lernoult, British Military Commandant of Detroit, 1774–1775." *Michigan Historical Review* 13 (1987): 47–82.

———. "Placing Proper Persons at Their Head: Henry Hamilton and the Establishment of the British Revolutionary-Era Indian Department at Detroit, 1777." *The Old Northwest* 12 (1986): 279–317.

Stevens, S. K., Donald Kent, and Autumn L. Leonard, eds. *The Papers of Henry Bouquet*. 6 vols. Harrisburg: The Pennsylvania Historical and Museum Commission, 1974–95.

Stevens, S. K., and Donald Kent, eds. *The Papers of Col. Henry Bouquet*. 19 series. Harrisburg: The Pennsylvania Historical and Museum Commission, 1940–43.

Stonequist, Everett V. *The Marginal Man: A Study of Personality and Culture Conflict*. New York: Russell and Russell, Inc., 1961.

Stotz, Charles Morse. *Outposts of the War for Empire: The French and English in Western Pennsylvania: Their Armies, Their Forts, Their People, 1749–1764*. Pittsburgh: Historical Society of Western Pennsylvania, 1985.

Sturtevant, William C., and Bruce Trigger, eds. *Handbook of North American Indians.* 20 vols. Washington, D.C.: Smithsonian Institute, 1978–.

Sullivan, James, Alexander Flick, Milton W. Hamilton, et al., eds. *The Papers of Sir William Johnson.* 14 vols. Albany: The University of the State of New York, 1921–65.

Sword, Wiley. *President Washington's Indian War: The Struggle for the Old Northwest, 1790–1795.* Norman: University of Oklahoma Press, 1985.

Szasz, Margaret Connell, ed. *Between Indian and White Worlds: The Cultural Broker.* Norman: University of Oklahoma Press, 1994.

Talbert, Charles Gano. *Benjamin Logan: Kentucky Frontiersman.* Lexington: 1962.

———. "Kentucky Invades Ohio—1780." *Register of the Kentucky Historical Society* 53 (1954): 291–300.

———. "Kentucky Invades Ohio—1782." *Register of the Kentucky Historical Society* 52 (1953): 288–97.

———. "Kentucky Invades Ohio—1786." *Register of the Kentucky Historical Society* 54 (1956): 203–13.

Tanner, Helen Hornbeck, and Erminie Wheeler-Voegelin. *Indians of Ohio and Indiana Prior to 1795: The Greenville Treaty, 1795 and Ethnohistory of Indian Use and Occupancy in Ohio and Indiana Prior to 1795.* 2 vols. New York: Garland Publishing, 1974.

Tanner, Helen Hornbeck. *Atlas of Great Lakes Indian History.* Norman: University of Oklahoma Press, 1988.

———. "The Glaize in 1792: A Composite Indian Community." *Ethnohistory* 25 (1978): 15–39.

Thompson, Charles N. *Sons of the Wilderness: John and William Conner.* Indianapolis: Indiana Historical Society, 1937.

Thornbrough, Gayle, ed. *Outpost on the Wabash: 1787–1791: Letters of Brigadier General Josiah Harmar and Major Francis Hamtramck and Other Letters and Documents Selected from the Harmar Papers in the William C. Clements Library.* Indianapolis: Indiana Historical Society, 1957.

Thurman, Lawrence S. "An Account Book of Baynton, Wharton, and Morgan at Fort Pitt, 1765–1767." *Western Pennsylvania Historical Magazine* 29 (1946): 141–46.

Thwaites, Reuben Gold, ed. *Early Western Travels, 1748–1846.* 12 vols. Cleveland: Arthur H. Clark Co., 1904.

Thwaites, Reuben Gold, et al., eds. *Collections of the State Historical Society of Wisconsin.* 31 vols. Madison: Democratic Printing Company, State Printers, 1854–1931.

Thwaites, Reuben, and Louise Phelps Kellogg, eds. *Documentary History of Dunmore's War, 1774.* Madison: State Historical Society of Wisconsin, 1905.

————. *Frontier Defense on the Upper Ohio, 1777–1778*. Madison: State Historical Society of Wisconsin, 1912.

————. *The Revolution on the Upper Ohio, 1775–1777*. Madison: State Historical Society of Wisconsin, 1908.

Tooker, Elizabeth. "The League of the Iroquois: Its History, Politics, and Ritual." In *Handbook of North American Indians*, edited by William C. Sturtevant and Bruce Trigger. 20 vols. Washington, D.C.: Smithsonian Institute, 1978. 15:418–41.

"Virginia Legislative Papers." *Virginia Magazine of History and Biography* 16 (1908): 53–55.

Volney, C[onstantin] F[rancois]. *A View of the Soil and Climate of the United States of America: With Supplementary Remarks upon Florida; on the French Colonies on the Mississippi; and Ohio, and in Canada; and on the Aboriginal Tribes of America*. Philadelphia: Conrad and Co., 1804.

Volwiler, Albert. *George Croghan and the Western Movement, 1741–1782*. Cleveland: The Arthur H. Clarke Company, 1926.

Volwiler, A. T. "The Imperial Indian Department and the Occupation of the Great West, 1748–1756." *Transactions of the Illinois State Historical Society* 32 (1925): 100–107.

————, ed. "William Trent's Journal at Fort Pitt, 1763." *Mississippi Valley Historical Review* 11 (1924–25): 28–57, 115–42, 390–413.

————, ed. "George Croghan and the Western Movement, 1741–1782." *Pennsylvania Magazine of History and Biography* 47 (1923): 28–57, 115–42.

Waddell, Louis M. "Expansion in Western Pennsylvania and the Upper Ohio Valley 1754 to 1800." In *Selected Papers From the 1985 and 1986 George Rogers Clark Trans-Appalachian History Conferences*, edited by Robert J. Holden. Vincennes: Eastern National Park and Monument Association and Vincennes University, 1986. 45–62.

Wainwright, Nicholas B. *George Croghan, Wilderness Diplomat*. Chapel Hill: University of North Carolina Press, 1959.

————, ed. "George Croghan's Journal, 1759–1763, from the Original in the Cadwalader Collection of the Historical Society of Pennsylvania." *Pennsylvania Magazine of History and Biography* 71 (1947): 305–443.

————, ed. "Turmoil at Pittsburgh: Diary of Augustine Prevost, 1774." *The Pennsylvania Magazine of History and Biography* 85 (1961): 111–62.

Wallace, Anthony C. F. *King of the Delaware: Teedyuscung, 1700–1763*. Syracuse: University of Syracuse Press, 1990.

Wallace, Paul A. W. *Conrad Weiser: Friend of Colonist and Mohawk*. Philadelphia: University of Pennsylvania Press, 1945.

————. *Indians in Pennsylvania*. Harrisburg: Pennsylvania Historical and Museum Commission, 1968.

————. *Indian Paths of Pennsylvania*. Harrisburg: Pennsylvania Historical and Museum Commission, 1965.

————, ed. *Thirty Thousand Miles with John Heckewelder*. Pittsburgh: University of Pittsburgh Press, 1958.

————, ed. *The Travels of John Heckewelder in Frontier America*. Pittsburgh: University of Pittsburgh Press, 1958.

Waller, George M. *The American Revolution in the West*. Chicago: Nelson-Hall, 1976.

————. "Target Detroit: Overview of the American Revolution West of the Appalachians." In *The French, the Indians, and George Rogers Clark in the Illinois Country*, edited by Thomas Krasean. Indianapolis: Indiana Historical Society, 1977. 47–66.

Weaks, Mabel Clare. *Calendar of the Kentucky Papers of the Draper Collection of Manuscripts*. Madison: State Historical Society of Wisconsin, 1925.

Weld, Isaac. *Travels Through the States of North America and the Provinces of Upper and Lower Canada during the Years 1795, 1796, and 1797*. 2 vols. London, 1799.

West, J. Martin, ed. *Clark's Shawnee Campaign of 1780: Contemporary Accounts*. Springfield, Ohio: Clark County Historical Society, 1975.

Wharton, Samuel. *Plain Facts: Being an Examination into the Rights of the Indian Nations of America . . . .* Philadelphia, 1781.

Wheeler-Voegelin, Erminie. *Indians of Northern Ohio and Southeastern Michigan*. New York: Garland Publishing Co., 1974.

White, Richard. *The Middle Ground: Indians, Empires, and Republics in the Great Lakes Region, 1650–1815*. Cambridge: Cambridge University Press, 1991.

Wickwire, Franklin B. "'Go on and Be Brave': The Battle of Point Pleasant." *Timeline Magazine* 4 (August/September 1987): 2–15.

Williams, Edward G. "Fort Pitt and the Revolution on the Western Frontier." *Western Pennsylvania Historical Magazine* 59 (1976): 1–37, 129–52, 251–87, 379–444.

————, ed. "The Journal of Richard Butler, 1775: Continental Congress' Envoy to the Western Indians." *Western Pennsylvania Historical Magazine* 46 (1963): 381–95; 47 (1964): 31–45, 141–56.

Wright, J. Leitch, Jr. *Britain and the American Frontier, 1783–1815*. Athens: University of Georgia Press, 1975.

UNPUBLISHED MANUSCRIPTS

Bridges, Diane. "In Defense of a Homeland: Indians at War along the Detroit Frontier, 1790–1815." Manuscript on file, Environment Canada–Parks, Ontario Regional Office, Cornwall, Ontario, 1986.

Couture, Paul. "War and Society on the Detroit Frontier, 1791–1815." Manuscript on file, Environment Canada–Parks, Ontario Regional Office, Cornwall, Ontario, 1989.

Davis, Patricia Talbot. "Alexander McKee, Frontier Tory, 1776–1794." Master's thesis. Bryn Mawr College, 1967.

Hinderaker, Eric Alden. "The Creation of the American Frontier: Europeans and Indians in the Ohio River Valley, 1673–1800." Ph.D. diss. Harvard University, 1991.

Hoberg, Walter R. "History of Alexander McKee, Noted Tory and Founder of McKee's Rocks." Master's thesis. University of Pittsburgh, 1928.

Ingham, John B. "Simon Girty: Degeneration Through Violence." Master's thesis. Bowling Green State University, 1981.

James, Peter. "Report on the British Indian Department in the Detroit-Amherstburg Region in the Period 1785–1812." Manuscript on file, Environment Canada–Parks, Ontario Regional Office, Cornwall, Ontario, 1989.

Lamm, Larry L. "The Early Life of Alexander McKee, 1740 to 1783." Master's thesis. John Carroll University, 1982.

Stevens, Paul L. "His Majesty's 'Savage' Allies: British Policy and the Northern Indians During the Revolutionary War, the Carleton Years, 1774–1778." Ph.D. diss. University of New York at Buffalo, 1984.

Walsh, G. Mark, "Your Humble and Obedient Servant, William Caldwell." Master's thesis. University of Windsor, 1984.

Wulff, Frederick. "Colonel Alexander McKee and British Indian Policy, 1735–1799." Master's thesis. University of Wisconsin-Milwaukee, 1966.

Index

A MAN OF DISTINCTION AMONG THEM
was designed & composed in 11.8/13.5 Fournier
by The Book Page, Inc.;
printed by sheet-fed offset lithography
on 50-pound Turin Book natural vellum stock
(an acid-free, totally chlorine-free paper),
Smyth sewn and bound over binder's boards
in Arrestox B cloth with Rainbow endpapers,
and wrapped with dust jackets
printed in three colors
by Thomson-Shore, Inc.;
and published by
THE KENT STATE UNIVERSITY PRESS
Kent, Ohio 44242